45 935 768 X

D1461377

The Battle of
The Wine Dark Sea

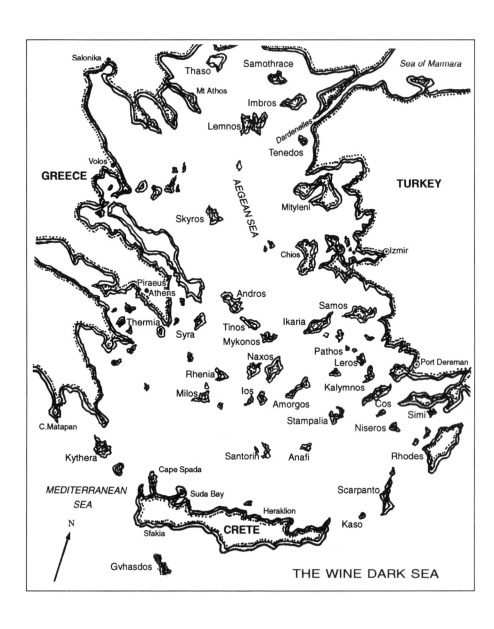

Salonika
Thaso
Samothrace
Sea of Marmara
Mt Athos
Imbros
Lemnos
Dardenelles
Tenedos
Volos
GREECE
TURKEY
AEGEAN SEA
Skyros
Mityleni
Izmir
Chios
Piraeus
Athens
Andros
Samos
Thermia
Ikaria
Port Dereman
Syra
Tinos
Mykonos
Pathos
Leros
Naxos
Rhenia
Kalymnos
Milos
Ios
Cos
Amorgos
Simi
Stampalia
C.Matapan
Niseros
Kythera
Santorin
Anafi
Rhodes
MEDITERRANEAN
SEA
Cape Spada
N
Suda Bay
Scarpanto
Heraklion
Sfakia
CRETE
Kaso
Gvhasdos
THE WINE DARK SEA

The Battle of
The Wine Dark Sea

The Aegean Campaign 1940–45

LEW LIND

Kangaroo Press

© Lew Lind 1994

First published in 1994 by Kangaroo Press Pty Ltd
3 Whitehall Road Kenthurst NSW 2156 Australia
P.O. Box 6125 Dural Delivery Centre NSW 2158
Typeset by G.T. Setters Pty Limited
Printed by Australian Print Group, Maryborough VIC 3465

ISBN 0 86417 562 0

Contents

Acknowledgments

No book, irrespective of the subject, is the work of one person. This particularly applies when the subject is historical and the events described occurred more than half a century before.

I am deeply indebted to the authors listed in the bibliography who, in almost every instance, were personally involved in the four years of operations in the Aegean Sea. Without their contribution, this book could not have been written.

Likewise, the contributions of the General Staff and the Naval History Section of the Hellenic Navy were vital in providing the official accounts of their respective operations. For arranging this cooperation I am indebted to Brigadier Ioannis Stouras, Defence Attaché at the Embassy of Greece, Canberra.

In addition to the official sources, I acknowledge information provided by Mr Markos G. Polioudakis, OAM, of Rethymnon for background information on Crete during the German Occupation and Mr Nicolas Katzabasakis, formerly of Temenia, for the translation of the history of the Greek Sacred Squadron.

My personal thanks are extended to Mr T.W. Ferrers-Walker of Worcestershire and Lieutenant Commander E.F. Baines, DSO, the former commanding officer of HMS *Talybont*, for their assistance in procuring photographic material.

The task of obtaining essential reference books was made much easier by the kind assistance of Mr Trevor Weaver, librarian of The Naval Historical Society of Australia, and by Mr Norman Rivett of the Garden Island Naval Museum.

Suggestions made by Mr A. Sheppard and Mr C. Harrison-Ford, who read the manuscript, were greatly appreciated.

Abbreviations

A/A	Anti-aircraft	LSI	Landing ship infantry
AB	Able Seaman	MAS-boat	An MTB built by Motoscafo
AC	Aircraft Carrier		Armato Svan in Italy
B	Battleship	MA/SB	Motor anti-submarine boat
BYMS	British yard minesweeper	MG	Machine-gun
CBE	Companion of the Order of	MGB	Motor gun boat
	the British Empire	MGB/MTB	An MGB armed with
C-in-C	Commander-in-Chief		torpedoes
CMB	Coastal motor boat	ML	Motor launch
C	Cruiser	MS	Minesweeper
Cor	Corvette	MTB	Motor torpedo boat
D	Destroyer	MVO	Member of the Victorian Order
DFC	Distinguished Flying Cross	NOIC	Naval Officer in Charge
DSC	Distinguished Service Cross	OBE	Order of the British Empire
DSM	Distinguished Service Medal	OS	Ordinary seaman
DSO	Distinguished Service Order	PO	Petty officer
EAC	Escort aircraft carrier	PT-boat	United States naval patrol
E-boat	A general term for S-boats		torpedo boat
	(Schnellboote) and R-boats	R-boat	Raumboote; a large German
	(Raumboote)		MTB
Elco	An MTB built by the	RAN	Royal Australian Navy
	Electric Boat Company of	RANVR	Royal Australian Navy
	America		Volunteer Reserve
EV	Escort vessel	RCN	Royal Canadian Navy
Fairmile	MLs built by the Fairmile	RCNVR	Royal Canadian Navy
	Boat Company, U.K.		Volunteer Reserve
F-lighter	German flak or anti-aircraft	RN	Royal Navy
	lighter	RNVR	Royal Navy Volunteer Reserve
FM	Fast Minelayer	RNZN	Royal New Zealand Navy
G	Gun boat	RNZVR	Royal New Zealand Navy
HDML	Harbour duties motor launch		Volunteer Reserve
HDPC	Harbour duties patrol craft	SAS	Special Air Service
Higgins	An MTB built by the	SBS	Special Boat Squadron
	Higgins Yard, U.S.A.	S-boat	Schnellboote; German MTB
HMAS	His Majesty's Australian	Sl	Sloop
	Ship	Sm	Submarine
HMS	His Majesty's Ship	TB	Torpedo boat
KG	Kampfgruppe	TT	Torpedo tubes
LC	Landing craft	U-boat	Undersea boat
LCA	Landing craft armoured	UJ	German prefix for an
LCG	Landing craft gun		auxiliary escort vessel
LCI	Landing craft infantry	USN	United States Navy
LCT	Landing craft tank	VC	Victoria Cross
LRDG	Long Range Desert Group	Vosper	An MTB built by Vosper's
LS	Landing ship		Yard, U.K.

Introduction

So many decisions made by Winston Churchill in two world wars reflected his deep and critical interest in history. In a long and often turbulent life this interest never flagged, and today there is an increasing realisation that the majority of his decisions were well based.

The Aegean Sea, as the strategic gateway to Central Europe, was already exercising his mind in 1900, following an intensive study of the campaigns of Xerxes and Alexander the Great. He was conscious, since the defeat of Napoleon at the Battle of the Nile, that the Mediterranean was a 'British lake' and a safe base for a drive northwards through the Bosphorus to the 'soft underbelly' of Europe.

Churchill appreciated the ease with which the British and French Fleets had entered the Black Sea to attack Crimea in 1852. After the First World War he likewise remembered the failure of the combined British and French fleets to penetrate the Narrows and the Bosphorus in 1914–15, a failure which cost him the post of First Lord of the Admiralty. Despite this painful failure, his confidence in the strategy never faltered. When fortune smiled on him in 1940 and he was appointed Prime Minister, the only ray of light he saw through the black situation in which he and Britain were placed shone in the Aegean.

Throughout his life Churchill also realised the importance of finding potential leaders and nuturing them, until the day they could lead a fleet or a army to a decisive victory. His choices included A.B. Cunningham, Bernard Montgomery, Philip Vian and William Slim.

Andrew Cunningham was the first. Their relationship commenced in 1900 when Churchill was a war correspondent covering the Boer War and Cunningham a junior lieutenant commanding a 12-pounder gun on an armoured train fighting its way through to Pretoria. The meeting fostered a relationship which lasted almost sixty years. Churchill steered Cunningham in his career, and many of the strategies the future admiral developed were those passed to him by his mentor. The importance of the Mediterranean and the Aegean were foremost amongst these.

The Aegean was never far removed from Admiralty planning. In 1852–55 the Royal Navy made the first comprehensive hydrographic survey of the Mediterranean. Charts prepared by Commander Brattan in the survey sloop *Spitfire* in 1852 were used in operations in 1941.

A Royal Navy intelligence presence in the wine dark sea may also be traced from this period. Greeks have loved intrigue since classical times and three generations of some families provided valuable information to the Directorate of Naval Intelligence in London.

In 1941, an estimated 80 per cent of the population of the Aegean Sea were of Greek extraction. Few had any love for the Italians or the Germans. The presence of these patriots was responsible for the successes of the Special Raiding Forces.

One of the few points of disagreement to exist between Cunningham and Churchill related to the use of irregular forces in the Mediterranean. To Cunningham, steeped in the traditions of the service, this was a reflection on the Royal Navy and the British Army. Yet, later in life, he was to admit that in those days when the Luftwaffe controlled the skies over large parts of the Mediterranean, the use of such desperadoes was the only means of striking at the enemy.

The two factors which had a strong bearing on Cunningham's change of opinion were: the first operation by irregular forces in his command, employing sailors of his fleet in an attempt to block the Danube; and the success of Italian sailors trained as 'charioteers' in sinking both battleships of his fleet in Alexandria Harbour.

Success in the Aegean following the surrender of Italian forces may well have shortened World War II, but the battles of Cos, Leros and Simi were lost for lack of air cover. Lightning long-range fighters, the only aircraft with the range to provide even an hour's cover over the battle areas, were withdrawn by the Americans at a critical part of the battles. There was a distrust of British intentions in the minds of senior United States officers, engendered by the fear that Churchill intended expanding British influence in the oil-rich Middle East.

In retrospect, however, the victories of Cos, Leros and Simi proved hollow to the Germans. The Special Boat Squadron, Long Range Desert Group and the Greek Sacred Squadron, aided by the Levant Schooner Flotilla, struck terror in the hearts of the garrisons isolated on hundreds of islands. In fact the Aegean Campaign created the last sailing flotilla used in war by the Royal Navy. The Levant Schooner Flotilla, later renamed the Anglo-Hellenic Schooner Flotilla, numbered 300 vessels in 1944. The commander of this reminder of a past age was one of Britain's last tall-ship captains, Commander Adrian Seligman.

In the wake of the heavy ship losses in the period September to November 1943, the larger units of the Royal Navy were withdrawn. Their place was taken by submarines and the ubiquitous MTBs, MGBs and MLs of Coastal Command. These elusive forces were responsible for the destruction of enemy naval forces and the sinking of the small ships which supplied its garrisons.

The Special Raiding Forces ranged from Rhodes to the Sporades in the far north, and when the enemy grip on the mainland loosened, they extended their operations along seaboard Greece. Athens and Salonika were liberated by SBS forces. Athens fell to a force led by Colonel, the Earl Jellicoe, and Salonika to one led by Major Anders Lassen, a Dane serving with the British.

In many respects, the campaign was an anachronism. The battles were fought with weapons of the past by small groups of men who arrived at their targets in ships little changed from those used by Xerxes. The actions were hit and run, often mounted at night, and designed to break the nerves of the garrisons.

The question of whether these operations precipitated the withdrawal of the enemy or whether the islands were abandoned when further resistance was of no avail is left to the reader to answer.

Waste not your Hour, nor in vain pursuit
Of This and That endeavour and dispute;
    Better be jocund with fruitful Grape
Than sadden after none, or bitter, Fruit.

—Edward Fitzgerald, *Rubáiyát of Omar Khayyám*, liv

1

The Aegean Architects

Three fighting leaders, all bearing the name Cunningham, made their impression on the war in the Mediterranean. They were Admiral Andrew Browne Cunningham, Commander-in-Chief of the Mediterranean Fleet, his brother, General Sir Alan Cunningham, Commander of the Desert Army, and Admiral Sir John Cunningham. Of the three, 'ABC', as he was widely known, was the master strategist. To him, the Mediterranean was the 'gateway to Europe'.

A.B. Cunningham was born in Dublin in 1883, the son of the eminent surgeon, Professor Daniel Cunningham, who at that time occupied the chair of anatomy at the Royal College of Surgeons. The family was of Scottish descent, from Hyndhope in Selkirkshire. ABC's elder brother, Alexander, followed his father's career and Andrew, following the custom of the period, joined the Royal Navy in 1897. He was entered into the training ship *Britannia* and soon distinguished himself for his pugnacity. His term mates remembered him as an inveterate scrapper—a quality he was to carry with him through a long and distinguished career.

Six months after entry as a cadet he participated in Queen Victoria's Diamond Jubilee Review at Spithead. It was the last royal review in which the ships of the fleet were to appear in a livery of black hulls, yellow masts and funnels, and brilliant white upperworks. Young Cunningham passed out of *Britannia* eleventh in his year with a first-class certificate in mathematics and navigation. Of the sixty-five cadets of his year, eleven reached flag rank, two won the Victoria Cross and five were killed in action.

The newly made midshipman opted for sea service and was posted to the Cape of Good Hope and West Africa Station. He joined the 4,320-ton Second Class cruiser *Fox* at Cape Town in July 1898. When *Fox* returned to England in May 1899, Cunningham was transferred to the flagship of the Station, HMS *Doris*. He was still serving in this ship when the Boer War broke out in October of that year. The midshipman's bearing and attitude to his career soon came to the attention of his commanding officer, Captain Reginald Prothero, who recommended Cunningham be posted as ADC to the commanding officer of the ship's Royal Marine contingent being landed to join the army fighting in Pretoria.

Opportunity played an important part in Cunningham's career and, soon after his arrival at Bloemfontein, he was introduced to the British Field Commander, Lord Roberts, who was a close friend of his father. Lord Roberts relieved him of his duties as an ADC and appointed him to command a naval 12-pounder gun mounted on an armoured train.

This field appointment was responsible for his meeting a round-faced war correspondent, some eight years his senior, who was reporting the important role of armoured trains in South Africa. The war correspondent was Winston Spencer Churchill. The association between the two men was to last for more than half a century and to survive two world wars in which, again, their paths were to cross.

Cunningham's first action took place in early June when his armoured train was ambushed by a commando of Boers north of Bloemfontein. The train's two 12-pounders engaged the Boers at close range and held them at bay until a squadron of British cavalry arrived and freed the train.

Two days later, two armoured trains, including Cunningham's, were cut off by a large Boer force commanded by the rebel leader, General Botha. The young midshipman fought off repeated attacks by the Boer, firing at one stage at point-blank range. Unwilling to accept more casualties, Botha turned his attack on the other train, which he captured. Among the prisoners taken in the engagement was Winston Churchill, who was taken to an enemy prisoner of war camp deep in enemy-occupied territory from which he later escaped and returned to the British lines.

Cunningham was involved in the intermittent skirmishing which continued until the Boers were defeated at Belfast in the last days of August 1900. This land fighting was to serve the future admiral well in his later career. He was one of the few British flag officers who could appreciate the problems of the army in battle.

The naval brigade was withdrawn in September 1900 and Cunningham rejoined HMS *Doris*. He returned to England soon after in the transport *Lake Eyrie*. ABC was seventeen years old, with his first campaign medal and four clasps representing the battles fought at Belfast, Diamond Hill, Orange Free State and Cape Colony.

During the next seventeen years he served in a succession of ships, many of which were commanded by officers who were to enjoy outstanding naval careers and to have an influence on his future career. In the battleship *Hannibal* he met Sub-Lieutenant Percy Noble, who later became the Royal Navy's most distinguished gunnery expert. His divisional officers in this ship were the future Admirals Jellicoe and Beatty. A short appointment in the sail training ship *Martin* followed this appointment. The Navy List at the turn of the century showed ten sail or sail auxiliary ships still in commission.

On his nineteenth birthday Cunningham was promoted to acting sub-lieutenant and posted to the 11,000-ton, First Class cruiser *Diadem*. In this ship he was intensively schooled in gunnery, torpedoes and navigation, the tools he was to use with great success in his later career.

His next appointment, on 14 March 1903, was to the new 15,000-ton battleship *Implacable*, which was commanded by the officer who had given him his first chance; Captain Reginald Prothero. This appointment introduced him to the Mediterranean, where he was to serve half of his long naval career. A year later Cunningham was promoted to lieutenant and received his first command. The training ship *Northampton* was a small barque-rigged frigate built in 1876. In her training role she was restricted to harbour cruising. Despite her age and the restrictions imposed on her, she was Cunningham's proudest command.

Between 1904 and 1908 he served in the 7,350-ton cruiser *Hawke*, which was later to be sunk by the German submarine *U9* in the North Sea, and *Scylla* and *Suffolk*. This last posting was fortunate, as the captain was Rosslyn Wemyss who later rose to the office of First Sea Lord. *Suffolk*'s commission was also served in the Mediterranean.

Lieutenant Cunningham received his first command of a fighting ship in May 1908. She was a torpedo boat, a typical young officer's command, a 26-knotter armed with two 12-pounder quick-firers and three torpedo tubes. *TB 14* was oil-fired, turbine-driven, and known throughout the fleet as the 'oily wad'. Cunningham soon made his mark as a TB skipper who took pleasure in high-speed manoeuvring, an essential for a potential destroyer commander.

Not surprisingly, Cunningham soon came under the eye of Captain Reginald Tyrwhitt, who in 1909 offered him command of the 30-knot oil-fired destroyer *Vulture* in his own squadron. He was commanding his second destroyer, *Roebuck*, when he was promoted to senior lieutenant in September 1910. The rank of senior lieutenant was changed to lieutenant and commander in 1914, and in the last year of World War I it became lieutenant commander.

On 8 January, 1911 he was appointed to command the new *Scorpion*, one of the last coal-burning destroyers built for the Royal Navy. A 27-knotter, *Scorpion* was four knots slower than most destroyers of her time, but her armament of one 4-inch and three 12-pounder guns and two 21-inch torpedo tubes was equal to any vessel of her class. The Beagle class destroyer was one of the most important ships Cunningham was to command. It was in her that he learnt the true meaning of command and served his apprenticeship in the Mediterranean. During his four-year command he was to get to know the Mediterranean as no other captain had done before or since and twenty-five years later he was still applying knowledge he had acquired in *Scorpion*.

In September 1913 Cunningham's flotilla was transferred to the Mediterranean Station in which he served for the next five years. This was the year when Winston Churchill became First Lord of the Admiralty, and the former war correspondent was quick to sound the dangers and potentialities of the Aegean to parliament. With Turkey coming under the influence of Germany and war drawing closer, Churchill ordered the Mediterranean Fleet to visit Constantinople. It arrived in the Bosphorus in the same week the Kaiser's delegation arrived to induce the Turks to enter the coming war on the German side. However, the presence of the British battleships, cruisers and destroyers in the Bosphorus cooled the Turkish war ardour.

Cunningham and other junior officers of the fleet were sure Britain would go to war with Germany in 1914 and German became the most popular language studied that year. However, the immediate enemy in the Mediterranean was Austria, and the powerful Austrian Fleet based in the Adriatic occupied the thoughts of the fleet commander.

The secondary threat was Turkey. Although her fleet was small and most of her ships were old, it operated in the narrow waters of the Dardanelles where it was protected by strongly fortified land batteries and minefields. To contain both enemy fleets, the Mediterranean Fleet of necessity would be divided and operate almost a thousand miles apart. To bring the Turkish fleet to battle, the Allies would first need to seize the Narrows.

War was declared soon after *Scorpion* arrived on the station, and action came to Cunningham in the first two weeks of hostilities. On the night of 6 August, the German battle cruiser *Goeben* and the cruiser *Breslau*, which had been trapped in the Mediterranean by the declaration of war, broke through a far superior line of British and French cruisers commanded by Admiral Troubridge, steamed through the Aegean and found succour in the Dardanelles. *Scorpion* was one of the flotilla of destroyers despatched to overtake the enemy, but the German vessels with their lead proved too fast for their pursuers.

Thus, in the opening days of the war, the Turkish fleet was strongly reinforced. Churchill reacted by sending a combined British and French fleet to the Aegean to contain the new threat. The First Lord was well versed in the campaigns of Xerxes and Alexander the Great in classical times and, strategically, little had changed in two thousand years. The Dardanelles was still the gateway to Europe. If Turkey entered the war on the German side, the Dardanelles offered an alternative front to break the deadlock already threatening in Europe.

Cunningham's first action against the enemy in the Mediterranean took place on 15 August, when Troubridge's cruisers and destroyers joined the French battle fleet in an attack on Austrian ships in the Adriatic. The Austrians, however, anticipated the attack and withdrew their heavy ships behind boom nets in their strongly defended base at Pola. The combined fleet met only one ship, the cruiser *Zenta* which had been patrolling to the south when the attack commenced. *Scorpion* was one of the first ships to fire on the cruiser, but to her captain's disappointment the *Zenta* was sunk in a smother of shells from battleships and cruisers.

Churchill's belief that the fighting in France would soon become a stalemate was quickly realised. By the end of October the two great armies on the Western Front had dug in for an extended trench war. However, the Russians had made important gains on the Eastern Front and a breakthrough south to the Dardanelles was a possibility. Churchill correctly reasoned that a British–French breakthrough in the Dardanelles would cause Germany to transfer some part of her army from France to meet the new threat.

Turkey entered the war while these plans were being discussed and the Allied fleet in the Aegean laid seige to the Dardanelles. The First Lord immediately laid plans before the War Cabinet to force the Narrows with a combined sea and land force which would advance through the Sea of Marmora to the Bosphorus and enter the Black Sea. The loss of the Sea of Marmora and the Bosphorus would force the Turks out of the war and allow the Allies to advance up the Danube through Central Europe. The armies of Britain, France and Russia would force the German High Command to withdraw large numbers of troops from the Western Front to meet this new threat.

Lord Kitchener rejected the plan out of hand, claiming land forces were not available, though it is more likely that he objected to the navy intruding on his responsibility as land commander. There was no love lost between Kitchener and the 'upstart' First Lord.

Undaunted by the rebuff, Churchill ordered an attack by the fleet. At 0915 on 19 February 1915, the British battleships *Vengeance, Albion, Cornwallis, Irresistible* and *Agememnon*, supported by four French battleships, opened fire with their 12- and 15-inch guns on the Turkish forts. The combined fleet was commanded by Rear Admiral John de Robeck. Two senior admirals had been offered the command but had declined.

Fire was maintained at point-blank range throughout the day and the return fire from the Turks was sporadic and far from accurate. At a conference of senior officers held that evening in the flagship, de Robeck expressed his opinion that the forts were heavily damaged and no longer posed a threat to an advance into the Sea of Marmora. Unfortunately, a heavy gale struck later that night and blew for six days. The fleet withdrew to safer waters, six miles from the entrance, and this delay was to cost the Allies the campaign.

During this period Cunningham's *Scorpion* was one of a flotilla of destroyers escorting minesweepers operating at the southern end of the Narrows. The destroyers had embarked Royal Marines and were under instructions to carry out probing landings on the bays at both sides of the entrance. The defenders, who were few, fled when the marines came ashore. A landing was made at the tiny fishing village of Krithia, at the foot of the 700-foot bluff called Achi Baba, and met with no resistance. Some months later, thousands of British lives were lost attempting to take the feature which was the key to Gallipoli. Detailed reports of the initial landings were made to the fleet commander, who attached no importance to the information. The opportunity to seize the Narrows and to avert the bloody campaign on Gallipoli was lost on that night.

The last bombardments of the Narrows commenced on 25 February and continued into March.

Far away in London, Churchill chafed at the lack of drive in the bombardments. When asked to act more aggressively, Admiral de Robeck resigned the command and Rear Admiral Rosslyn Wemyss, Cunningham's commanding officer in HMS *Suffolk* in 1908, was appointed Senior Officer, Aegean. A renewed attack was launched on the morning of 18 March, but disaster struck the bombarding battleships from the onset. Six battleships were mined in the entrance. The mines, the last held by the Turkish Navy, had been laid two nights before. In three hours *Inflexible, Irresistible, Ocean, Gaulois* and *Bouvet* were either sunk or run ashore.

British and French minesweepers, based at nearby Tenedos, had not been called in to sweep the waters before the attack commenced. Even more mortifying was the fact, which became known only days later, that the forts the battleships intended attacking had exhausted the ammunition for their guns and the garrisons had withdrawn.

The failure of the navy to force the Dardanelles was responsible for the resignation of Churchill as First Lord of the Admiralty and Admiral Lord Fisher as First Sea Lord in May 1915. The horrifying losses suffered by the army at the landings at Gallipoli and Sulva Bay caused Churchill to don uniform and join his regiment on the peninsular.

In hindsight, the lack of forceful direction and leadership by the naval commanders cost the Allies a victory which would have forced Turkey out of the war and probably reduced the conflict by at least a year.

The *Scorpion* remained in the Mediterranean until January 1918, except for refits. In this period Cunningham won the DSO and a bar for his aggressive support of troops ashore at Gallipoli. His gun support and spotting of guns endeared the *Scorpion* to the army command. The ship likewise came to the attention of the Commander-in-Chief for her successful actions against German submarines. This service was to hold Cunningham in good stead in his later service in the Aegean and the Eastern Mediterranean generally. His apprenticeship was complete.

When Turkey surrendered in October 1918, a British fleet swept through the Aegean and entered the Black Sea to operate against German units withdrawing from eastern and southern fronts. Five ships of the Royal Australian Navy, including the new cruiser *Brisbane* and the destroyers *Huon, Parramatta, Warrego* and *Yarra*, were a part of this fleet.

Cunningham, who knew these waters better than most officers of the period, had been transferred to the Home Fleet. He returned to England in early 1918, assumed command of the destroyer *Termagant* and spent the last year of the war commanding a flotilla in the North Sea. His last operation was transporting the newly appointed First Sea Lord, Admiral Sir Rosslyn Wemyss, across the Channel to sign the Armistice.

Cunningham was now one of the substantial band of Royal Navy officers who found peacetime routine hard to endure. It was not surprising, therefore, that he jumped at the opportunity of joining the naval force being prepared for operations against the Soviet Army in the Baltic. The commander of the force was Rear Admiral Walter Cowan, who had served with Cunningham in South Africa eighteen years before and was to meet him again in another war under vastly changed circumstances.

Cowan's orders were to prevent the Soviet Army and the few former Russian Imperial Navy ships under its control from interfering with the democratic parties establishing governments in Lithuania, Latvia and Estonia. It was the Royal Navy's first fleet venture in the Baltic since the days of Nelson. The British government preferred to call the operation a police action. Cunningham in HMS *Seafire* found his share of excitement in the campaign, although he missed the two fleet actions. Employing a rare mixture of diplomacy and muscle, he prevented the army under General von der Goltz from seizing the port of Libau. The last action won him a second bar to the DSO.

He was promoted captain a few days after his thirty-seventh birthday in 1920. A short appointment followed in the Naval Inter-Allied Commission of Control in which he was responsible for the destruction of German fortifications in Heligoland. This command was followed in April 1922 by appointment as Captain (D) of 6th Destroyer Flotilla. Eight months later he was back in the Mediterranean commanding the destroyers of the 1st Flotilla in Turkish waters.

To Cunningham's delight, he was not only back in familiar waters, but in a war zone. War between Turkey and Greece had broken out in 1919 when Greece attempted to seize Thrace. The Aegean Squadron's task was to ensure Turkish forces did not cross the Bosphorus. ABC's plan to thwart any such attempt was to steam the flotilla at high speed through the restricted waters of the Bosphorus to swamp the boats carrying the invasion force. This service was to give Cunningham an expert knowledge of the waters of the Black Sea, the Caspian, the Sea of Marmora and islands of the Aegean. His Letters of Proceedings of the period, carefully preserved by the Admiralty, were consulted on frequent occasions twenty years later when the Royal Navy was again operating in these waters.

The promotion ladder was now opening for ABC. His next appointment was captain-in-charge of the important destroyer base at Port Edgar in the Firth of Forth and, once more, he served under Admiral Cowan. When the admiral was transferred to command the North American Station, Cunningham accompanied him as commanding officer of the cruiser, HMS *Calcutta*. In 1941 he was to grieve the loss of this fine ship when she was sunk by German dive-bombers off Crete.

January 1930 found him serving in the battleship *Rodney* and later in that year, when promoted to commodore, he took the ship on a flag-showing cruise to Iceland, Denmark and Sweden. During this cruise he made valuable diplomatic and service contacts which were to serve him well in his later career.

Cunningham returned to the Mediterranean in January 1933 as Rear Admiral, Destroyers. Eighteen years had passed since he joined the station as commanding officer of HMS *Scorpion*. This command was to be of the greatest importance in his later career. The junior officers serving under him were to be his destroyer commanders in 1941 and 1942. Foremost among these were Lieutenant Commander Lord Mountbatten and Lieutenant Commander Philip Vian.

Both of these young officers had the greatest admiration for their admiral's skill in ship-handling. Mountbatten later wrote: 'I watched this absolute wizard handle thirty-six ships entirely by himself. In spite of his red and watery eyes he always saw everything first—no move escaped his eagle eye. At that time his fame in the destroyer world was legendary throughout the Navy.'

While Cunningham rose to the highest posts in the navy, Winston Churchill remained in the political wilderness. The only light to brighten this black period in his career came in 1935, when for a few brief months he returned to his old post of First Lord of the Admiralty. However, Churchill used his time to good effect. He had an implicit belief in his return to office and during this period he prepared for that event. His interest in naval matters never flagged and, encouraged by his old friend, the Director of Naval Intelligence, Rear Admiral Hall, he became interested in naval intelligence and gathered around him people who had skills which could be applied in this field at a later date. One of these was William Stephens, another protégé of Hall's, who was responsible for unravelling Enigma and laying the foundations for Britain's greatest weapon in the Second World War, ULTRA.

It was on Stephens' suggestion that Churchill formed a club in London, membership of which was restricted to people who had skills useful in intelligence work. Over the years this club was to bring together a number of distinguished scientists, linguists, archaeologists, explorers, missionaries and adventurers, the majority of whom were to make important contributions when war came in 1939. He named the group the Golf, Cheese and Chess Club. Churchill never lost interest in the new generation of naval, army and air officers. By 1936 he had prepared a list which included almost every outstanding senior officer in the Second World War.

Cunningham was now one of the most experienced senior officers in the Royal Navy. By 1936, when the Italians invaded Abyssinia, his future was clearly defined. His appointment gave him a clear insight into the aspirations of the Italians in this vital region and he soon became aware of the superiority of the cruisers and destroyers of the new Italian Navy. These vessels were faster and better armed than ships of the same class in the Royal Navy.

Two events occurred during his visit to England in 1935 to attend King George V's Jubilee Review which were to have great influence on his future career. Vice-Admiral Sir William Fisher, Commander-in-Chief, Portsmouth, died, and Vice-Admiral Sir Geoffrey Blake fell seriously ill in Malta. Cunningham was offered command of the battle cruiser squadron in the Mediterranean Fleet.

Cunningham immediately reported to the Commander-in-Chief, Mediterranean at Valetta. Admiral Sir Dudley Pound was in his bath but nevertheless ordered ABC to hoist his broad pennant in the HMS *Hood*. He was now a vice-admiral.

The newly appointed squadron commander was soon involved in events in the western

Mediterranean, where General Franco was attempting to seize power in Spain. Germany and Italy were supporting the insurgents and Britain faced serious problems. British ships were being attacked by unidentified submarines and aircraft but Cunningham knew the aggressor was Italy. He solved the problem by introducing a convoy system for all British and French ships passing through the dangerous waters. However, the situation remained serious and more destroyers from the Home Fleet were transferred to the Mediterranean. The Royal Air Force deployed flying boats to the danger area to provide additional cover for the defenceless ships.

How close Britain came to declaring war on Italy in 1937 was appreciated by the Service Chiefs of Staff. In August 1937 the Italian submarine *Iride* narrowly missed the

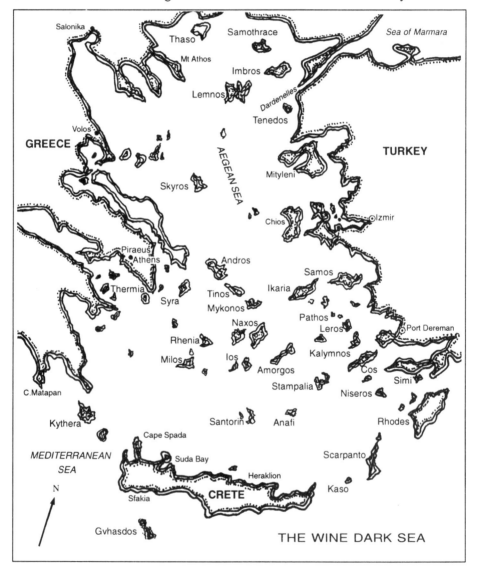

destroyer HMS *Havock* in a deliberate torpedo attack. Had the ship been hit, the two nations may well have gone to war. *Havock* was lost in June 1942 off Tunisia while serving under Cunningham's command.

ABC was transferred back to England in 1938 to obtain administrative and higher command experience. His arrival coincided with the cold war between England and Germany which, only a month before his arrival, had been responsible for the mobilisation of the fleet. The eight months Cunningham spent in England were applied to the study of planning, armaments and rearmament, modernising the Fleet Air Arm and the anti-aircraft defence of ships and ports. No admiral in modern times received such a compacted course in higher command.

Admiral Sir Dudley Pound was appointed First Sea Lord on 9 May 1939 and Cunningham became Commander-in-Chief, Mediterranean with the temporary rank of admiral. Soon after hearing of his new appointment, ABC wrote: 'I probably knew the Mediterranean as well as any naval officer of my generation. I had spent about ten and a half years there in eight different ships, a goodish slice of a lifetime.'

Cunningham assumed his new command on 5 January 1939 and eight months later, on the outbreak of the Second World War, Prime Minister Neville Chamberlain, appointed Winston Churchill First Lord of the Admiralty. Thus the two leaders who believed the Mediterranean held the key to the war in Europe came together once again.

Churchill shared with the great prophets of history the power to identify great leaders and inspire them with a mystique and zeal which bordered on fanaticism. He wrote in 1940, soon after accepting the burden of leading Britain in war: 'I felt I was walking with destiny and that all my past life had been but a preparation for this hour and for this trial'.

It was not surprising that Cunningham, Montgomery and Tedder fell under Churchill's spell and responded to his mystique. He was the great precursor of the Second World War. His emergence as spiritual leader was responsible for the inspirational upheaval that lifted Britain at that time. 'There was a white glow, overpowering, sublime, which ran through our island from end to end.'

2

First Rounds in the Mediterranean

Fifty-six-year old Temporary Admiral A.B. Cunningham (he was not confirmed in the rank until January 1941) was above average height, of athletic build and fitter than most senior officers of the period. His bright eyes were set in a well-lined face moulded and etched by thirty-nine years of sea service. There was a bird-like quickness about his movements which reflected, to the observant, a sharpness of mind honed and disciplined for command. In every respect, he was the popular image of the aggressive seadog, and in the five years ahead that image remained unchanged.

On his arrival at Malta in 1935, at that time the base for the fleet in the Mediterranean, he reported to Admiral Sir Dudley Pound whom he was to relieve as commander-in-chief. Pound had the utmost confidence in Cunningham, and not once in the bitter years which lay ahead did he have cause to lose it. In later years, in the office of First Sea Lord, Pound described ABC as 'a dynamic leader not afraid of delegating responsibility'. On his death bed, Pound recommended Cunningham as his successor in the Royal Navy's highest post.

ABC likewise had sublime confidence in his own ability to carry out the duties entrusted to him. His seniority, his service and proven ability, not only to command but to win the respect of those both junior and senior to him, was known in all quarters. He was undaunted by the challenges he knew lay ahead. There were no waters between Gibraltar and Suez in which he had not served, and the new Commander-in-Chief used the last days of the Indian summer before the outbreak of war to good effect. He visited Alexandria, which was being fitted out as the Royal Navy's Mediterranean base, Palestine, then in the throes of a civil war, Syria, Turkey and the islands of the Aegean.

Like Churchill, Cunningham had a strong sense of history. In selecting Alexandria for his fleet base he was not unmindful of the fact that this was the port built and named by Alexander the Great. It was from here the great war galleys of the Macedonian sailed to conquer the world. The capital ships of the Mediterranean Fleet were moored in the ancient Western Harbour which was known from antiquity as Eunostos Haven, the Greek 'Harbour of Safe Return'.

Cunningham well appreciated the importance of the base. With Gibraltar to the west and Alexandria to the east, the Mediterranean and Mussolini's fleet were contained by jaws of steel. Alexandria faced the Aegean and was only fifteen hours steaming from Crete and nine from the Suez Canal. As well, it was the pivot for Wavell's Desert Army.

Hostilities with Germany had little immediate effect on his command, whose main duty was to provide escorts for the British and French shipping passing through the Mediterranean. However, within a few months there was a sharp reduction in the number of ships in his command. Operations in the Atlantic and Norwegian waters caused a stream of destroyers and cruisers to be withdrawn to support the Home Fleet. Even his flagship, the battleship *Warspite*, sailed for the frozen waters of the north, where she soon won distinction at Narvik. *Warspite* was a lucky ship, which saw action in both World Wars. During the Narvik Campaign she was hit by three torpedoes and survived. All three were duds. Later in the war she was the first battleship to be hit by a guided missile and again survived. ABC's pride in *Warspite* knew no bounds and he delighted in telling visitors to the flagship that the first *Warspite* served in the Aegean in 1592.

Initially, the Commander-in-Chief was alarmed at the whittling down of his fleet, but reports from the excellent intelligence system established in Italy soon allayed these fears. The Italian Navy was far from being prepared for war and its building program was timed for hostilities to commence in 1942.

In addition to his own fleet, a small French fleet consisting of the battleship *Lorraine*, three 8-inch cruisers, *Suffren, Duquesne* and *Tourville*, the 6-inch cruiser *Duguay-Trouin* and three destroyers, commanded by Rear Admiral R.E. Godfroy, was also based at Alexandria. This force, when combined with the British fleet, offered more than sufficient deterrent to the Italians.

During the bitter winter of 1939 and the early spring of 1940, Cunningham was handicapped by a shortage of destroyers for use as convoy escorts. However, this was somewhat relieved by the arrival of the Australian Destroyer Flotilla commanded by Commander Waller. The six ships of the flotilla were old V and W class vessels built during the First World War for fleet work. Despite these limitations they were immediately pressed into service convoying French transports from Syria to Marseille. The Australian crews suffered purgatory in sub-zero temperatures and Spartan living conditions.

The most significant event of the first year of war was the return of Winston Churchill to his old post of First Lord of the Admiralty. His ebullient presence in the War Cabinet ensured that the Royal Navy retained its rightful importance in the minds of his fellow politicians. The new First Lord was responsible for the Mediterranean Fleet making a special visit to Turkey in early 1940. The timing of the visit was perfect. Uncannily echoing events at the beginning of the First World War, it coincided with a visit by a German diplomatic delegation bent on enticing Turkey to enter the war on the side of Germany. The foreknowledge of this visit was undoubtedly known by Churchill.

Churchill's decision to use Cunningham to head the mission, normally a reserve of career diplomats, was more than a coincidence. He was well aware of the Commander-in-Chief's experience in Turkish and Aegean waters from his First World War service, while Cunningham shared the First Lord's belief that the gateway to Europe was through these vital waters.

Cunningham was later to comment on the perfect timing of the visit. The Mediterranean Fleet arrived in the Bosphorus three hours before the German delegation. The sight of the battleships, cruisers and destroyers flying the Union Jack at the main berths nullified the German diplomats' suggestion to the Turks. Cunningham returned to Alexandria with the Turkish President's warm assurances of continued friendship with Great Britain. Cunningham also made good use of the visit by holding exercises off the

Italian bases on Leros and Rhodes. On several occasions Italian aircraft were sighted approaching the fleet, but on each occasion they turned away when the cruisers launched their aircraft.

The 'phoney war' in Europe ended in April when German armoured divisions rolled across the frontiers of Belgium, Holland and France and added a new word to the English language, blitzkrieg. The British and French armies were driven back to the Channel coast. The French government sued for an armistice and the British Army withdrew to Dunkirk, from where a major proportion of it was evacuated. On 10 June, to a fanfare of trumpets, Mussolini announced that Italy had entered the war on the side of Germany. The Mediterranean was now an active theatre of war.

Admiral Cunningham was not alarmed with the situation he now faced. In the three months before Italy entered the war his fleet had been heavily reinforced. It now consisted of the battleships *Warspite, Ramillies, Royal Sovereign* and *Malaya*, the small aircraft carrier *Eagle*, 9 cruisers, 26 destroyers, 2 sloops, 15 submarines and a large number of auxiliaries. At the western end of the Mediterranean, a second fleet, soon to take the name of Force H, commanded by Admiral Somerville, was also prepared. It consisted of 2 battleships, a battlecruiser, the new aircraft carrier *Ark Royal*, 11 destroyers and 12 submarines.

The combined British fleets were more than a challenge to the Italians, who at this stage had only two battleships ready for service. However, four more were being modernised although not all would be in service for another year. Nineteen cruisers, 50 destroyers and 115 submarines were already at their war stations. The two aircraft carriers on which Mussolini had placed his faith were far from complete on their cradles at Genoa.

Cunningham's main concern was the disparity in the strength of the two air forces. The Italians could muster more than 2000 aircraft of all types, while the Royal Air Force and the Fleet Air Arm had fewer than 500. Enemy air bases stretched in an unbroken arc from Pantellaria in the west to Rhodes in the east. The entire Mediterranean, including the Suez Canal and the northern approaches of the Red Sea, was within range of Italian bombers. Air bombardment of Malta commenced on 11 June and continued uninterrupted for three bitter years before the Allies gained command of the air over the Mediterranean.

The operation plan for the war in the Mediterranean Command was completed by Cunningham and his Chief of Staff, Rear Admiral Willis, two weeks before hostilities commenced. Admiral Godfroy and the French squadron, the battleship *Lorraine*, four cruisers and three destroyers, sailed on 11 June on the first operation. It was a sweep of the Aegean.

Cunningham, in the battle fleet, sailed four hours later for the waters north of Crete. No enemy ships were sighted, but as the fleet was withdrawing on 12 June the light cruiser *Calypso* was torpedoed by the Italian submarine *Bagnolini* and sank off Crete. The destroyers immediately closed the area of the attack and dropped depth charges without any evidence of success. However, several days later intelligence agents on the island reported the submarine *Uebi Scebeli*, which was operating with *Bagnolini*, had been sunk close to where *Calypso* was lost.

This report was responsible for the first secret operation carried out by the navy in the Mediterranean. A team of divers arrived in the area of the sinking on 28 June and commenced a search for the *Uebi Scebeli* on the next night. They found the submarine lying in 75 feet of water, with its conning tower open, and the divers entered. Their search enabled the Royal Navy to obtain an Italian version of the Enigma cyther machine and the enemy's secret naval codes. However, the Italians learnt of the operation, and on 1 October 1940 new codes were introduced. These were never broken by the British.

At this period of the war, Cunningham knew more of the Italian war plans than he did of those of the British War Cabinet. Even while the Mediterranean Fleet was returning from its first operation, the Combined Chiefs of Staff and the War Cabinet in London were discussing the total evacuation of all British air, sea and land forces from the Mediterranean to bolster Britain's defences against a German invasion. The plan was strongly opposed by the First Sea Lord, Admiral Sir Dudley Pound, who threatened to resign if it was adopted. The War Cabinet withdrew its proposal. ABC was not to learn how close he came to losing his command in the first week of the war against Italy until three years later, on his appointment as First Sea Lord in October 1943.

Cunningham knew all national leaders believed they were the grand strategists in time of war. During the Second World War, both Churchill and Hitler were guilty of making decisions which were rightly the prerogative of the admirals or generals appointed for the purpose. Luckily for the outcome of the war, the British Chiefs of Staff ignored directives they considered wrong.

On his return to Alexandria, Cunningham was confronted by a crisis that was to test his powers of diplomacy. On his desk was a signal from the War Cabinet instructing him to seize the French fleet. The signal read: 'The French Fleet must not fall into the hands of the enemy. An ultimatum is to be made to Admiral Godfroy to comply with one of the following alternatives: 1. Surrender all units of your squadron. 2. Proceed to sea and scuttle all units. If Admiral Godfroy refuses both options, immediate action is to be taken to render the French Squadron unserviceable.'

Cunningham was not surprised at the instruction and he delivered the ultimatum to Admiral Godfroy later that day. The French admiral was requested to make his decision by the evening of 3 July. However, this deadline was extended for forty-eight hours as negotiations continued. Godfroy was cordial throughout the distressing period and, in confidence, he intimated to Cunningham that should the decision to scuttle be reached, the action would be carried out in a manner convenient to the British.

On the morning of 5 July the Italians launched a heavy air attack on Alexandria and all ships, including the French, opened fire on the enemy aircraft. It was this action, combined with the British commander's diplomacy, which influenced the French decision to surrender. Disarmament of the French ships commenced soon after the 'all clear' was sounded. 'I can think of no more suitable salute to surrender,' ABC commented to his officers that evening.

Two days after this momentous event, the submarine *Phoenix*, patrolling east of Malta, reported that an enemy fleet consisting of two battleships, twelve cruisers and a large number of destroyers was standing north of Benghazi, providing cover for a large supply convoy. Cunningham immediately despatched a flying boat from Malta to shadow the enemy fleet and ordered the battle fleet to sea. At 1145 the aircraft reported the Italians ninety miles to the northwest of HMS *Warspite* and, a few minutes later, a second force of six cruisers and eight destroyers twenty miles north of the main fleet.

Cunningham ordered the carrier *Eagle* to fly off her reconnaissance aircraft. Two hours later these aircraft reported the main enemy fleet, which included the battleships *Conte di Cavour* and *Giulio Cesare*, had turned north and joined sixteen cruisers and three flotillas of destroyers. The British fleet, with the battleships *Warspite, Royal Sovereign* and *Malaya*, the aircraft carrier *Eagle*, eight cruisers and eighteen destroyers, was stronger than the Italians.

Soon after receiving this report, Italian high-level bombers appeared over the fleet and attacked. Bombs fell close to the speeding fleet and the cruiser *Gloucester* was hit on the bridge by a heavy bomb. Eighteen of her crew, including the captain, were killed and twelve wounded. The cruiser fell out of the formation and was ordered to return to Alexandria.

The presence of aircraft caused Cunningham to decrease speed and wait until nightfall before closing the enemy. However, it was not until 1508 on 8 July that contact was made. The cruisers *Orion* and *Neptune* sighted the enemy and sent Nelson's historic signal: 'Enemy battle fleet in sight'. The Australian destroyer *Stuart* was also in the van of the fleet, and one of her officers described the sighting: 'In perfect visibility, blue sea and cloudless sky, the cruisers on the wing and the destroyers in a semi-circular formation screening in front of the battleships, made a picture no one who saw it can ever forget'.

Minutes later, *Warspite*'s 15-inch guns opened fire at a range of 26,400 yards. Great water spouts were seen rising around the enemy flagship, *Giulio Cesare*, and smoke from a hit was seen rising from her superstructure. It was later learnt that twenty men were killed and six boilers knocked out by this hit.

The Italian admiral ordered smoke and changed course drastically. Despite the damage, *Giulio Cesare* and her sistership *Conte di Cavour* replied with accurate salvos from their main armament. Two British battleships and a cruiser were straddled and the enemy destroyers, trailing long plumes of grey smoke, closed at high speed to launch their torpedoes. They were met by heavy and concentrated fire from the British cruisers and destroyers. *Hyperion* and *Stuart* engaged the Italian *Zeffiro* at close range and smothered her with a hail of shells. She sank soon after. While this action was being fought, the main enemy force retired at high speed behind the smokescreen. They were later reported passing through the Straits of Messina.

This first battle fleet action in the Mediterranean was called the Battle of Calabria.

Cunningham broke off his pursuit when enemy bombers appeared overhead. The Commander-in-Chief never underestimated the Italian airmen in this type of attack. 'Italian high-level bombing,' he wrote, 'was the best I have ever seen, far better than the German.'

Four days after the smoke of the Battle of Calabria cleared, HMAS *Sydney* gave the morale of the Mediterranean Fleet another boost. The Australian cruiser, commanded by Captain John Collins, and the four destroyers under her command, *Hyperion, Ilex, Hero* and *Hasty*, engaged the Italian cruisers *Bartolomeo Colleoni* and *Biovanni delle Bande Nere* off Cape Spada, Crete. In the battle which followed, the Australian cruiser and her destroyer consorts won a resounding victory over the two fastest cruisers in the world. *Sydney* sank the *Barolomeo Colleoni* and heavily damaged the *Biovanni delle Bande Nere*.

This second victory coming so soon after Calabria pleased Cunningham greatly and when *Sydney* proudly steamed into Alexandria he sent the following signal to all ships: 'Give her a rousing cheer'. When Collins reported on board the flagship, the Commander-in-Chief greeted him: 'Well done. How did you get there?' Collins had his reply ready. 'Providence guided me, Sir', he said, and ABC's repartee was equally appropriate: 'Well in future, you can take your orders from Providence'.

In London, Winston Churchill was equally loquacious in announcing the naval victories in the Mediterranean to the House of Commons. The Prime Minister had been in office for three months and the two victories were the first flashes of light to pierce the gloom.

These successes were no doubt responsible for Churchill raising the question of seizing the small Italian island of Pantellaria at the Combined Chiefs of Staff meeting soon after. The Chiefs of Staff opposed the operation, as they believed a combined assault could take the poorly defended island but could not hold it without strong air support.

Churchill was not satisfied, and shortly after asked Cunningham for his comments. ABC was well aware he was skating on thin ice, particulary as the First Sea Lord had opposed the operation, and did not comment on Pantellaria. Instead, he suggested an operation to capture the tiny Italian island of Casteloriso in the Eastern Mediterranean. He added that this island threatened the line of enemy air bases in the Aegean. The Prime Minister proposed the capture of Casteloriso at the next Combined Chiefs of Staff meeting and, surprisingly, it was approved without demur.

August brought welcome reinforcements to the Mediterranean Fleet. These were the new armoured deck fleet carrier *Illustrious*, which replaced the small *Eagle*, the battleship *Valiant* and the anti-aircraft cruisers *Calcutta* and *Carlisle*. *Illustrious*' complement of new Fulmar fighters soon proved their worth, shooting down three enemy shadowers and a high-level bomber in their first week on the station.

The arrival of the ships was as timely as it was welcome. Mussolini was implementing his plans to expand eastward through Albania to invade Greece. To intimidate the Greeks, who were passing through a period of political instability, he ordered the sinking of the cruiser *Helle* at Tinos in the Cyclades on Assumption Day. The attack was carried out by the Italian submarine *Osiro*, but Mussolini denied responsibility for the sinking. Italian forces were also strongly established on the Egyptian border and in Abyssinia, Massawa and Eritrea. However, the greatest threat to British control of the vital convoy routes were the air bases on Kythera, Kasos, Scarpanto and Rhodes in the Aegean.

This threat was never far from Cunningham's mind and on 27 July he initiated the first of a series of sea and air strikes against the enemy bases. The cruiser *Orion*, destroyers *Vampire* and *Vendetta*, and the armed boarding vessels *Fiona* and *Chakla* were despatched to stage a simulated landing on the island of Casteloriso in conjunction with a bombing raid launched from Palestine.

The operation was carried out with no opposition from the enemy. The boarding vessels lowered their boats and the destroyers fired star shells. No enemy ships were sighted and the captain of *Orion* recorded in his report that 'to all intents and purposes the island could have been uninhabited'.

This raid was in fact staged as a cover for the passing of a convoy through Kythera Channel to Alexandria. Escort for the operation consisted of the cruisers *Sydney, Liverpool* and *Neptune* and three destroyers. However, the convoy was attacked by Italian high-level bombers as it passed south of Kasos and both *Sydney* and *Neptune* were near-missed by bombs. The two cruisers were detached from the escort when the aircraft departed and turned north. They reached Thermia Channel close to Athens seven hours later and intercepted the enemy transport *Ermioni*, which was carrying supplies and personnel to the enemy Aegean bases. The vessel was sunk by gunfire after the crew and passengers were removed.

On 2 September, the radar stations and airfield on Scarpanto were the target for *Sydney* and *Orion* and the destroyers *Dainty* and *Ilex*. The ships stood off the coast and shelled Makri Yala airfield, destroying hangars, fuel dumps and workshops. Three aircraft were either damaged or destroyed on the tarmac. Later *Orion* moved to Pegadia where she set on fire and wrecked further installations. The Italian reacted with an attack on MAS-boats. *Ilex* engaged the elusive high-speed torpedo craft in the dark, sinking two and leaving the third burning like a beacon.

A month later, on 2 October, the two cruisers and their consorts bombarded the airfield at Maltazana on Stampalia, destroying aircraft on the runway and damaging the barrack buildings.

Italian naval forces in the Aegean at this period were considerable. Based on Leros were the fast fleet destroyers *Francesco Crispi* and *Quintino Sella* and the torpedoboat destroyers *Solferino* and *San Martino*, eight submarines *(Gondar, Scire, Neghelli, Asciangi, Durbo, Tembien, Beilul* and *Lafole)* and twenty MAS-boats.

Cunningham's ships were also in action against enemy light forces off Crete. The cruisers *York* and *Ajax* intercepted the destroyer *Argliere* and the torpedo-boat destroyers *Airone* and *Ariel* in these waters on 12 October. *York* sunk the *Argliere* in a running engagement off the south-west point of the island, and *Ajax* damaged both torpedoboat destroyers, which near-missed her in a combined torpedo attack.

A week after this action Mussolini issued his ultimatum to Greece. Transfer Salonika and Crete to Italy as naval bases or suffer the consequences. The Greeks refused, and on 28 October an Italian army attacked Greece through Albania.

The Admiralty reacted by ordering Cunningham to occupy Suda Bay in Crete and develop the excellent port as an advance base for the Mediterranean Fleet. Three days later a convoy consisting of oil tankers, store ships and the netlayer *Protector* was escorted into the bay by the Australian destroyers *Vampire, Voyager* and *Waterhen*. A week later a second convoy arrived, carrying anti-aircraft guns and troops. The fleet now had its advanced base covering the main convoy routes from east to west.

To Mussolini's surprise, the poorly armed Greek Army halted the Italian advance twenty miles inside Greece and in the months which followed drove the enemy back into Albania.

While these events were taking place, the carriers *Illustrious* and *Eagle*, with a strong escort of cruisers and destroyers, launched two heavy air attacks on the enemy base at Leros. The first struck Porto Laki, causing heavy damage to the dockyard, and the second destroyed fuel tanks. In his report on this operation ABC commented: 'The presence of *Illustrious*'s Fulmar fighters discouraged retaliation from enemy fighters over the target, but unfortunately the Fleet was heavily bombed by his high-level bombers as it withdrew and the cruiser *Newcastle* was severely damaged by a torpedo bomber south of Crete'. Two years later *Newcastle* was again torpedoed off Malta by the German torpedo-boat *S 56*.

In November the Mediterranean Fleet made its most crippling blow on the Italians. On the night of Armistice Day, *Illustrious* launched a force of twenty Swordfish aircraft against the important enemy naval base at Taranto. The reconnaissance for the attack was carried out by Australian-born Flight Lieutenant E.A. Whiteley, RAF, in a Glen Martin aircraft of No 431 Flight. The raid caught the defences unprepared. Three battleships, *Littorio, Conti di Cavour* and *Caio Dulo*, and a cruiser were sunk at their moorings. The port facilities were severely damaged, as were three smaller warships. Two of *Illustrious*' aircraft were lost in the raid. Cunningham expressed his elation at the success: 'Twenty aircraft had inflicted more damage on the Italian Fleet than was inflicted on the German High Seas Fleet at Jutland'.

By a strange coincidence, on the night of the attack on Taranto, Italian aircraft made their first attack on London.

Illustrious did not rest on her laurels. On 26 November, with the small carrier *Eagle*, she launched a second attack on Maltazana airfield on Stampalia. The Italian forward base in the Aegean had not recovered from the previous attack and was put out of action for many weeks.

The year ended on a bright note for the Mediterranean Fleet, but there were already sinister omens of what awaited it in 1941. Cunningham knew a German anti-shipping air armada was being transferred to the Mediterranean in support of the Italians. This message, one of the first ULTRA intercepts relating to the Mediterranean, was forwarded by Admiral Pound at the beginning of Christmas week. However, all news was not bad news and on 3 January 1941 Cunningham was confirmed in his rank of admiral.

Illustrious' first meeting with aircraft of the Luftwaffe's Flieger Korps X took place on 10 January while she was escorting a convoy east of Malta. The carrier was singled out by a squadron of fifteen Stuka dive-bombers which plunged out of the sky and screamed down towards the vessel's broad flight deck. In less than nine minutes she was hit by six 1,000-pound bombs which penetrated the flight deck to the hangars below and turned the ship into a blazing inferno.

The Commander-in-Chief described the attack in his report: 'The attacks were pressed home to point blank. I saw her hit early on, just below the bridge, and in all, in something like ten minutes, she was hit by six 1,000-pound bombs, to leave the line badly on fire, her steering gear crippled, her lifts out of action, with heavy casualties.'

When the Luftwaffe left the scene the carrier was still afloat and under way. It took five hours to repair the steering gear. She was still on fire and later in the day the German aircraft found her again, but on this occasion her Fulmar fighters, which had flown back to Malta after the first attack, were overhead and shot down five of the Stukas and drove the rest off. *Illustrious* reached Malta late that night and repairs were undertaken immediately. She survived many more attacks before she was patched up and sailed for an American shipyard to be permanently repaired. She later re-entered service and rendered valuable support in other campaigns.

There were other victims of this operation. During the same afternoon and fifty miles to the east, the cruisers *Gloucester* and *Southampton* were hit by the Stukas. The damage sustained by *Southampton* was so heavy she was later torpedoed and sunk.

On land Wavell's army was scoring success after success. Bardia, Tobruk and Derna fell to the Desert Army and the Italians withdrew into Cyrenaica. In two months they left behind 130,000 prisoners of war, 400 tanks, 850 field guns and several thousand motor vehicles.

Unfortunately for Cunningham, similar victories did not come to the Royal Navy. In February the gunboat *Terror* and the destroyer *Dainty* were sunk by dive-bombers on the Libyan coast. Even more ominously, Luftwaffe aircraft operating from the Italian airfields in the Aegean were laying mines in the Suez Canal.

Early in the new year Churchill remembered the Commander-in-Chief's suggestion to seize Casteloriso for use as a springboard for knocking out the enemy's bases. He ordered Wavell to launch a commando attack for this purpose and his signal arrived within days of an unsuccessful attempt by No. 50 Middle East Commando to seize the island of Kasos.

Preparations for the Kasos operation had been hurried and bore the hallmark of failure. The commandos were embarked on the minelayer HMS *Derby* at Suda Bay in late January and arrived off Kasos unsighted. The boats were lowered but almost immediately filled with water. It was later learnt they had lain ashore on Crete for several months and the seams had opened.

Undeterred by this failure, the commandos were embarked in the destroyers *Hereward* and *Decoy* on 23 February and, escorted by the cruisers *Gloucester* and *Bonaventure* and the gunboat *Ladybird*, arrived off Casteloriso on the 25th. The commandos landed and, after a day of fighting, succeeded in taking the island. After dark, the naval support sailed for Cyprus to embark the garrison for the island, the Sherwood Foresters, and return on the night of the 26th. They failed to arrive, and during that night the Italians landed a strong force which recaptured Casteloriso on the following day.

When the ships arrived on the night of the 27th, it was soon discovered the island was in enemy hands. The naval commander of the operation was later removed from his command.

On a brighter note, a week later *Illustrious'* replacement, HMS *Formidable*, arrived. It was an opportune arrival for Cunningham as a decision had been reached to send British troops to Greece and the aircraft carrier and her planes were desperately needed to provide air cover for the convoys.

The first convoys sailed on 4 March, bound for the ports of the Piraeus and Volos on the east coast. In addition to providing escorts for the ships, Cunningham knew he would have to keep the battle fleet in the waters to the west of Crete to meet any threat from the Italians. Lighter forces were also required to patrol the western side of the island to guard against enemy light forces based in the Aegean. While the Commander-in-Chief was preparing these dispositions, he received news he had been made a Knight Grand Cross of the Order of the Bath. When congratulated by one of his staff, he remarked: 'I would rather have been given three squadrons of Hurricanes'.

ABC's next catastrophe came from the sea and not the air. Early on the morning of 26 March he learnt the 8-inch cruiser *York* had been sunk during the night by Italian explosive motor boats in Suda Bay. It was a loss he could ill afford. The Achilles' heel of Cunningham's battle fleet was the shortage of these hard-hitting ships which filled the gap between battleships and the 6-inch cruisers. His battleships, all of which were laid down early in the First World War, were a poor match for the Italian ships. *Warspite, Barham, Valiant* and *Malaya* all fought at the Battle of Jutland.

As March slowly passed, Cunningham's fears of an attack on the Greek convoys by the Italian fleet increased. An intelligence report, another ULTRA decrypt relating to the Mediterranean, reported a meeting between Admiral Raeder, the German Commander-in-Chief, and his Italian opposite number, Admiral Riccardi, and confirmed his fears. On the morning of 27 March a Malta-based Sunderland reconnaissance aircraft sighted enemy cruisers south of Sicily. Cunningham sailed the battle fleet from Alexandria that night to rendezvous with the cruiser squadron commanded by Vice-Admiral Pridham-Wippell south-west of Crete, in the vicinity of Gavdhos Island, at 1700 on the 28th.

Admiral Iachinio, with the Italian battle fleet, was already at sea and steaming east for Gavdhos. Aircraft from the *Formidable* reported four cruisers and six destroyers close to the rendezvous, astride the convoy route to Greece, at 0800 on the 28th. While Cunningham was waiting for confirmation of the identity of this sighting, his own fleet was found by a German reconnaissance aircraft which sent off a report to Iachino at 0900.

The enemy cruisers sighted by *Formidable*'s aircraft were the 8-inch ships *Trento, Trieste, Bolzano* and *Pola,* all of which were superior to the British cruisers in armament, speed and range.

At 0910 the opposing squadrons were in sight of each other. Admiral Pridham-Wippell's squadron—the cruisers *Orion, Ajax, Perth* and *Gloucester* with the destroyers *Ilex, Hasty, Hereward* and *Vendetta*—endeavoured to draw the enemy south towards the rapidly closing British battle fleet, but at 0912 he opened fire and engaged the cruisers.

Although the range was almost thirteen miles, shells fell close to *Gloucester.* The captain of the British cruiser held his fire hoping to entice the Italian ships to close the range, which they did very cautiously. At 0929 they altered course away and *Gloucester* fired a full salvo which unfortunately fell a mile short. Pridham-Wippell now realised his ploy had failed. The enemy was on a northerly course, opening the distance from Cunningham's battle fleet, and he took up a shadowing position. His destroyer force was reduced to three when the *Vendetta* signalled she was having engine trouble and was detached to fall back on the main fleet.

Cunningham, who was seventy miles south of the cruisers, was confused by the signals he was receiving from Pridham-Wippell. There were discrepancies in accounts of the strength of the enemy squadron. At 1030 the Commander-in-Chief was convinced the cruisers sighted by Pridham-Wippell were the only force at sea. However, at 1100 he was electrified by a series of emergency signals: 'Make smoke by all available means', 'Turn together to 180 degrees' and 'Proceed at your utmost speed'. It was evident the cruisers had stumbled onto something big.

Pridham-Wippell's signal to Cunningham followed several minutes later. He reported two battleships with destroyer escort were sixteen miles south of his squadron and he was steering south at 31 knots to join the battle fleet. Minutes later the Commander-in-Chief learnt that, in addition to the cruiser force originally sighted and the enemy battleship force, a third squadron consisting of five cruisers and a flotilla of destroyers was closing the enemy battleships. Cunningham was now like a blind man in a room without lights. The enemy held the initiative. If all three enemy forces closed the battle fleet or the cruiser force simultaneously, the Italians would have victory in their hands.

At 1100 Pridham-Wippell's squadron was steaming south at 31 knots, closely pursued by Admiral Iachino's flagship *Vittorio Veneto.* Minutes later, the cruisers *Orion* and *Gloucester* were straddled by 15-inch salvos from the battleship.

When the Commander-in-Chief received Pridham-Wippell's engagement signal he ordered *Formidable* to launch her torpedo bombers. The Swordfish delivered their first attack at 1127 and one probable hit was reported. Iachino was surprised by the appearance of carrier aircraft and turned away.

At 1148 Pridham-Wippell reported the enemy was no longer in sight, and accordingly reversed his course to the north. Fleet Air Arm and RAF aircraft were despatched from Maleme airfield on Crete and soon located the battleship and her escorts. The aircraft attacked the battleship, which had slowed down as a result of the earlier hit. No further damage was inflicted on *Vittorio Veneto* and she was joined by the other two enemy forces at 1915. The fleet was steaming north and its position was reported to be forty-five miles north of the British battle fleet.

Cunningham now ordered the 14th Destroyer Flotilla under Captain Mack to circle north and launch a torpedo attack on the enemy ships soon after dark.

Meanwhile, aircraft of the Fleet Air Arm launched the last air attack of the day. This attack was to decide the outcome of the battle. The cruiser *Pola* was torpedoed in the engine-room and was left stopped in the water. At 2015, Pridham-Wippell picked up radar contact with a large ship stopped six miles to the north. The Commander-in-Chief ordered the battle fleet to close the vessel. However, unknown to Cunningham, Admiral Iachino had detached the 8-inch cruisers *Zara* and *Fiume* and four destroyers to find the *Pola*. At 2200 the two forces were converging on the hapless cruiser at 25 knots.

For sixty tense minutes the battle fleet pounded through the darkness and then, at 2225, two large cruisers of the *Zara* Class were sighted stopped in the water by *Warspite's* lookouts. The enemy was within point-blank range of the battleship's 15-inch guns.

As the guns fired their first salvo, the scene was illuminated by the searchlights of a destroyer. Five of the six shells fired in the first salvo tore into the nearest cruiser's side several feet below the waterline. It was later learnt that the officer in charge of the destroyer's searchlight was Lieutenant, Prince Phillip of Greece and Denmark, and later the Duke of Edinburgh.

When the cruiser sank, Cunningham ordered his destroyers in to sink the other two cruisers which had also been hit by the *Warspite's* fire. In the wild melee which followed racing destroyers crisscrossed the battle scene firing torpedoes and raking their victims with point-blank gunfire. The three cruisers *Pola*, *Fiume* and *Zara*, along with an enemy destroyer which came to their aid, were all sunk.

Fifty years were to pass before it became known that Admiral Cunningham's victory at Matapan owed much to ULTRA. Full details of the Italian battle plans were in the hands of the British Commander-in-Chief before he sailed from Alexandria. The intercept of the plans were made by the secret British Intelligence team at Bletchley Park in England seventy-two hours earlier. The decrypt was a message to the Luftwaffe to enable them to launch air attacks on the British fleet. With this information, Cunningham despatched a reconnaissance aircraft to sight the enemy cruiser squadron which was to operate north of Crete. This sighting decided Iachino to concentrate his full force south of the island.

Both Churchill and Cunningham expected greater rewards from the Battle of Matapan. They had been dealt the perfect gambler's hand and yet, had not *Pola* been damaged by the Swordfish's torpedo, the results may well have been nil. Such are the fortunes of war. Nevertheless, Matapan saved the troop convoys to Greece from heavy losses. Of more importance still, it demoralised the Italian Fleet, dealing it a blow from which it never recovered.

Vice-Admiral Weichold, the German Naval Representative in Italy, commented at the time: 'The unhappy result of this action, the first offensive operation which the Italian

Fleet had undertaken through German pressure after nine months of war, was a shattering blow to the Italian Navy and its prestige'.

The dash and aggressiveness of the Australian ships in his command had impressed Cunningham from the outbreak of hostilities in the Mediterranean and it was no surprise Australian volunteers were selected for an operation deep in the heart of Europe.

3

Operation Iron Gates

The eastern Mediterranean has long lent itself to intrigue and special operations. Small groups of men have appeared unheralded from the desert or the sea, or even fallen from the skies, and vanished just as covertly. Their origins and their destinations were known only to a few. The purpose of their strange perambulations were rarely reported in official records and their names found no place in official histories, not even when their activities influenced the outcome of battles or the future of nations.

Operation Iron Gates was planned and refined by Commander Ian Fleming, RNVR, later the author of the James Bond series of spy novels. In October 1939 Fleming was an aide to Admiral Roger Bellairs, the recently appointed Co-Ordinator of Secret Intelligence. At one of the first meetings of the War Cabinet, he proposed an operation to block the Danube River at Kazan Gorge in Rumania, where the river narrows to pass between great granite cliffs known as the Iron Gates. Through this gorge passed Germany's main oil supplies and a variety of raw materials, such as copper and chrome, for her war industries.

It is certain that Winston Churchill, recently appointed First Lord of the Admiralty, and Admiral A.B. Cunningham, Commander-in-Chief, Mediterranean, were involved in or were aware of the plan, but neither man referred to it in their autobiographies.

The man who made the plan possible was Britain's leading Grand Prix driver and an amateur spy, Merlin Minshall, who in 1933 undertook a voyage from the North Sea to the Black Sea, which carried him up the Rhine and down the Danube. Soon after entering the Rhine, he came under the eyes of the German secret police who warned him he risked physical and other dangers if he persisted with the voyage.

The veiled threats did not deter Minshall, although several attempts were made to sink his old Dutch river barge early in the adventure, and two attempts were made on his life shortly after he entered the Rumanian stretch of the Danube. Despite the threats and the attempted violence, Minshall continued.

The Rumanian police then placed a writ on the barge, claiming the vessel was not licensed to sail in their waters. This ploy had been foreseen by Minshall, who had obtained an international license for ships undertaking scientific research. The writ was withdrawn.

When he arrived at Kazan Gorge, the reason for the German concern became obvious. It was difficult for him to avoid it. A large fleet of tankers and bulk cargo vessels, the majority of more than 5,000 tons displacement, were passing out of the gorge which was marked on the river chart as 'navigatable for vessels of less than 1,000 tons displacement'. The German secret was a great lock in the gorge, built into the granite walls of the

Iron Gates, to allow large vessels to bypass the rapids. A railway had been built on the Rumanian side of the river, along which immense locomotives towed the ships against the current. The impassable barrier to large ships was no longer impassable.

On his return to England, Minshall presented a report on his discoveries to the Admiralty.

A plan to block the Danube in the eventuality of war was prepared by Naval Intelligence in 1938, but was rejected by the conservative Admiralty as impractical. However, it was revived in early 1940 and the new First Lord, Winston Churchill, gave it immediate approval. Commander Fleming was appointed project leader.

In February 1940 the British Ambassador at Ankara sought permission from the Turkish government for a company of Royal Engineers to be stationed at the Black Sea entrance of the Danube to study river siltation. The request was approved and the troops set up their base, but German reaction was immediate and the Turks were forced to eject the engineers. Commander Fleming, who had proposed the use of Royal Navy personnel, now asked Churchill to obtain fifty volunteers from the Mediterranean Fleet. Admiral Cunningham asked Captain Waller to provide the volunteers from the Australian destroyers.

When Waller called for volunteers, ten times the number required came forward. The winter of 1939–40 on the monotonous convoys from Marseilles to Haifa had been sheer misery for the sailors. Their old ships were classified as 'hard lying' and the crew were paid an allowance of sixpence a day as recompense for the complete lack of amenities. Chief Petty Officer Fred Thompson summed up the feelings of all his shipmates in a desultory diary entry at this time: 'Cold and gray for the most part. Spotted a portion of Corsica—snow fell.'

With the withdrawal of the army, Fleming recast his plans for the operation. Minshall, now a lieutenant, was to command the operation in Rumania. He was already in Bucharest on the staff of the ambassador as a vice-consul and the appointment provided him with excellent cover and ample freedom to make arrangements for the operation.

Fleming's plan was two-pronged. He had found six large river vessels at the nearby port of Braila, six hours steaming from the Iron Gates, which were British-owned. These he arranged to be secretly chartered to the Royal Navy. The German skippers were paid off with a handsome bonus and six British officers were appointed in their place. In mid-February, twelve regular service engine-room petty officers arrived at Braila as distressed Russian seamen and were smuggled on board the ships. They were responsible for maintaining the ships' engines and guarding the vessels.

The second prong was provided by six river steamers at the Black Sea end of the river. These vessels, when their crews arrived, would sail up the river to the Iron Gates and be scuttled on river bars at the downriver end of the Kazan Gorge.

The Australian volunteers, kitted out as merchant seamen, sailed from Malta in a disreputable Turkish-owned tramp. They passed through the Italian-garrisoned islands of the Aegean without arousing suspicion and arrived at the river mouth. All six vessels were waiting and the sailors transferred to them at night. Each steamer had a river pilot aboard and three Turkish crewmen. The cargo was already loaded in the holds, layer after layer of tinned fish oil and, at the bottom, two layers of TNT.

When Minshall's activities in Bucharest attracted the attention of the Rumanian secret police, he soon discovered they were distracted by large bribes paid in British gold sovereigns. However, unknown to him, a member of the British Ambassador's staff was in the pay of German Intelligence.

Minshall's duties required him to travel on the Orient Express to carry diplomatic mail from France. Included in each consignment were a number of bags which contained cartons labelled 'Mackintosh Toffee'. Each carton contained twelve large slabs of Torpex explosive cast in the factory moulds and identical in appearance to the genuine slabs of toffee. These consignments were the scuttling charges for the ships at Braila.

On one of these courier journeys, Minshall returned to his compartment and surprised a man slitting open the toffee cartons. Minshall throttled the intruder, stripped him of all clothing and threw the body out of the toilet window. A bribe of 5,000 gold sovereigns bought the silence of the Rumanian police.

In the last week of March, Minshall's preparations were almost complete. The Australians were well on their way and the ships in the harbour at Braila had their scuttling charges in place. Each member of the crew had his escape clothes, passports and permits, rail tickets and a considerable sum of money.

Minshall had acquired a fast motor launch through the embassy and he used this to maintain contact with the ships. The launch would also carry him into the gorge on the night of the operation. On 29 March the Australians were forty miles downstream and Minshall decided to carry out the blocking operation on the 30th. That day, things went wrong.

At 1000, a confidential telephone call informed him the six barges coming upriver had been seized by the Rumanian secret police. There was nothing Minshall could do without compromising the other prong of the operation, so he waited until darkness, then slipped down to the launch and set off downriver to Braila and the other six ships.

Everything appeared normal on board and there was nothing to arouse Minshall's suspicions. He checked that the scuttling charges were still in place and told the senior officer on each ship he would return at 2330 and they would then move into the gorge. As Minshall went over the side, the senior Royal Navy petty officer thanked him for providing overnight leave to all hands on the previous night. The words stopped him in his tracks. No such concession had been granted.

A quick search of the ship's hold showed all of the detonators had been removed from the charges and Minshall knew at once that the Germans had been warned of the operation. He was not beaten, however. In the next thirty minutes he had all six ships ready to cast off. They were to follow him in the launch and be run aground on the river bar below the lock. The current would swing the sinking vessels across the entrance of the channel.

The first vessel eased out of the harbour and silently turned upstream. Two hundred yards from the river entrance, her engines stopped. Minshall went alongside, but he already knew the explanation. The fuel tanks of all six ships had been drained. Minshall returned to the launch and set off upstream at full speed. In his duffle bag was the last package of Torpex. This he would use on the secondary target, the towing locomotive on the lock side.

As the launch turned into the main stream of the river, two large Rumanian patrol boats swept out from the shore on an interception course. As Minshall's launch was ten knots faster, he swung between the boats and drew away upstream. Two hours later he was well into the gorge and nearing the lock. The current was running so fast he was forced to close the bank. One hundred yards short of the locomotive wall he crashed the launch into the rocks and leapt ashore.

The huge locomotive towered above him. It was claimed to be the largest of its kind in the world, two powerful diesel traction engines on one great chassis with driving cabs at both ends. Fleming had told Minshall that destruction of the engine would close the lock for months.

A light in the cab at the south end of the locomotive told him the crew were still on board. Minshall climbed the rough bank and when he reached the railway track he lay still, recovering his breath and listening for possible sentries. He waited five minutes, then crawled along the track until the open door of the occupied cab was immediately above him.

Minshall drew his pistol and noiselessly climbed the ladder, stopping at floor level. Three men in blue overalls were lounging in front of the control panel. He aimed carefully, and shot all three. He now opened the Mackintosh Toffee carton and set charges behind the control panel, under the diesel engines and in the gigantic fuel tank. Hurrying back to the control cab, he stepped over the dead crew, started the engines, pulled the throttle to maximum, released the brakes and dived out of the landside of the cab.

He climbed the embankment and lay under a bush. The locomotive was roaring down the track to a slight bend where the waterway changed direction. Normally, it would have been travelling at walking speed, hauling a ship of 5,000 tons, but now there was nothing to stop its flight. One minute it was travelling through the air, then the front end dipped and the whole roaring mass plunged into the racing waters of the Iron Gates. A huge pillar of purple-hued flame rose a hundred feet into the air, illuminating the cliffs as the fuel tanks exploded.

Lieutenant Minshall, wearing the uniform of an officer of the Rumanian Customs, left Rumania in a first-class compartment of the Orient Express. Ten days later he reported to Commander Fleming in London.

The Australian sailors were removed to a police barracks where, after an interrogation, they were well cared for. Twenty-four hours later they walked out of the unlocked doors of their rooms. No attempt was made to take them back into custody and several months later they returned to their ships in the Mediterranean, Minshall's contingency fund having paved the way for their escape.

All fifty sailors were interrogated later at Alexandria by British Intelligence officers and swore an oath of secrecy. No record of Operation Iron Gates appeared in the Official History of the Navy in the Second World War. However, the following small item did appear in the *Adelaide Advertiser* of 25 July 1941, under the headline 'VAMPIRE'S MEN IN DANUBE EXPLOIT/THRILLING STORIES BY MEN ON LEAVE':

'A dangerous eight months journey along the Danube, before which members of the expedition had been told that if their job was done properly, many might not escape alive, was among heroic adventures described by seven South Australian seamen from HMAS *Vampire* who reached Adelaide yesterday.

'Able Seaman J. Dix of Port Lincoln told of a call for 50 volunteers for a party to proceed up the Danube with the object of blasting away its cliff banks at the spot known

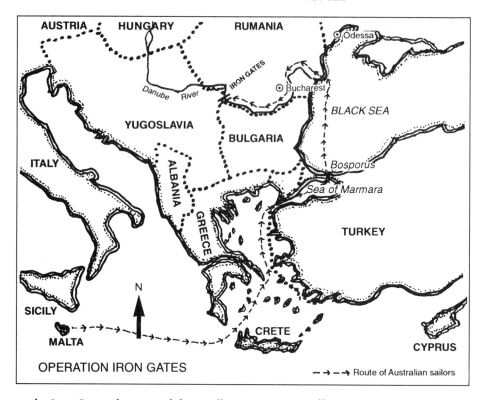

OPERATION IRON GATES

— → — → Route of Australian sailors

as the Iron Gates, thus immobilising all German river traffic. Starting from Malta, the sailors made their way through the Dardanelles and started up the Danube in flat-bottomed oil lighters laden with 100 tons of explosives.

'Rumanian [river] pilots, however, recognised them 150 miles from the German border and 50 miles from their objective, and reported them to the German Consulate. Their equipment was seized, but they managed to escape down the river.

The blocking of the Danube was one of a number of operations bordering on the fantastic undertaken by British Intelligence in the first years of the war. Another was the seizure of three German passenger and cargo vessels held in the Vichy French port of Dakar. This operation was undertaken by a small group of amateurs and succeeded beyond all expectations. Two of the ships were sunk and the third, a large passenger cargo ship, was steamed to an Allied port.

In 1939 only a small number of people outside Germany were aware the Danube was navigatable by large ships for the whole of its length and the bulk of Germany's war materials were being shipped by this route. Indeed, it was only thanks to Merlin Minshall's bizarre voyage in 1933 that this knowledge was obtained by British Intelligence.

The locks at the Iron Gates were unusable for several months and cargoes of vital oil were unloaded at Braila and transferred by road around the blockage. The effect of these delays on German plans for the assaults on Holland and France in May was considerable.

Merlin Minshall was involved in other strange activities before and during the Second

World War. Not the least of these was an expedition he undertook to find a passable passage from the Western Desert to Central Africa. Aware that a normal vehicle, dependent on water cooling, could not traverse the waterless sand areas, he designed a water-cooled three-wheeled truck for the purpose and succeeded in finding a route, despite attempts by French and German authorities to stop him. The maps he made on this epic journey were available for British generals in the Western Desert Campaign.

As with so much of Minshall's life, little else is known of his service in the war, but in early 1944 he arrived in Yugoslavia. The former Grand Prix driver spoke the Yugoslav language fluently and he was appointed special liaison officer to General Tito's headquarters. In this capacity he organised a successful gun-running operation to supply the Partisans with much needed arms. MLs *361, 368* and *386* were used in this vital and dangerous service. When hostilities ended, General Tito admitted he distrusted the British and American officers who were sent to him on liaison duties, but there was one exception, Lieutenant Commander Merlin Minshall, RNVR.

4

The Glorious Failure of Greece

To most nations, winning is the golden fleece, but to Britain and Greece, to fight against great odds and to fight to the end was the stuff of heroes. And so it was in Greece in 1941, when three British divisions joined the battle-weary Greek Army to rattle their shields in the face of the thirty-one division German Army. And when it ended in inevitable defeat the Greeks did not castigate their allies—they deified them.

In one of the last battles of the campaign, when Australian troops were fighting with their backs to the sea at Markopolous near Porto Rafti, the author heard a Greek peasant remark: 'And now the blood of Australians and New Zealanders is mingled forever in the sacred soil of Greece'.

When Mussolini issued his ultimatum to Greece in October 1940, Winston Churchill saw the opportunity of re-establishing a British Army on the continent. A British–Greek alliance could bring other European nations into the war against the Axis powers. This possibility became a reality when the Greeks hurled the Italian Army back into Albania, where the exhausted armies remained locked in a stalemate for five months.

In December, Churchill learnt through ULTRA of Hitler's plans to follow in the footsteps of Napoleon and invade Russia. He also learnt the capture of Turkey was a prerequisite of the plan. Finally, American sources informed him Yugoslavia would resist any Axis move against Greece. Acting on this information, he made the decision to offer assistance to the Greeks. Seven weeks later, the British Foreign Minister, Sir Anthony Eden, and Field Marshal Sir John Dill opened negotiations to provide aid to the Greeks if they were attacked. The Greek government was reluctant to accept such aid, fearing it would precipitate an attack.

However, three weeks later, Admiral Cunningham was ordered to prepare plans for transporting an army of 60,000 troops and their equipment to Greece. The logistics of the operation were daunting. The army would require 8,588 trucks, 300 field guns of all calibres, 80 tanks, 30 armoured cars, 5 field hospitals, 3 field workshops and many thousands of tons of ammunition and rations to last the force three months. The number of ships required to carry the force and its equipment would require the transfer of shipping from the Red Sea and India. Escort vessels could only come from the battle fleet, which would be left without its vital cruisers and destroyers.

Cunningham knew the Royal Air Force lacked the aircraft to provide air cover for the convoys which must pass within 100 miles of enemy air bases. The arrival of the Luftwaffe in the Mediterranean only months earlier had already cost him valuable ships.

Passage through the Suez Canal could not be guaranteed with enemy aircraft laying mines in the vital lifeline. Even the fleet base at Alexandria was within range of enemy bombers.

The Commander-in-Chief appreciated the gamble he was taking in running the convoys to Greece. If the Italian battle fleet intervened his fleet would be at a disadvantage. He remembered Nelson's precept—'Victory does not necessarily go to the strongest fleet, but to the fleet which makes the least mistakes'—and ordered the convoys to commence.

The first convoy, AG 1, sailed from Alexandria on 4 March 1941. It consisted of five transports escorted by the cruisers *Gloucester, York* and *Bonaventure*. All ships, including the escorts, carried troops. It was followed a day later by AN17, with six transports escorted by the cruiser *Coventry*, the destroyers *Stuart* and *Hereward* and the corvette *Hyacinth*. AG 1 reached Piraeus safely, but AN 17 was sighted by enemy aircraft and came under attack. *Stuart* was near-missed but was able to proceed. Her commanding officer, Captain Waller, later remarked: 'The last aircraft was after my blood'.

The first loss occurred on 21 March when Convoy AN 21, thirteen merchant ships with a destroyer escort, was attacked by a force of Stuka dive-bombers and Dorniers as it was passing through the narrow Kythera Channel. The 8271-ton *Marie Maersk* was hit close to the bridge by a heavy bomb which set the ship on fire. Casualties were heavy among the crew and passengers. *Waterhen* went alongside the ship, which had stopped, and took off thirty-two of the crew. When Commander Swain noticed the ship was not sinking he placed a steaming party, led by Lieutenant C.G. Hill, RANR, a former merchant officer, on board.

Assisted by *Marie Maersk*'s second engineer, Hill rigged hoses to confine the fire and the engines were restarted. However, soon after getting under way the steering gear failed and Hill steered by the engines until hand-steering was rigged. The fire was brought under control during the night and Hill worked the ship up to full speed. At noon, as they were approaching Suda Bay, an aircraft was sighted overhead. Hill recorded in his log: 'We all greatly appreciated one of our own fighters overhead'.

Marie Maersk was saved with the loss of only 500 tons of her cargo of 10,000 tons of oil. Hill was made a Member of the Order of the British Empire for his salvage of the ship.

On 25 March, Cunningham learnt from intelligence sources the Italian battle fleet was putting to sea. He immediately withdrew some of his cruisers and destroyers from the convoys to reinforce his battle fleet, which had been weakened on the 21st when one of his two 8-inch cruisers, *York*, was sunk at Suda Bay by Italian explosive motor boats. It was a loss he could ill afford.

The battle fleet put to sea at noon on 27 March to patrol the waters between Crete and the Greek mainland. On the night of the 28th the Battle of Matapan was fought and not only was the *York* revenged three times over, but the threat of Italian attacks on the convoys was reduced.

Cunningham's exhilaration following Matapan evaporated when he returned to Alexandria. On that day, Rommel launched his attack on Cyrenaica and within hours Wavell was calling for navy gunfire support along the coast road. The Desert Army was no match for the Panzer army, which soon swept them back to the Egyptian border. A scratch force of sloops and gunboats was diverted to Benghazi and Tobruk, but there was little they could do to stop the revitalised Axis armies.

On 27 March the Germans struck south into the Balkans.

Convoy AG 9 was approaching Crete, steaming into the path of the two fleets which were sparring for positions south of Cape Matapan. Cunningham ordered it back to Alexandria and GA 8, the southward-bound convoy, was held in Piraeus. GA 8, escorted by the destroyers *Stuart, Hereward* and *Griffin*, sailed on its interrupted voyage on the 29th and was joined by the cruiser *Bonaventure* off Crete. All went well with the convoy until 0300 on the 31st, when midway between Crete and Alexandria. The Italian submarine *Dagabur* was laying athwart the convoy's course and fired two torpedoes which hit the *Bonaventure*. The cruiser sank in minutes, taking 210 or her crew with her.

Stuart, the next in line, increased speed and ran down the torpedo tracks dropping depth charges. When the second pattern exploded, *Dagabur* was forced to the surface. Unfortunately, there was no vessel backing up, and by the time *Stuart* had turned the submarine had dived deep and contact was lost. A disappointed Captain Waller joined the other escorts picking up survivors from the cruiser. In all, 310 were saved.

The last supply convoy to Greece was AN 27, which came under heavy dive-bomber attacks in the Cretan Sea, during which the 6,098-ton tanker *British Lord* was hit and sunk. Twenty-four hours later the southbound Convoy AS 23 was attacked south of Gavdhos Island and the 5,324-ton *British Homefield* and the 4,914-ton *Couloutos Xenos* were sunk.

Between 22 March and 18 April, a total of twenty-five merchant ships were lost, only seven while in convoy.

Many of the escorts were handicapped by their poor anti-aircraft armament and had little defence against massed air attacks. Commander Walsh of the Australian destroyer *Vampire* wrote in a report: 'We had a 12-pounder H.A. gun fitted in Alexandria when the after torpedo tubes were removed. I gather it was a German World War I piece with the marking "Pietermaritzburg 200". The ammunition provided was 10 rounds. I claim we got a torpedo bomber south of Crete with our last round—nobody else claimed him when he crashed in the Kythera Channel.'

Cunningham did not wait for the army to reach the decision to evacuate. Ten days before this came about, his officers were requisitioning every merchant ship they could find in the eastern Mediterranean capable of a return voyage to Greece. He immobilised the battle fleet and ordered its cruisers, *Orion, Ajax, Perth, Phoebe, Calcutta, Coventry* and *Carlisle*, to join the destroyers and sloops in preparing to bring the army back. On board the flagship *Warspite*, swinging around her buoy in Alexandria's old Western Harbour, Cunningham studied the relative dispositions of his ships, the enemy air bases and the shrinking line of the troops in Greece. It was a depressing sight. Nelson's dictum was not far from his mind: 'I wish there were twice as many, the easier the victory, depend upon it.'

The first rescue convoy, AG 13, arrived at Suda Bay on 23 April when the army's front line was a few miles south of Lamia. On that day the Australian and New Zealand governments approved the renaming of the British, Australian and New Zealand force the Anzac Corps. For ten long days they had carried out a classic retreat. There was no sign of rout, despite the overwhelming superiority of the enemy. The positions they defended were selected to deny the enemy the use of his greater strength. They fought their actions in narrow mountain passes through which the enemy could advance only on one-lane roads. During the long and bitterly contested withdrawal, the Germans failed to turn a single Allied position. The Anzacs exacted a high toll in enemy casualties.

Movement on the winding mountain roads was restricted to the hours of darkness. From dawn until dusk the Luftwaffe was in undisputed command of the skies. The least movement on the ground attracted relays of dive-bombers and strafing fighter-bombers. The last of the RAF Hurricanes had pulled back to protect Athens and the beaches from which troops were already being evacuated.

The Greek government warned the Commander-in-Chief on 21 April that their forces could not continue resistance for more than twenty-four hours. Cunningham immediately alerted the evacuation armada. At 0900 on the 22nd, the first evacuation convoy—the cruiser *Calcutta*, destroyers *Stuart* and *Voyager* and the landing ships *Glengyle* and *Glenearn* and the transport *Ulster Prince*—sailed from Alexandria. The ships were bound for Nauplia where 5,000 troops were already assembled. During the day they were joined by the cruiser *Phoebe*. At Suda Bay the convoy was broken into two divisions: *Calcutta*, *Perth*, *Glengyle* and *Salvia* sailed for Porto Rafti; *Phoebe*, *Stuart*, *Voyager*, *Hyacinth*, *Glenearn* and *Ulster Prince* for Nauplion.

The Porto Rafti force arrived at the small resort before midnight on the 23rd, where they were joined by the sloops *Auckland* and *Grimsby*. Four thousand New Zealand troops were embarked and the convoy sailed at 0200. At 1200 on the 24th they were found by a flight of Ju 88 fighter-bombers and came under attack. The barrage put up by the ships, supported by the mass fire of machine-guns and rifles of the New Zealanders, proved too much for the enemy. One aircraft was shot down into the sea and two others were hit. The convoy arrived at Suda Bay without loss at 1750.

The second force was off Nauplia at 1700 on the 23rd, and thirty minutes later was attacked by a large number of Stuka dive-bombers. *Glengyle* was hit on the stern by a 500-pound bomb which blew her 4-inch gun and its platform into the sea. Luckily, it exploded at deck level and the propeller and rudders were not damaged. One and a half hours later, a flight of Heinkel 111 torpedo bombers arrived. The ships, which were under way, turned to face their attackers and the torpedoes ran down their sides. One aircraft was hit and was last seen low to the sea, trailing a long plume of black smoke.

The ships entered Nauplia Bay at 2000, but *Ulster Prince*, the largest, ran aground on a reef. *Voyager* was nearby and passed a tow. The ship was freed. *Glengyle*'s landing barges were soon in the water and, assisted by ships' boats and two caiques, soon had a continuous stream of troops moving from the shore to the ships. Several enemy aircraft circled the bay at 2030, but no bombs were dropped.

Many acts of bravery were performed by naval personnel during the evacuation. One of the first occurred that night, when a caique was transferring Australian Army nurses to *Voyager*. A steep swell rolling in from the open sea was causing the two vessels to grind together. The caique swung away from the destroyer's side as one nurse was jumping across the gap and she plunged into the water between the grinding hulls. AB C.J. Webb immediately jumped into the turbulent water and dragged the heavily clad nurse deep beneath the surface before the hulls came together again. Alternately diving and swimming, the young sailor swam the nurse to the stern of the destroyer, where both were dragged aboard.

By 0330, a total of 3,500 troops were embarked and the ships weighed anchor. All went well until *Ulster Prince*, manoeuvring to pass out of the bay, once more ran aground. *Voyager* went to her assistance but the heavy vessel was firmly held by the reef. The cruiser *Phoebe* closed the stricken transport and took off her passengers and crew. Dawn was close at hand and the convoy increased speed to clear the coast before the enemy aircraft arrived. At daybreak they were joined by *Perth* and Suda Bay was reached at 1750 without further loss. *Ulster Prince* was found by German bombers soon after first light and was bombed until she became a blazing wreck.

On 25 April, celebrated as Anzac Day in Australia and New Zealand, Convoy AN 29, consisting of the transport *Pennland* and the escorts *Griffin, Decoy, Hasty, Waterhen* and *Vendetta*, came under heavy air attack north of Crete. The 16,032-ton transport was hit by a heavy bomb and immediately lost speed. She was detached and sent back to Crete, escorted by *Griffin*.

The remainder of the convoy reached Megara at 2100 and *Vendetta* was sent into the bay to contact the troops ashore. She glided through the dark waters with her guns trained on the shore but found no sign of the 7,000 troops awaiting evacuation. The destroyer stopped off a small jetty and sent an officer ashore in one of the boats. When the boat was twenty yards off the jetty, the officer hailed the shore. An unmistakably Australian voice replied out of the dark: 'Who in the hell do you think you are?'

Vendetta embarked 350 troops and sixty wounded, using her whaler and smaller boats, and then moved out into the stream to allow *Waterhen* to come alongside the jetty. Commander Swain sent his whaler in, but there were no troops on the beach. Leading Seaman R.E. Smyth volunteered to go ashore and make contact. He was landed beside the jetty, walked twenty yards and blundered into a patrol of German soldiers. Smyth escaped in the darkness and several minutes later found the first British perimeter guard.

The whaler had followed Smyth and took him and the first troops back to the destroyer. *Waterhen* took off 400 soldiers and rejoined *Vendetta*. Both destroyers then stood out of the bay to rejoin the convoy, but as they passed the entrance a caique with 250 wounded aboard was sighted aground on the northern headland. Commander Rhoades of *Vendetta* signalled the command ship *Coventry* for permission to embark the wounded but permission was refused. It was a painful decision, but correct in the circumstances, as delay would prevent the convoy from clearing the coast by first light.

The convoy came under air attack soon after daylight, but once again the dive-bombers were held at bay by the combined fire of the ships' guns and the soldiers' weapons. It arrived at Suda Bay at 1800.

On that night, 600 miles to the south, Cunningham and his staff in *Warspite* were assessing the results of the previous night's evacuation. At the conclusion of the meeting, the Commander-in-Chief turned to his staff and said: 'The Battle Fleet will not let them down. Another *Warspite* opened the Levant to British ships in 1694 and later took Gibraltar for Britain. This ship and her consorts will do everything to maintain that fighting tradition.' The admiral was informing his officers the fleet would put to sea to support the evacuation.

Convoy AG 15, transports *Iowia, Corinthia, Itria* and *Comliebank* escorted by the destroyers *Kimberley* and *Vampire* and the sloop *Auckland*, sailed from Alexandria on 24 April and on the morning of the 26th was passing through Kaso Strait when it was ordered to lend assistance to the *Scottish Prince*. The ship had been heavily damaged by enemy aircraft and abandoned. *Vampire* was detached to assist. The Australian destroyer found the transport north of Crete and put her engineer aboard to assess the damage. It was soon discovered the ship was not sinking and could steam at reduced speed.

Commander Walsh put a steaming party aboard and soon the small convoy, joined by the sloop *Grimsby*, was heading for Suda Bay where it arrived safely at 0610 on the 27th.

The German airmen soon discovered the transports were a more vulnerable and less dangerous target than the warships. At 1640 on the 26th, Convoy AG 14 was found by a flight of Stukas which concentrated their attack on the landing ship *Glenearn* and the *Khedive Ismail*. *Glenearn* was hit and severely damaged and the destroyer *Griffin* was detached to escort her to Kisamos Bay.

Cunningham now despatched the cruisers *Orion* and *Perth* to reinforce the threatened AG 14, which was bound for Nauplion. Since the destruction of *Ulster Prince*, Nauplia Bay embarkation of troops had become more hazardous. The larger ships could not enter and stood off the coast while the troops were ferried out. *Calcutta, Diamond, Isis, Hotspur, Slamat* and *Khedive Ismail* arrived off the bay at 2000 on the 26th and embarkation commenced immediately, using ships' boats and caiques. Loading proved slow and, when *Orion* and *Perth* joined the ships at 2300, only 1,000 troops had been taken off.

The slow ships sailed at 0300 on the 27th. Four hours later they came under heavy air attack. *Slamat* was hit by two bombs and set on fire. Casualties were heavy and the survivors were taken off by *Diamond*. The other destroyer, *Wryneck*, was left to escort the damaged transport to Suda Bay. All three ships failed to arrive at Suda Bay. At 1025, a signal was received from *Wryneck* requesting fighter protection. This was the last message from the destroyer. A raft from the ship, containing a few survivors, was picked up by *Griffin* on the 28th. German records show the two destroyers and the transport were sunk by dive-bombers on the afternoon of the 27th. Cunningham added three more names to the 'butcher's bill' for Greece.

Hero and *Hereward* were despatched to Kalamata on the night of 26–27th to make arrangements for the embarkation of 10,000 troops known to be in the area. Commander H.W. Biggs was put ashore to investigate the position and was surprised to find only 400 RAF personnel and 150 soldiers. However, the remainder of the force was some miles inland. The two destroyers took 3,000 troops out to waiting ships and another 3,800 were ferried out in ships' boats and caiques. When the convoy sailed at 0340 on the 27th, it was estimated another 9,000 were still in the area.

On this day, several convoys were heading south for Crete. Convoy GA 14, which included the transports *Salween, Khedive Ismail, Dilwara, City of London* and *Costa Rica* escorted by the destroyers *Defender* and *Hereward* and the landing ship *Glengyle*, was within seventy miles of Suda Bay. At 1500 it was found by three dive-bombers which screamed down on the convoy and near-missed the *Costa Rica*, opening her seams. The destroyers took off the passengers and crew before she sank.

The effectiveness of the small arms and machine-guns of the troops surprised both sailors and the enemy airmen. The captain of the *City of London* recorded his anti-aircraft defence was increased by 84 Vickers, Bren and Hotchkiss machine-guns, 30 anti-tank rifles and more than 500 rifles.

On 0925 on 27 April, German motorised units entered Athens as British troops were withdrawing through the city. The 2/3rd Australian Field Regiment had the unique experience of moving down one of the city's thoroughfares as enemy motorised infantry was moving up a parallel street. The Australians were en route for Markopoulon, east of the city, to form the last defence line around the embarkation port of Porto Rafti.

The position of the large number of troops in the Kalamata area was still confused on the 28th. Throughout the day strong German forces closed on the port, compressing the British in a narrow strip of beach and the port area. Brigadier Parrington, the senior officer in the area, signalled Rear Admiral Pridham-Wippell he was trying to marshal the 8,000 troops adjacent to the town. His task was made more difficult by the large number of non-English speaking soldiers in the force. These included Indian mule drivers, Palestinian and Cypriot labourers and a large group of Yugoslav and Lascar survivors from sunken ships. His fighting troops, Australian and New Zealand, numbered about 1,000.

Pridham-Wippell replied a final embarkation would be undertaken on the night of 28–29 April. Less than an hour after this signal was received, German motorised troops were seen approaching the town. Before Parrington could move his force, tanks and motorised artillery captured Kalamata. Parrington rallied his remaining fighting troops and launched a fierce counter-attack at 2015. Heavy fighting ensued around the port area, but after determined bayonet attacks by the Australians and New Zealanders, the enemy was driven back, abandoning their mobile guns. Enemy casualties were high: 41 killed, 60 wounded and more than 100 prisoners.

Although the position was still unknown, Pridham-Wippell had ordered his ships to Kalamata. *Hero* was sent ahead to try to contact the troops and at 2015, when approaching the evacuation area, received a signal from Parrington warning German troops were in the port.

Hero's commanding officer was not satisfied and landed his first lieutenant, Lieutenant Commander R.F.G. Ellswort, to establish the position. Heavy tracer fire was observed in the town, but Ellswort landed at the quay and contacted Parrington. It was agreed to attempt the evacuation. *Hero* made her report and immediately commenced taking off the wounded. At 0100 she was joined by *Kandahar, Kimberley* and *Kingston*, which had been sent to escort *Hero* clear. These destroyers embarked another 100 wounded and 300 troops before they left at 0300.

At first light, Parrington marshalled his force and informed them the evacuation was ended. He gave them the options of surrendering or scattering in the countryside. At 0530, the gallant force at Kalamata surrendered. Pridham-Wippell, alarmed at the number of troops still at the port, sent in destroyers on the next night, but only 250 stragglers were found.

The final evacuation from Greece took place on the night of 30 April–1 May. *Hotspur* and *Havock* rescued 700 British troops from the island of Milos and landed them at Suda Bay.

And so, the Royal Navy honoured its pledge to take the Expeditionary Force to Greece and bring it back again. By sunset on 1 May a total of 50,662 had been evacuated, but 14,861 remained to be taken prisoner of war or to make their own way home. More than 1,000 chose the latter.

Cunningham had expected the Italian fleet to make a sortie in the closing days of the evacuation and during the afternoon of 29 April the 1st Battle Squadron, the battleships

Barham and *Valiant*, the aircraft carrier *Formidable* and the five old Australian destroyers *Stuart, Vampire, Vendetta, Voyager* and *Waterhen* sailed from Alexandria to patrol the Kaso Strait. The Italian fleet was not sighted and Admiral Rawlings brought his fleet back to Alexandria on 2 May to find he could not enter—German aircraft had mined the port.

Several days later, Cunningham commented: 'The Army's faith in the Navy was purchased by the loss of some valuable ships and lives of many brave sailors'. This faith was confirmed on the following day when a New Zealand private presented to him £900 for distribution to navy charities. The money was donated by New Zealand soldiers evacuated from Greece.

5

The Holocaust in Crete

The Führer's conference held in Berlin on 21 April 1941 approved the plan submitted by Goering for an airborne seizure of Crete. However, Hitler had reservations on the ability of the paratroopers to overcome the British forces on their own and when final approval was given on the 25th, the day the British agreed to withdraw their Expeditionary Force from Greece, it included a sea landing by the Mountain Division. Overall command of the operation, which was called Merkur, was given to General Student. The forces to be committed were the Fourth Air Fleet, the VIII and XI Air Corps and the mountain troops of the Twelfth Army. Sea command was given to the Admiral Commanding the South-Eastern Area, Aegean Sea.

The German naval commands in the Mediterranean had been established in February 1941 and comprised an Admiral Commanding Balkans and naval shore commanders at Piraeus, Salonika and Volos—the last-named posts to become effective when Greece was captured. The new command for the Aegean Sea was an operational one. Later in the year, a submarine command was approved for the base at Salamis.

When the British established their naval base organisation at Suda Bay in October 1940, little consideration had been given to defending the island against a full-scale assault involving the use of airborne troops. The garrison, which was mainly concentrated in the naval base area, consisted of two British battalions and some batteries of anti-aircraft guns. The normal garrison for the island was the 5th Cretan Division, which had been lost in Albania, and in April 1941 the Greek forces in Crete consisted of one partly trained infantry brigade of 3,733 men armed with only 659 rifles.

Churchill called a meeting of the Chiefs of Staff Committee in the first week of May which agreed Crete could be held for the present only to the extent of denying it to the enemy. Later, when the defences were strengthened, it could be developed as an operational base similar to Malta. This somewhat nebulous assessment was made, not only to formulate plans for the island's defences, but to placate the Dominion governments whose troops were soon to be committed to the task.

General Bernard Freyberg, the New Zealand commander, was placed in command of Crete on 29 April. General Wavell had arrived on the island on the same day, and in the evening informed Freyberg it was the Prime Minister's wish he assume the command. Freyberg declined on the grounds that his duty was to reorganise New Zealand forces in Egypt. Wavell informed him it was his duty to accept and there was nothing else he could do. The New Zealand government overrode Freyberg's objections and accepted the command.

A Greek caique of the Levant Schooner Flotilla base at Casteloriso.

Caiques berthed at Hydra, 1969.

The Greek Sacred Squadron patrolling the Western Desert, 1942. *(Greek Staff College)*

The Commander of the Greek Sacred Squadron, Colonel Tzigantes, in the Western Desert, 1942. *(Greek Staff College)*

Churchill sincerely believed that Crete could be held. On the island at this time were two understrength New Zealand brigades and a slightly smaller component of the Australian 6th Division, the 14th British Brigade and part of the 1st Armoured Brigade. Cunningham's fleet, after its heavy losses in Greece, was reinforced by the 5th Destroyer Flotilla, *Kelly*, *Kipling*, *Kelvin*, *Kashmir*, *Jackal* and *Jervis*, two new Australian destroyers, *Napier* and *Nizam*, and the cruiser *Dido*. At the end of April, the battleship *Queen Elizabeth* and the cruisers *Fiji* and *Naiad* arrived.

The weak link, however, was air support. Two squadrons of Hurricane fighters were stationed at Maleme, the island's main airfield, and a second squadron and five obsolete Gloster Gladiators was divided between the secondary airfields at Heraklion and Rethymnon. This inadequate force was soon reduced by continual enemy air attacks on Suda Bay, and the last serviceable Hurricanes were flown back to Egypt on 18 May. The Gloster Gladiators lacked the range and so remained on the island until they were decimated by the Messerschmitts and Junkers. The last four took off from the airfield at Rethymnon on the morning of the 19th to attack a strong formation of Dornier bombers. All four of the ancient biplanes were shot down in the action, but not before they had accounted for two of the bombers. One of the Gladiator pilots was an American volunteer serving in the Royal Air Force.

Churchill was aware of the inadequate defences, but believed he held the trump card to save Crete. This was ULTRA, which gave the British access to the German top secret codes. The Prime Minister believed Freyberg, armed with a foreknowledge of the enemy's plans, could counter his every move. However, during the battle, the New Zealand general made little use of the information passed to him. Some critics believed he was overawed by ULTRA, but in reality his hands were tied, as he could use the information only if its use in no way compromised its origin.

While the land forces were making their last preparations to meet the assault, Cunningham was at sea escorting the Tiger Convoy with a vital cargo of tanks and guns for Wavell's Desert Army. On 10 May, when between Malta and Alexandria, Churchill asked the Chiefs of Staff Committee to divert the cargo vessel *Fort Lamont* to Suda Bay and land part of her cargo of tanks. The committee refused, but within a matter of weeks the tanks were lost in Operation Battle-Axe.

In a lighter vein, on 12 May, ABC was delighted when he received a signal from the commander of Force H, Admiral Somerville. It read: 'Fancy twice a knight at your age'. Somerville was referring to the award of the KCB to Cunningham, who had received the KBE some years earlier.

The admiral, however, was more moved by the arrival of two additional flag officers for the Mediterranean Fleet. They were Rear Admirals King and Rawlings and their arrival relieved him of the burden of commanding three divisions as well as the fleet itself. Vice-Admiral Pridham-Wippell now assumed command of the battleship squadron, Rear Admiral King the cruisers and Rawlings joined Glennie with the destroyer flotillas. He now could direct all his energy to the duties of Commander-in-Chief.

At this time ABC renewed his acquaintance with his former commander in the Baltic operations of 1919, Admiral Sir Walter Cowan, Ret., who now, despite his seventy years, was serving as a private soldier with the commandos in the Western Desert. Soon after the meeting, Cowan was captured while attempting to destroy two German tanks. The old warrior was taken to Germany, but later escaped and returned to the Mediterranean. Cowan was awarded a bar to the DSO he had won in South Africa in 1900.

Initially, Hitler nominated 15 May for the assault on Crete, but the difficulties of concentrating the 6,000 parachutists, the glider troops and the fleet of Junkers transports on the primitive Greek airfields caused him to move the date to 20 May.

This information came to the British through ULTRA, but the grace of five extra days was insufficient to allow completion of all defence positions. The three airfields were underequipped with anti-aircraft and field artillery; the infantry were well below their allowance of machine-guns and mortars and more than 50 per cent of the troops on the island lacked arms of any kind. Freyberg begged Churchill to despatch a squadron of modern tanks and 25-pounder field guns to equip the artillery, but these vital arms were not forthcoming. The Army Commander-in-Chief, Wavell, did not share the Prime Minister's confidence that Crete could be held.

Two large convoys carrying three British battalions, ammunition, twenty obsolete Italian field guns, without sights, which had been captured earlier in the Desert Campaign, and 10,000 American First World War rifles, arrived at Heraklion. Wavell had no intention of parting with valuable equipment which most certainly would be lost.

Cunningham risked the three valuable transports, *Rawnsley, Dalesman* and *Logician*, in transporting these meagre reinforcements and supplies to Crete. He was now feverishly repairing ships damaged in the Greek Campaign and had appealed to the First Sea Lord for cruisers and destroyers to replace those which had been lost. Likewise, he needed more aircraft for HMS *Formidable*, now reduced to four serviceable planes.

Despite the shortages, he was determined to prevent any enemy ships reaching Crete. On 18 May Vice-Admiral Pridham-Wippell led the 1st Battle Squadron, composed of the battleships *Barham* and *Queen Elizabeth* and a flotilla of destroyers, on a sweep of Kaso Straits while Rear Admiral Rawlings with the 2nd Battle Squadron, *Warspite* and *Valiant*, covered the eastern and western approaches of the island.

The German High Command was applying heavy pressure on the Italians to commit their battle fleets in the waters around Crete. Mussolini refused a personal request from Hitler to place his fleets under the command of the Admiral Commanding Balkans. However, on 15 May he relented and Italian light forces in the Aegean were temporarily transferred to German command. This force of destroyers, destroyer escorts and MAS-boats, commanded by Captain Count Peccori-Giraldi, was deployed to provide close support for the seaborne assault forces. Cunningham became aware of this decision through an ULTRA intercept and moved his ships to meet this threat.

At daylight on 20 May, a great circle of British ships which included *Warspite, Valiant, Dido, Gloucester, Orion, Fiji, Naiad, Perth, Napier, Kimberley, Isis, Janus, Griffin, Imperial, Kandahar, Nubian, Kingston* and *Juno* was deployed from the Antikythera Straits in the west to Kaso Strait in the east. To reach Crete, the enemy seaborne armada must breach this line.

Meanwhile, on Crete, Freyberg made his final dispositions. His main force was dug in around Maleme airfield at the western end of the island. This force consisted of the three New Zealand battalions with the 1st Welch in reserve. Two batteries of Bofors anti-aircraft guns ringed the airfield and an under-strength squadron of the Hussars was under cover in nearby gullies. On the airfield proper a scratch force of RAF personnel, commanded by Squadron Leader Howell, waited to engage the enemy before he could reorganise after landing.

Seven miles to the east of the airfield, a second force was disposed to defend the approaches to the city of Canea and the base at Suda Bay. On the high ground overlooking the anchorage were several batteries of 3.7-inch anti-aircraft guns. Three understrength batteries equipped with captured Italian field guns were disposed to give support to both areas.

Midway between Maleme and Heraklion at the eastern end of the island was the Australian 19th Brigade, entrusted with the defence of the small fishing port of Georgioupolis and the airstrip and harbour at Rethymnon. The four battalions of the brigade were divided, with the 2/1st and 2/11th at Rethymnon and the 2/7th and 2/8th at Georgioupolis. A battery of artillery was dug in to cover the airstrip.

At Heraklion, another infantry brigade, composed of the 2nd Black Watch, 2nd York and Lancasters and the Australian 2/4th Battalion, was responsible for the defence of the airfield and the harbour. A light anti-aircraft battery and a battery of field artillery were sited to cover the airfield.

Smaller forces were deployed at various locations along both the north and south coasts. At Timbaki, south of Heraklion, was stationed the 1st Argyll and Sutherland Highlanders and six light tanks. Three Greek battalions were disposed in the hills around Kastelli to protect an emergency landing strip and on the north-east point of the island was the partly trained 1st Greek Regiment.

Freyberg had arms for only half of the troops on the island, and in the hills south of Canea were 9,000 soldiers who could not be committed to the battle. These troops later created a problem when the fighting force withdrew to positions along the road to Sfakia.

By the morning of 20 May, Freyberg was as prepared as the circumstances would permit. The New Zealand general had not wanted the command, but was determined to do his utmost in denying the island to the enemy. In his final address to his troops on 19 May he revealed his concern at the shortages which were apparent in every area. 'Just fix your bayonets and go at them as hard as you can,' he said.

At 0615 on the bright, sunny morning of 20 May, the first flights of Junkers 52 transport aircraft rumbled down the tarmacs at three airfields around Athens. They rose in the air in a great cloud of reddish dust and soon vanished low over the sea. Each of the aircraft carried sixteen lightly armed parachutists and six containers carrying their heavy weapons and supplies. From other fields nearby, sixty more transports with troop-carrying gliders were taking to the air. The first assault armada was on its way to Crete.

Over the sea they were joined by swarms of Messerschmitt fighters, and as the misty blue mountains of Crete rose out of the sea they were passed by a vast fleet of bombers and dive-bombers returning from the softening-up attacks on the airfields. The great air fleet of more than 150 Heinkel, Dornier and Junkers bombers had dived out of the sky soon after dawn and struck the defences around Maleme and Suda Bay. Wave after wave dived down from the mountains, carpet bombing the slit trenches and gunpits. As they vanished out to sea, the dive-bombers screamed in and laid their bombs in a mathematical pattern across the airstrip. The third wave flattened out at ground level and strafed the defences with cannon and machine-guns.

Casualties from this fiery onslaught were surprisingly low. The majority of slit and weapon pits were dug under the olive trees which rose in serried ranks from the edge of the airfield to the crests of the hills. However, the attacks did succeed in laying an impenetrable screen of stinging red dust which masked the approach of the transport aircraft now circling at sea before dropping the first gliders and parachutists.

An eerie silence, lasting ten minutes, followed the air bombardment. The swishing sigh of the gliders, which had now been released, was not heard by the shocked ears of the defenders. Suddenly, lookouts posted on the high ground sighted the gliders turning for their run in. They swept low overhead, like a flock of black vultures, and were met by a fusillade of small-arms fire. Two faltered in flight, dipped their noses and plunged into the trees on the side of the hill. The remainder straightened up and crash landed into the rock-strewn bed of the Tavronitis River which formed the western perimeter of the airfield. The survivors of the crash landings crawled from their splintered aircraft and opened a ragged fire on the airfield. More than half of the force was killed on landing.

Even as this macabre event was taking place in the river bed, a second and much larger armada arrived over the airfield. The great Junkers approached in flights of three, flying level at approximately 250 feet, and as they crossed the edge of the field released their troops in strings of sixteen. When the parachutes opened, they burgeoned into a bizarre cloud of confetti.

The awesome sight mesmerised the defenders momentarily, but then they stood up in their trenches and picked off the swaying targets like duck shooters. This deliberate, aimed fire wrought carnage in the first wave. One after another, as they were hit, they plummetted to earth in a tangle of silk and cords. Those who landed on the open airstrip were torn to pieces by sustained bursts of machine-gun fire as they struggled to release their parachute harness. Still others, who had the misfortune to land in the trees close to the defensive positions, died on the point of the New Zealanders' eighteen-inch long bayonets.

It was estimated that two-thirds of the first drop died in the first minutes of the battle. The survivors who were fortunate enough to land close to the western perimeter joined the remnant of the glider battalion in the river bed. The fate of this first drop was not known to General Student in Athens for twenty-four hours.

Four drops were made in the Maleme and Suda Bay area on the first day of the battle. One group fell in the Prison Valley south of Canea and was attacked by prisoners who had been released from the civil prison. Others fell victim to Cretan villagers who streamed down from the hills and armed themselves with German weapons.

Similar scenes were re-enacted later in the day at Heraklion and Rethymnon. The Australian and British troops at these airfields fought with great ferocity and enemy casualties exceeded 50 per cent. At Rethymnon, the two understrength battalions killed 400 in the first hour and took more than 250 prisoners, including the German commander, Colonel Sturm.

When darkness fell all three airfields were securely held by the defenders. On that night, General Student, in his headquarters in Athen's Grande Bretagne Hotel, was close to admitting defeat. Some 8,500 airborne troops had been landed on the island, 1,860 at Maleme, 2,460 at Suda Bay, 2,360 at Heraklion, 1,380 at Rethymnon and 72 at Kastelli.

In addition, 330 glider troops had landed in the Tavronitis River. Casualty figures already at hand suggested half the force had been destroyed.

However, while Student was assessing his losses, the New Zealanders withdrew from the vital ridge which commanded Maleme airfield from the south. This action remains unexplained, even today. Puttick, the commander, claimed his ammunition was exhausted and he had lost his communications but these reasons were not borne out by the evidence. It was to cost the British Crete. At first light on the 21st, Student received a signal informing him the ridge was in the parachutists' hands and, with it, the airfield. One hour later, a Junkers transport landed on a road beside the airfield and one of Student's staff officers conferred with the senior German officer on the ground. The decision was made to land reinforcements directly on the airstrip. Three hours later the first aircraft landed and the battle was won.

At sea on 20 May, Admiral Rawlings' 2nd Battle Squadron was patrolling to the west of Crete. Admiral Glennie's cruiser and destroyer force was to his north, withdrawing from the Anti-Kythera Straits, and to the east Admiral King's squadron was south of Kaso Strait. The enemy's seaborne fleet had not been sighted, although reports of the airborne landings had been received.

Soon after noon an aircraft made the first sighting report of the enemy armada. It consisted of approximately twenty-five vessels battling headwinds on passage from Piraeus to the island of Milos, which had been selected by the enemy as his advanced base. A second report described the armada as a mix of small motor coasters, caiques and fishing boats. All were loaded with troops. On receipt of these reports, Cunningham ordered Admiral King to cover the approaches to Heraklion and Glennie the Suda Bay area. Rawlings, with the battleships, was to bar the approach of the Italian fleet from the west. All three forces were in position by dusk on the 20th.

King's force was sighted by a Heinkel reconnaissance aircraft soon after taking up its position and came under attack by torpedo bombers. The aircraft swept in from the starboard quarter, but all ships turned in unison and the torpedoes streaked down their sides and missed. Some hours after dark they came under attack by Italian MAS-boats. These, too, were driven off without loss.

While the three squadrons were waiting to intercept the enemy ships, a fourth group consisting of *Jervis*, *Nizam* and *Ilex*, under the command of Captain P.J. Mack, was nearing the enemy island of Scarpanto to the east of Crete. At 0130 on the 21st, the destroyers opened fire on enemy airfields at Pegadia Bay. The bombardment lasted twenty minutes and when the ships withdrew, hangars, workshops and aircraft on the tarmac were burning brightly. The destroyers returned to Alexandria without loss.

The three squadrons positioned off Crete made no enemy sightings on that night. They remained on station and soon came under heavy air attack. At 1100 next day, the cruiser *Ajax* was near-missed by a heavy bomb. She was severely damaged, but remained with her squadron. Two hours later the destroyer *Juno* received a direct hit and sank in five minutes. She was the second ship of her class to be sunk in two weeks, *Jersey* having been lost at Malta, also from enemy air attack.

During the long, cloudless day the ships were in constant action fighting off attacks from medium and dive-bombers. By late afternoon the anti-aircraft ammunition of all vessels was running low. Admiral Rawlings warned his ships to economise in its use, but for some ships it was too late and this shortage was to be responsible for some of the losses suffered in the twenty-four hours ahead.

At the German base on Milos, a second flotilla of ships intended for the landing at Heraklion had arrived. The German Admiral Southeast was now under pressure from General Student and OKW in Berlin to expedite his movement of troops, and the two flotillas were alerted to sail for Maleme. During the morning, air reconnaissance reported the British naval squadrons had withdrawn to the south, and at 1700 the two flotillas, escorted by the Italian destroyer escort *Lupo* and a squadron of MAS-boats, sailed for Maleme.

The German report on the withdrawal of the British ships was incorrect. At dusk on the 21st, all ships were in position. They came under heavy attack soon after and six enemy aircraft were shot down. At 2330 the destroyer *Janus*, in Glennie's squadron, sighted the enemy force buffetting strong headwinds thirty-five miles north of Crete.

Glennie immediately alerted the cruisers which increased speed and swept around to attack the enemy from the north and so prevent him from turning back. As the line of cruisers bore down on the melee of small ships, the little *Lupo* bravely interposed herself between the flotilla and the cruisers and laid a smokescreen. Her course brought her hard alongside *Dido*'s starboard and she came under light-calibre fire. *Lupo* then turned away and, as the range increased, fired two torpedoes at the cruisers. The torpedoes missed and the Italian destroyer was exposed to the combined fire of *Orion* and *Ajax*'s 6-inch guns. She was hit by two salvos and reduced to a smoking wreck. *Ajax* turned and rammed the plucky ship.

All nine ships of the cruiser squadron now raced into the confused mass of small ships. They fired at point-blank range with guns fully depressed. In the light of cruisers' searchlights, the surviving vessels were reduced to a raft of splintered timber among which floated the bodies of the men of the German Mountain Regiment. Admiral Glennie wrote in his Letters of Proceedings: 'In all, one or two steamers, at least a dozen caiques, a small pleasure steamer and a steam yacht were engaged and either sunk or left burning'.

The commanding officer of III Mountain Regiment was in one of the caiques and recorded the following graphic description of the attack in *Mountain Troops in Crete*: 'A hard jolt lifts the ship for seconds and a huge explosion shatters the silence. The ship's sails stand out white like a magnesium torch lit up by the beam of the searchlight. Black shadows glide by to port. Shells come screaming at us—there are hits, steel splinters, wrecked timbers, yells from the wounded. Dinghies and lifeboats are got ready to launch but a fresh hit sets the ship alight. Some men are flung overboard by the blast. The ship sinks with a huge tongue of flame.'

The carnage continued for three hours. By 0200 on the 22nd, no enemy craft remained afloat in the immediate area. The cruisers knived through a sea covered in shattered timbers and floating bodies. However, as more anti-aircraft ammunition had been expended in the engagement, Glennie ordered the fleet to withdraw south to rendezvous with Admiral Rawling's battle fleet and replenish.

While Glennie's squadron was engaged in destroying the Maleme flotilla, to the east Admiral King was patrolling off Heraklion, but having met with no success he turned north soon after dawn. At 0830, to the south of Milos, a single caique loaded with troops was sighted. The Australian cruiser *Perth* immediately closed the unlucky vessel and sunk it with a fusillade of gunfire. King had already despatched his destroyers to search to the north, and within minutes they reported a large fleet of small craft heading south.

This sighting coincided with a heavy air attack which continued unabated for two hours. At 0945, King decided to break off the chase and withdraw to safer waters. The cruisers *Naiad* and *Carlisle* had been hit but were able to continue and *Perth* was near-missed as she was rejoining the fleet.

King was bitterly criticised for not closing the enemy. Cunningham wrote of his action: 'King's situation was a difficult one but it appears that no diminishing of the risk could have been achieved by retirement and that, in fact, the safest place for the squadron would have been among the enemy ships'. Nelson's dictum was still applicable in modern warefare, but as later events would show, King's action did stop the seaborne force reaching Heraklion. The Germans withdrew the flotilla to Piraeus and the Mountain Battalions were airlifted to Crete.

Enemy records examined after the war reveal that seventy men of the Maleme flotilla sunk by Glennie's squadron did reach the island, but the heavy equipment so desperately needed by the parachutists remained at the bottom of the sea. Five weeks after the battle ended, bodies and wreckage from the lost flotilla were still being washed ashore.

When Admiral Glennie's ships returned to Alexandria to replenish ammunition stocks, Mountbatten's destroyer flotilla and Waller's detached group of three ships took their place. While these changes were taking place, an appeal was received from Admiral King for air cover. His squadron was under savage air attack in Kythera Channel. Air cover was not available and Rawlings went to his aid with the battle fleet. At 1330, when the two forces were within sight of each other, the flagship *Warspite* received a direct hit on her starboard batteries amidships. All four 6-inch guns and the 4-inch anti-aircraft guns were knocked out, one boiler room was put out of action and water flooded her lower compartments. One officer and thirty-seven men were killed instantly and another thirty-one wounded.

Thirty minutes later, the destroyer *Greyhound* was hit by two bombs and sank immediately. The cruiser *Gloucester* was next. Hit by a large bomb, she stopped dead in the water, burning furiously. Rawlings ordered *Fiji* to go alongside and drop boats and Carley floats, and when the survivors were clear, to sink her with torpedoes. The destroyers *Voyager* and *Vendetta* later picked up the survivors.

The blackest day in the history of the Mediterranean Fleet had not ended. Soon after 1800, the cruiser *Fiji* was hit repeatedly by dive-bombers and sank within minutes. Mountbatten's flotilla, which joined the battle fleet at 1830, was ordered to pick up survivors. *Kandahar, Kingston, Kipling, Kashmir* and *Jackal* arrived on the scene of the sinking as darkness was falling and found the survivors scattered over a wide area. In three hours *Kingston* and *Kandahar* rescued 530.

When darkness fell, the air attacks which had continued for more than twelve hours ceased. The destroyers *Hero* and *Decoy* were despatched to Ayia Roumeli, on the south coast of the island, to rescue the King of Greece and members of his parliament and the British Ambassador to Greece. Mountbatten's flotilla patrolled off Suda Bay and Maleme, searching for enemy seaborne troops, while King's squadron and the damaged *Warspite* withdrew to Alexandria for replenishment and repairs.

The night of 22 May found the land forces in the Maleme area confronted with a stalemate. The defenders had yet to mount a concerted attack to drive the Germans off the airfield, and the enemy was still building up his strength to drive the British into the sea. Throughout the long day, a shuttle of troop-carrying aircraft had landed reinforcements for the Mountain Division. Major General Ringel, the divisional commander, now assumed command of all German troops in Crete.

At Heraklion, the British force had driven the enemy survivors from the airfield area and the city. Thirty-nine miles to the west, at Rethymnon, a similar situation existed. The two Australian battalions had split the enemy survivors into small groups, and these were pinned down until the battle ended. However, inertia was settling over the main Allied force at Maleme. Freyberg's forces still greatly outnumbered the Germans, but German air mastery more than counterbalanced this. The initiative, with few exceptions, was passing to the enemy.

Cunningham deployed his forces during the night of 22–23 May to patrol off Maleme and Heraklion. Captain Mack's destroyer flotilla, *Jervis, Ilex, Nizam* and *Havock*, made a sweep of Kaso Strait to the east and early on the 23rd, returned to Alexandria to replenish. *Kelvin* and *Jackal* made a reconnaissance of Canea Bay while the destroyers of Mountbatten's flotilla bombarded Maleme airfield, sinking two caiques loaded with troops.

This flotilla retired south of Crete and at 0755 came under attack from thirty dive-bombers off Gavdhos Island. *Kelly* and *Kashmir* were singled out by the Stukas, but the planes were driven off after two of their number were shot down. The destroyers increased speed to escape to sea but *Kashmir* was hit by two bombs and rolled over and sank. *Kelly* turned to cover her sister ship and, a minute later, was hit by a 500-pound bomb which struck just abaft of the engine-room. The ship was steaming at maximum speed and heeled over with the sea flooding through a great rent in her side, her momentum driving her down.

Kipling, which was closely following her leader, reduced speed to pick up survivors, and she too came under heavy attack. More than forty enemy aircraft circled her as she dropped boats and Carley floats. In a space of half an hour, between attacks, she picked up 279 officers and men including the flotilla commander, Captain Mountbatten. In the next hour, as she steamed south with her decks crowded with survivors, she was close-missed by eighty-three bombs. *Kipling* reached a point fifty miles north of Alexandria before running out of fuel. She was towed into the port on the 24th.

The lesson, established at high cost in Greece, that troops could not operate without air cover, was still to be learnt by British staff officers. On the 22nd, General Wavell ordered more ground troops to be despatched to Crete. A battalion of 900 troops were embarked in the fast minelayer *Abdiel* and the sloops *Auckland* and *Flamingo* to be landed at Timbaki on the night of 23–24 May but Cunningham, fearing further ship losses, cancelled the operation. In fact, Freyberg had more troops on the island than he could use. However, the army Commander-in-Chief persisted and *Abdiel* landed 200 commandos at Suda Bay on the following night.

On the same night and sixty miles to the east, the cruisers *Ajax* and *Dido* and the

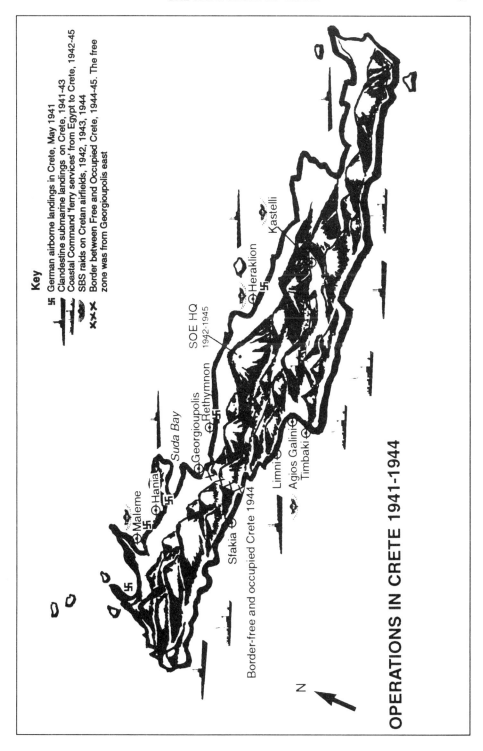

Key

🇩🇪 German airborne landings in Crete, May 1941
Clandestine submarine landings on Crete, 1941-43
Coastal Command 'ferry services' from Egypt to Crete, 1942-45
SBS raids on Cretan airfields, 1942, 1943, 1944
××× Border between Free and Occupied Crete, 1944-45. The free zone was from Georgioupolis east

OPERATIONS IN CRETE 1941-1944

destroyers *Kimberley* and *Hotspur* were patrolling off Sitia on the north coast to intercept an Italian seaborne force which had sailed from Rhodes. Italian records show the convoy turned back and did not reach the island until 28 May. British forces in eastern Crete were evacuated twenty-four hours earlier.

The position of Freyberg's troops in the Maleme area deteriorated even further on the 25th. Spearheaded by the 100 Mountain Regiment, the enemy reached Galatos, three miles west of Canea. During the day Brigadier Puttick signalled Freyberg: 'Am exceedingly doubtful on present reports whether I can hold the enemy tomorrow'. The field commanders were losing their drive, and on that night the British line withdrew to the suburbs of Canea.

Early next morning Freyberg signalled Wavell, suggesting evacuation of the entire force from Crete. Wavell approved the evacuation on 27 May and ordered Freyberg to conduct a fighting withdrawal southward over the mountains to the small fishing port of Sfakia. Preference for embarkation would be given to the fighting units. The Allied defenders at both Heraklion and Rethymnon, who had improved their positions and had contained the surviving enemy forces, were to be taken off at other ports on the eastern end of the island.

Despite the worsening position ashore, the navy was doing its utmost to reduce the scale of the enemy attacks. By the 25th, the carrier *Formidable* had built up her aircraft to twelve machines, and Cunningham decided to use these and the guns of the battleships to hit the German airfields on Scarpanto. The 1st Battle Squadron, *Queen Elizabeth* and *Barham* with *Formidable* and eight destroyers, sailed from Alexandria late on that day and launched the attack from Kaso Strait on the following morning. The enemy was caught off-guard and several aircraft were destroyed on the ground, while five more were shot down in combat. Hangars and workshops were damaged but the airfield was in service again within twelve hours.

However, the cost of success was high. *Formidable* was hit by two bombs: one holed her on the starboard side and started fires and the other caused damage to her landing deck. *Barham* was hit by a heavy bomb and one of her main turrets was put out of action. The destroyer *Nubian* had her stern blown off but reached port.

On the night of 26–27 May, *Abdiel* landed another 400 commandos at Suda Bay and evacuated 930 merchant seamen and naval personnel. This was the last reinforcement to the island.

While the ships were preventing the enemy from reaching Crete by the sea, an estimated 4,000 Mountain troops arrived at Maleme by air. This infusion of fresh troops with their heavy arms enabled the enemy airborne forces to maintain pressure on the tired defenders. A convoy of more troops had sailed from Pireaus and landed near Suda Bay during the night of the 27–28th. The Royal Navy had now lost control of the sea north of Crete.

Captain R.A. Morse, RN, Naval Officer in Charge, Crete, had maintained a tenuous contact with the beleaguered forces at Rethymnon with a landing barge commanded by Lieutenant R. Haig, RN, who had evacuated many of the troops from the beachhead in Greece only a month before. This intrepid officer and his crew made three voyages to Rethymnon, travelling at night and hiding in caves during daylight hours to avoid enemy aircraft. The dangerous 50-mile voyage took eighteen hours.

Haig made three voyages carrying vitally needed ammunition, medical supplies and food. On the third he carried evacuation orders for the force, but unfortunately, and for the second time, these did not reach the force commander, Lieutenant Colonel Campbell.

Landing in the British lines at night was difficult as the fighting ashore was fluid. The author was a member of one of the reception committees at a feature called Wadi Pigi, 200 yards from the German lines. Enemy flares were fired every five minutes and a machine-gun was being fired on fixed lines along the beach.

On the third voyage Haig did not return to Suda Bay, but sailed his barge around to the south coast where it provided valuable service at Sfakia ferrying troops out to the evacuation fleet.

When the decision to evacuate Crete was made at the Chiefs of Staff meeting in Cairo, Cunningham wrote in his diary: 'We now wearily turned to planning another evacuation with fewer ships, far less resources, and in circumstances much more difficult. Our seamen and ships were torn to the point of exhaustion, and now they were asked for more.'

Cunningham knew all too well the problems and risks which faced the fleet in attempting to evacuate more than 20,000 troops from the island. There were no safe harbours on the south side of the island and the troops would need to be taken off in small craft and ship's boats to the fleet standing offshore. The ships would be under heavy air attack from the time they left Alexandria until they returned. Of necessity, the main load of evacuation would fall on the long-suffering destroyers whose numbers had already been severely reduced in providing support to the army during the battle.

ABC was not a highly religious man but, like so many men of Scots descent, he possessed a simple faith. His favourite prayer, copies of which he frequently passed to his staff, was the 'Angler's Prayer', which reflected much of the simplicity of his character:

> I pray that I may live to fish
> Until my dying day,
> And when it comes to my last cast,
> I then most humbly pray:
> When in the Lord's great landing net,
> And peacefully asleep:
> That in his mercy I be judged,
> Big enough to keep.

6

Now They Were Asked for More

'The Army cannot be left to its fate. The Navy must carry on.' These were brave words from a Commander-in-Chief who had just assessed the cost of his fleet's ten days of sacrifice to hold Crete—two cruisers and four destroyers sunk; two battleships, the fleet's only aircraft carrier, five cruisers and four destroyers damaged beyond the ability of Mediterranean dockyards to repair. On 23 May the five MTBs commanded by Lieutenant Commander E.C. Peake, which had been sent to Suda Bay to counter enemy seaborne landings, were sunk at their moorings by marauding Me 109 fighters. The MTBs and two MLs and ten other small vessels which had met the same fate accounted for the navy's small craft. The admiral knew the evacuation of the army would cost even more in ships and sailors' lives.

Cunningham was not a man to be daunted by the cost. On the afternoon of 27 May he told his staff officers: 'Our seamen and our ships are worn to the point of exhaustion and now they ask for more'. In the recesses of his mind stirred memories of another evacuation twenty-six years previously, when a greater number of men were taken off Gallipoli. 'It takes three years to build a ship,' he said, 'but it would take three hundred to build a new reputation. The evacuation will continue.'

There were 22,000 troops on the island, of whom at least 2,000 were wounded. The majority of these would have to be taken off from open beaches under both ground and air attack. The First Sea Lord suggested the use of the three infantry landing ships but Cunningham, aware of the easy target they presented and their slow speed, opposed their use. However, unknown to him when he arrived at the decision, *Glengyle* had already sailed for Crete and it was too late to turn her back to Alexandria.

The only good news to reach the Commander-in-Chief's ear on that dismal day was a signal from Churchill informing him the German super battleship *Bismarck* had been sunk by units of the Royal Navy in the Atlantic.

Heraklion, on the north-east coast of the island and the only port held by the defenders, was chosen for the first big lift of troops. From here, the survivors of the 5,000 British and Australians who had held the airfield could be taken off in one night. Cunningham signalled his plan to the NOIC, Heraklion, Captain M.H.S. MacDonald, RN.

To command the operation, he appointed Rear Admiral Irvine Glennie, who was later to command the largest destroyer fleet of the Second World War at Normandy. The evacuation fleet consisted of the cruisers *Orion*, *Ajax* and *Dido* and the destroyers *Decoy*, *Jackal*, *Imperial*, *Hotspur*, *Kimberley* and *Hereward*. It sailed from Alexandria late in the afternoon of 28 May. Two hours after this force departed, a second one, consisting of the destroyers *Napier, Nizam, Kelvin* and *Kandahar,* commanded by Captain S.H.T. Arliss, brother of the film star George Arliss, sailed for Sfakia.

Rawlings expected to come under air attack from 1200 on the 29th, but they were not sighted by a German reconnaissance aircraft until 1600. Dive-bombing attacks commenced at 1700 and continued unabated for three hours. In spite of the concentrated umbrella of fire put up by guns of all calibres, the Stukas repeatedly skimmed over the ships at masthead level. At 1910, *Imperial* was near-missed but continued, unaware she was heavily damaged.

Fifty minutes later, a large bomb fell hard alongside the cruiser *Ajax,* wounding twenty of the crew and inflicting serious hull damage. Small fires were started amidships, but these were extinguished. Suspecting the ship was more seriously damaged than her captain claimed, *Rawlings* ordered her back to Alexandria.

Meanwhile, at Heraklion, Captain MacDonald had arranged for the garrison to be withdrawn from the airfield they had held so staunchly for nine days. By 2100 they had formed an inner defence line around the small harbour. This withdrawal was accomplished despite attacks by enemy ground forces and a 200-plane raid late in the afternoon.

The first ships, *Hotspur, Decoy, Jackal* and *Hereward,* slipped silently into the old Venetian harbour at 2330 and berthed at the stone mole. The troops were waiting, three deep and separated into groups of thirty men. Each destroyer embarked 500 soldiers, slipped, and passed out of the harbour undetected by enemy lookouts on the city wall three-quarters of a mile away. *Imperial* and *Kimberley* followed and loading proceeded smoothly. *Hotspur* and *Jackal* returned for a second loading after transferring their troops to the cruisers. *Decoy* and *Hereward* took off the rearguard of 900 men.

By 0300 on the 29th, the entire force of 4,500, less the seriously wounded who remained in the hospital with their orderlies, had been evacuated. The battlefield was left to the enemy. Admiral Rawlings, on the bridge of *Orion,* estimated 4,080 were embarked but knew the travail of his squadron lay ahead. In less than three hours it would be daylight, the ships would be seventy miles off the hostile coast and forty minutes flying from the German airfields.

At 0345, *Imperial*'s steering failed. The destroyer circled out of control with her rudder jammed hard over. She narrowly missed ramming *Kimberley* when she attempted to go alongside to lend assistance. Rawlings ordered *Hotspur*'s commanding officer, Lieutenant Commander C.P.F. Brown, to take off *Imperial*'s passengers and crew and sink the crippled vessel with a torpedo. At 0446, with the first glow of day in the sky, *Imperial* rolled over and sank.

Hotspur, with 900 soldiers on board, turned south and increased to full speed. The squadron was out of sight, twenty-five miles over the horizon, and the first German aircraft were taking off from their airfields in the Peloponnese and Scarpanto. However, fate was in one of her capricious moods, and instead of seeking out the lone overloaded destroyer, the Luftwaffe vented its fury on Rawling's squadron to the south. Soon after 0625, two groups of Ju 87 dive-bombers and Ju 88 fighter-bombers found the speeding ships and attacked.

The first victim was *Hotspur*'s sister ship, *Hereward.* A Stuka bomb hit the destroyer's overcrowded deck amidships. When the smoke cleared, it was seen the destroyer could still steam and Rawlings ordered her to turn back to Crete. She was last seen, surrounded by a forest of bomb spouts, weaving and twisting in the distance. *Hereward* sank before she reached land, but the survivors of her passengers and crew were rescued and taken prisoner by a flotilla of Italian MAS-boats which had been attracted by the aircraft milling above her.

At 0815, *Decoy* was near-missed by a heavy bomb and her speed fell to 17 knots. On the port wing of the squadron the cruiser *Dido* was singled out by five dive-bombers. One aircraft failed to pull out of a power dive and splashed into the sea under her bows. The explosion from its bomb severely damaged A and B turrets and reduced the ship's firepower drastically.

A few cables ahead of *Dido*, Rawlings' flagship *Orion* was also near-missed. A minute later a second bomb hit close under the bridge, killing the cruiser's commanding officer, Captain G.R.B. Back, instantly and wounding Admiral Rawlings. Command of the *Orion* passed to Commander T.C. Wynne.

However, *Orion*'s ordeal was not over. At 1045, when the sorely pressed squadron was 100 miles south of Kaso Strait, eleven yellow-nosed Stuka bombers plunged down on the flagship in a mass attack. In flights of three, they alternated in attacks from the stern and the flanks. As the second wave passed over the ship's masts, a 500-pound bomb speared through the bridge and penetrated to the mess deck below, in which more than 500 soldiers were packed. When the smoke and dust of the explosion cleared, 260 were dead and 280 more were wounded.

The cruiser was now half-obscured by rolling clouds of yellow and black smoke. She was out of control, steaming in circles. Communications between bridge and engine-room were severed, the steering gear was knocked out and three of her boiler rooms were out of action. Several of her oil tanks were ruptured and sea water was reaching the fuel.

Petty Officer Ron Atwill led one of the first damage control parties to enter the mess deck. He was horrified by the charnel house in which he worked. Atwill had been awarded the DSM for a similar task he performed in HMS *Exeter* following the Battle of the River Plate, eighteen months earlier.

Despite her own damage and her crowded decks, *Hotspur* closed the flagship to render aid, but *Orion* straightened up and returned to her rightful place at the head of the squadron. The destroyer was thanked for her intentions and ordered to return to her place in the convoy.

This was the last air attack of the passage and the battered ships arrived at Alexandria some hours after dark. A total of 3,486 troops of the 4,080 embarked at Heraklion eighteen hours earlier were landed. Some 600 were either dead, wounded or prisoners of war. The Black Watch Regiment, which had fought so stoutly in the battle, lost 200 on the voyage home. Rear Admiral Rawlings later wrote in his action report: 'The conduct of the military units embarked in my flag was admirable. I very much regret the heavy casualties they sustained.'

Cunningham visited *Orion* soon after she berthed at Alexandria. His sharp eyes took in the wrecked blackened bridge, the scarred hull with half of its paint blistered and streaked, the overworked guns bared to the metal, and the guys of the foremast slack and broken. He saw the rows of silent dead on the decks and the endless stream of stretchers passing down the brow to the long line of ambulances on the wharf. Not least, he saw the grim, strained faces of the ship's complement and the thought passed through his mind: 'If this is the first, what will it be like at the end?'

Captain Arliss' destroyers arrived off Sfakia at midnight on 28 May. The ships were carrying rations for 15,000 troops and 150,000 rounds of small-arms ammunition for the rearguard, which were landed by the ships' boats before evacuation began.

Lieutenant L.M. Hinchcliffe, RAN, was landed from *Napier* as beachmaster. He found there was only a short stretch of shingle beach suitable for embarkation. A strong undertow was present, and this necessitated the use of a line of sailors and soldiers to help the soldiers being taken off keep their feet while reaching the boats. Behind the beach, a 400-foot cliff rose into the gloom, and down this zigzagged a rough donkey track. The area for marshalling the troops on the beach was extremely limited. The beachmaster found his manifold duties of coordinating the boats and the passengers difficult in the extreme and was awarded the DSC for the efficient manner in which he carried out his task.

Captain Arliss had hoped to embark 1,000 troops, but at 0300—the deadline for ships to clear the coast before daylight—only 744 had been taken aboard. On his return to Alexandria he suggested the number of checkpoints being used by the army to identify personnel moving down the escarpment to the beach should be reduced.

The checkpoints were far from efficient, as *Napier*'s log later revealed. Her total of 313 embarked was made up of 36 officers, 260 other ranks, 3 women, 2 children, 10 merchant seamen, 1 Greek and 1 Chinese, as well as a dog.

Arliss' destroyers were lucky on their return passage, suffering only one attack at 0905 when the ships were 125 miles south of Crete. Four bombers, identified as Heinkels, made five runs over the ships in a space of thirty-five minutes. None of the destroyers was hit, although *Nizam* was near-missed. They arrived at Alexandria at 1700 on the 29th and disembarked their passengers.

The position on shore continued to deteriorate. Freyberg's decision to evacuate was made on the afternoon of 27 May and the news spread like wildfire through the non-fighting troops in the valleys south of Suda Bay. During the night, many of these undisciplined groups started climbing the narrow, winding road which led south over the mountains to Sfakia. In twenty-four hours, their numbers increased to many thousands and were to block the road for the rearguard when it withdrew to new positions.

Freyberg later wrote in his report: 'The road from Suda Bay over Crete to Sfakia was well described by someone that night as the Via Dolorosa! Never shall I forget the disorganisation and almost complete lack of control of the masses on the move as we made our way slowly through that endless stream of trudging men.'

On 27 and 28 May, Australian and New Zealand infantry and artillery counter-attacked in the Stilos area to the south of Suda Bay. These well executed attacks prevented the strongly reinforced enemy from cutting the vital road to Sfakia. On the 28th, the force withdrew through a strong rearguard consisting of units of the New Zealand 5th Brigade, the Australian 19th Brigade and commandos of Layforce which inflicted heavy casualties on General Ringel's force of parachutists and the Mountain Regiment.

A second line was established on the edge of the Askifou Plain, deep in the White Mountains. When the Australians and New Zealanders attempted to fall back from this line, the crush of undisciplined troops forced them to leave the road and reach their next position by crossing rough mountain terrain.

The final rearguard position, on ridges overlooking passes to the south of Imvros, was manned by Australians on the 29th. This position, supported by two field guns, was held until the final evacuation on the night of 31 May.

With the evacuation of the Heraklion force on the night of 28 May, the only other organised Allied force on the island was the 1,200-strong garrison at Rethymnon, commanded by Colonel I. Campbell. This small force fought valiantly for ten days and reduced the 1,600-strong parachute brigade to 250 men, now dug in at a roadblock close to Rethymnon.

Two attempts were made to inform Campbell of evacuation plans. The first message was dropped by a long-range Hurricane fighter sent from Egypt, but the message container is believed to have fallen in the enemy lines. A second, sent by Lietenant Haig's landing barge, also failed to reach Campbell. The gallant Rethymnon force surrendered on the morning of the 30th when attacked by a strong tank and motorised force which had fought its way east from Suda Bay.

Rear Admiral King commanded the force which sailed from Alexandria at 2100 on 28 May. It consisted of the cruisers *Phoebe, Perth, Calcutta* and *Coventry*, the destroyers *Jervis, Janus* and *Hasty* and the landing ship *Glengyle*. As *Glengyle*'s maximum speed was only 26 knots, its inclusion in the squadron was to add eight hours to both the outward and return passages. Cunningham was far from happy about the use of *Glengyle* in Cretan waters and some hours after the squadron sailed he despatched the destroyers *Stuart, Jaguar* and *Defender*, commanded by Captain Waller, to meet King's force on the morning of the 30th to provide additional support on the return passage.

King's squadron arrived off Sfakia at 2330 on the 29th and embarkation commenced immediately. *Glengyle*'s landing craft expedited the transfer of the troops from the shore to the ships. These craft had the additional advantage of running up on the beach for loading and carried more passengers than the ships' boats. This resulted in 6,000 troops being lifted in less than four hours.

The squadron sailed at 0320 and was met off Gavdhos Island by Waller's destroyers. Two hours later they came under air attack from a large force of dive-bombers and fighter-bombers. Almost immediately the cruiser, HMAS *Perth* was hit. The 500-pound bomb carried away the radar aerial on the foremast, passed through the deck at the back of the bridge and exploded in No 1 boiler room. The cruiser was seriously damaged, but casualties were surprisingly light. Although the ship had 1,188 troops on board, only seven of the crew and seven soldiers were killed. After a short delay *Perth* was able to get under way again, but was the target for three more attacks between noon and 1300. On the last, the cruiser was near-missed. Fortunately, damage from the attack did not impair the ship's speed.

Two different figures are quoted in records for the number of troops embarked by King's force. Captain Morse, NOIC, Crete, placed the number at 3,410 and King, 6,029. The latter figure is regarded as correct.

On the afternoon of the 29th, Morse signalled Cunningham the number of troops likely to be available on each night up to 31 May. These were 6,000, 5,000 and then 3,000. Unaware that Freyberg's messages had not been received by Campbell at Rethymnon, he advised Cunningham that this force would be embarked from Plakia Bay on the 31st.

Captain Arliss' force, now reduced to the destroyers *Napier* and *Nizam*, sailed from

Alexandria at 0915 on the 30th, passed King's squadron late in the afternoon and soon after came under air attack. At midnight they were standing off Sfakia and thirty minutes later troops were swarming over their rails. The army ashore had allocated a maximum of 250 men to each destroyer, but Arliss soon corrected their estimates of his ship's carrying capacity. By 0300, with 1,403 safely bedded down in the two destroyers, they sailed on the return passage.

Arliss' departure was delayed for thirty minutes when two Sunderland flying boats took off from the bay. The aircraft were taking Generals Freyberg and Weston and Captain Morse to safety.

Three hours after leaving Sfakia, the crews of *Napier* and *Nizam* were surprised by the appearance of a flight of long-range Hurricane fighters overhead. They were the first Allied aircraft they had seen over enemy waters since the battle had started. The fighters remained with them for thirty minutes, until their fuel reached the danger level. As they dipped their wings, the sailors gave them a spontaneous cheer. It took courage of a high order to operate so far from land, knowing the odds of being picked up alive were negligible.

Soon after the fighters departed, the ships were attacked twice by enemy bombers, but the attacks were not pressed home.

At 1430, *Napier*'s engineering officer, Commander Oliver, reported a broken oil pump and the ship stopped for thirty long minutes while repairs were effected. One of the ship's crew recorded in his diary the feelings of the destroyer's crew and passengers when the ship got under way again: 'At 1500, seven hundred sighs of relief went straight up to heaven'.

When the ships arrived at Alexandria, Arliss reported to Cunningham: 'There are roughly 6,500 men still on Crete who could still be rescued. Most of these are at Sfakia.' However, in Crete on that night, there were close to 14,000 men.

The last rescue convoy sailed from Alexandria at 0600 on 31 May. It was commanded by Rear Admiral King and consisted of the cruiser *Phoebe*, the minelayer *Abdiel* and the destroyers *Kimberley, Hotspur* and *Jackal*. Their destination was Sfakia, although during the night the Commander-in-Chief came under army pressure to divert it to Plakia Bay where the gallant 1,200-strong garrison from Rethymnon was believed to be waiting. The garrison, including the author, had surrendered twelve hours earlier. Fortunately, Cunningham did not bend to the pressure.

King arrived off the now-battered little fishing port at 2320 on that night. The ships were carrying large quantities of food and medical supplies for those who would be left behind. These were landed before the troops were embarked. The admiral soon learnt German troops had completely surrounded Sfakia during the day. Fighting had taken place within half a mile of the beach and, even now, the ships were within small-arms range of the shore.

However, embarkation was slow. By 0300, departure time, only 3,900 troops had been taken off. The beachmaster reported to King that personnel not listed for evacuation had attacked the control officers and disrupted the marshalling of troops. As a result of this, the Australian rearguard troops who had held the Germans at bay for three days and were given priority for the last convoy, did not reach the beach and were taken prisoner of war. It was a sad ending for a courageous evacuation.

The return passage to Alexandria was free of enemy air attacks and once more RAF Hurricanes met the squadron soon after daylight. To further ensure their safe return, Cunningham despatched the anti-aircraft cruisers *Calcutta* and *Coventry* to patrol midway between Crete and Egypt. At 0900, five hours before they were to meet the squadron, the two ships were attacked by a large force of Stuka dive-bombers and fighter-bombers. Thirty of the Stukas concentrated their attacks on *Calcutta* and the veteran of Norway and many other battles was hit by two bombs and sunk.

Coventry stood by her sister ship and, despite the continuing attacks, picked up twenty-three officers and 232 sailors from her crew. *Calcutta* was the last Royal Navy ship sunk in the Battle of Crete.

With the arrival of King's squadron at Alexandria, the results of the evacuation could be assessed. A total of 16,511 troops were rescued from the island, but 13,000 were left behind to become prisoners of war.

Crete cost the navy dearly. Ship losses were 3 cruisers, 6 destroyers, 2 sloops, 1 minesweeper and 7 Coastal Forces vessels. Two battleships, an aircraft carrier, 3 cruisers and 2 destroyers were damaged beyond the repair capacity of the Mediterranean dockyards.

No account of the Royal Navy's participation in the Battle of Crete would be complete without reference to the Suda Bay Local Patrol. An odd mixture of small vessels under the command of Captain Morse, it was responsible for defence of the base and adjacent coastal waters. The patrol was made up of five MTBs, three MLs and a dozen or more small auxiliaries such as boom-defence vessels, minesweepers and landing craft. The strangest of this unusual force were two whale-chasers, *KOS 21* and *KOS 22*.

The auxiliary patrol vessel *Syvern* was the first of the SBLP ships to engage the enemy. On 21 May she was on patrol to seaward of Suda Bay, guarding against possible enemy seaborne landings. At 1345 the small vessel was sighted by a Ju 88 fighter-bomber which immediately launched on attack. The three gunners on *Syvern*'s deck opened fire on the aircraft as it zoomed down in a power dive. Regardless of the hail of machine-gun and cannon fire, they continued firing until all were shot down. The vessel was now defenceless.

During the next ten minutes the Junkers made six low-level attacks and, on the last, hit the ammunition locker which immediately exploded, hurling shards of torn metal into the sky. One jagged shard struck the aircraft's port engine, causing it to sideslip and crash into the sea hard alongside the patrol vessel.

Syvern's luck deserted her on the 27th May when she sailed from Suda Bay for Alexandria. At sunset she came under a second attack from aircraft and was sunk by a 250-pound bomb. Her survivors reached the shore and were later evacuated to Alexandria.

Two days later Captain Morse despatched *ML 1011* to Sfakia on the south coast of the island to set up a base for possible evacuation. On reaching the south-west point of the island the ML met heavy weather and sought shelter behind Selinos Kastelli. Soon after first light on the next day she was sighted by a force of seven Me 109E fighters and two Ju 88s. Like *Syvern*, her gunners manned the single Lewis gun and endeavoured to fight off her attackers. The gunners were hit by the first burst of cannon fire from the aircraft. Seconds later a heavy bomb landed close alongside and the vessel rolled over and sank. *ML 1011*'s survivors crossed the mountains and were later evacuated from the base which they had failed to establish.

The remaining two MLs of the patrol, *1030* and *1032*, sailed for Alexandria early on the 28th. Several hours later they were off the small island of Gavdhopoula and there they were sighted by a flight of Ju 88s. The two vessels closed and engaged their attackers with machine-guns and rifles. *ML 1030* received the full fury of the strafing attack and was soon reduced to a sinking wreck. *ML 1032* was luckier than her sister ship. She was not hit and drifted behind a low headland which protected her from further attacks. She later continued her voyage and reached Alexandria on 29 May.

The stubby whale-chasers *KOS 21* and *KOS 22* sailed from Suda Bay on the evening of 26 May but at daylight were still in the outer reaches of the large bay. They took refuge in a small inlet, intending to lay up until dusk, but late in the afternoon two German aircraft dived on them and both ships were hit by bombs and set on fire. *KOS 22* was totally wrecked but *KOS 21*, although fire-blackened and with her superstructure reduced to splintered timber, was still afloat and with the engine undamaged. The survivors of the other ship boarded her and at 0600 on the next day they sailed south for Alexandria.

Within an hour of getting under way they were under attack. A Junkers 87 swooped out of the sky and lashed the small ship with machine-gun and cannon fire. The crew fought back with the single Lewis gun and succeeded in driving the aircraft off. One man was killed and a second seriously wounded. *KOS 21* resumed her voyage but two hours later the Luftwaffe found her again. Four Heinkel 111 bombers strafed the battered whale-chaser in consecutive attacks from both sides. Two more men were killed in the fifteen-minute attack.

The ship was now out of sight of Crete but still within range of its tormentors. The last attack was suffered at 1220 and two men were wounded. *KOS 21* was leaking in three places along the waterline and the vessel was listing. However, there was no thought of abandoning ship and they continued. Forty-eight hours later they sighted the coast of Africa, altered course to the south-east and closed the coast, but ran hard aground on a submerged reef. All hands turned to and baled the hull until the water level fell to two feet. The tired old craft trembled down her length and floated free. Three hours later it was sighted by the escort vessel *Flamingo* and towed to Alexandria, where it arrived late on 1 June.

HMS *Lanner*, the fourth and last ship of the Suda Bay Local Patrol to escape, was a small trawler of indefinite age which had been commissioned as a minesweeper. She was manned by a Maltese crew and commanded by an Aberdeen captain, Skipper W. Stewart, RNR. This unusual combination, described in Captain Morse's commendation as 'a fearless and determined ship's company', had survived continuous bombing and strafing for over a month before being despatched to Alexandria on 27 May.

Skipper Stewart sailed north from Suda Bay before turning east. On several occasions enemy aircraft flew low over the old trawler but did not attack, confused by the course it was following. Under cover of darkness Stewart turned south and by morning on the 29th was well clear of Crete. *Lanner* arrived at Alexandria at 0300 on the 30th.

The one other vessel of the Suda Bay Local Patrol, the landing ship *A 16*, was sunk on the same day in Cretan waters. It required thirty-seven dive-bombing attacks to sink her. The crew were picked up by the minelayer *Abdiel*.

The navy lost more than 2,000 men—twice the number suffered by the army.

Cunningham wrote in his dispatch to the Admiralty: 'Losses and damage were sustained which would normally only occur in a major fleet action. The Mediterranean Fleet paid a heavy price for its achievement and I trust that it will not be lightly forgotten.'

The finest tribute paid to Cunningham and his fleet was that of Colonel Utz, who commanded the German 100th Mountain Regiment during the assault on Sfakia: 'We had no knowledge the British were evacuating troops from the beach. My first knowledge of the successful rescue of 13,000 troops from Sfakia was on the morning of 1 June when captured British officers were interrogated.'

7

The Phantom Armies

The German conquests of Greece and the islands of the Aegean were never complete. Of all the campaigns fought in the Second World War, the ratio of evaders and escapees in this theatre was the highest. This large number of Allied troops, integrated with the local populations, tied down more than two German divisions for almost four years.

Conservative estimates, made soon after the main campaigns ended, placed the number of Allied troops still free close to 6,000. In Greece there were more than 3,000, in Crete 2,000 and in Leros in 1944 some 300. Postwar studies suggest these estimates were low. Reductions caused by the capture of escapees and evaders, and the continual stream of those who returned to friendly territory and those who died were topped up by more escapees joining the phantom army.

German occupation authorities were well aware of the large number of enemy troops being sheltered by the local inhabitants, but there were restraints to mounting full-scale operations against them. Foremost in these was the danger of sparking an open conflict with the countless resistance groups which thrived in the rough terrain. The German occupation forces knew vast quantities of arms and ammunition had fallen into Greek hands after the battles and were afraid of the powerful Greek Orthodox Church leading a resistance campaign against them. Memories of the church's role in the uprisings against the Turks a half century earlier were fresh in German minds. Consequently, direct action, when it was resorted to, was somewhat subdued.

Large-scale drives were initiated in Crete in the second half of 1941 but brought few results. In October a division of 15,000 troops, supported by aircraft, launched a well-organised drive through the mountains of western Crete, where it was known that 2,000 Allied soldiers were being sheltered by villagers. It netted fewer than 100 escapees and evaders, the majority of whom were either seriously ill or disillusioned. When direct action failed, 100,000 leaflets were dropped from the air, threatening death to any civilian found harbouring British soldiers. The results were negligible. This was followed by a poster campaign offering substantial rewards for information leading to the capture of escaped enemy soldiers.

Frustrated by all this effort, the Germans resorted to infiltrating English-speaking German soldiers posing as British escapees into the more troublesome areas. The author met one of these agents in the village of Livados in late 1941. Fortunately, for both the Greeks and escapees, few were deceived and a number of the German agents vanished without trace.

Allied Headquarters in Cairo learnt of the existence of the phantom army when the first escapees reached safety in 1941. General Wavell ordered Special Operations Executive, which already had small intelligence networks operating in the occupied areas, to organise rescue missions. SOE recognised Crete as the easiest area to begin. An intelligence network had been established on the island before the war under John Pendlebury, a distinguished archaeologist who was leading British Museum excavations at the Minoan sites near Heraklion.

Unfortunately, British Intelligence was not aware that Pendlebury's network had been penetrated by the Germans before the attack on Crete. The archaeologist was wounded and captured by paratroopers on the first day of the assault on Heraklion, treated at a German casualty station and later interviewed by enemy intelligence officers. It is believed Pendlebury was executed that night and buried near the airfield. His body was exhumed twice during the occupation for identification.

Pendlebury lives on in Cretan legends, in which he is known as Colonel Cyclops because he lost an eye early in life and wore an eye glass. During the occupation, when fighting was heard in the mountains mothers would turn to their children and say: 'Ah, Colonel Cyclops'.

Major Ian Fielding replaced Pendlebury, and within a few months established a headquarters in a cave on the heights of Mount Ida. He was later joined by Major A.M. Rendel, Captain T.J. Dunbabin and Captain Patrick Leigh-Fermor. These officers established more networks, which within a few months covered the whole of Crete. All five SOE operators were awarded the DSO at the end of the war.

The new organisation's first task was to locate the escapees and evaders and establish their numbers. This was a considerable task in the rugged mountain terrain, but they soon discovered the heaviest concentrations were in western Crete. By early August, a fair estimate was made and arrangements were put in train to take them off. The story of these organised escapes is related in the next chapter but, before they were organised, and indeed for several years after, enterprising soldiers and airmen were responsible for some of the most remarkable individual escapes in history.

Two Australian corporals, Ken Clift and Jim Cochrane, were cut off from their battalion when German tanks attacked on the Pinios River in Northern Greece on 18 April 1941. They escaped capture and moved into rough country near the coast. Here they met other Australian soldiers in a similar plight, and together they set out for the coast where they hoped they would be picked up by the navy. They walked for two days through rough country and reached a small fishing village south of Volos. Their welcome was friendly, but the villagers were terrified of a surprise visit by the Germans and hid the Australians in a small church some distance from the village.

One of the men in the party had a map which showed a small naval base on the island of Skia, twenty miles to the east. Next morning they returned to the village and explained their plan to reach Skia. The villagers lent them a small barge fitted with an old semi-diesel engine. They put to sea at 0700, but on clearing the land found themselves in a choppy sea and spent the four hours needed to reach the island baling continually.

The naval base was on the western side of Skia and as they closed the shore it became obvious German bombs had reduced it to a deserted waste of rubble, collapsed jetties and workshops, twisted cranes and the shells of burnt-out buildings. The only vessels they found were two rusting hulks against the jetty wall. Their presence was observed by some of the few residents of the island, who told them there were no boats and precious little food on the island. However, they shared with them part of a goat they were cooking.

Clift and his comrades discussed sailing on to Turkey, but this was obviously impractical. The barge had little fuel and was not equipped with a sail. They returned to the fishing village where they were greeted by another party, made up of two New Zealand infantrymen, along with the British attaché at Salonika and his daughter. A conference was held in the little church next morning, and all agreed they must move on, as the villagers were short of food. The attaché suggested they press on to the south, where the battle was still being fought, and they would eventually reach their own lines. There were no dissenters to the proposal.

Two hours later, after thanking their hosts, they set off again in the little barge which they agreed to hide wherever it ran out of fuel. The voyage ended ten miles south of the village and they ran the barge into a small bay and covered it with bushes. Next day they set out inland. Soon after noon they reached a road which passed through dense forest and they rested. However, an hour later they heard a truck approaching. Cochrane identified it as a Greek armoured car. They flagged it down and the Greek officer in command offered them a lift south.

Three hours later they stopped beside a railway marshalling yard where they were set down by the armoured car. The Greeks were heading inland. An abandoned train was on a siding and two of the New Zealanders and Clift walked over to it. The firebox was still warm and, as luck would have it, one of the New Zealanders had been a train driver in civilian life. The party was set to work searching for anything combustible and twenty minutes later they steamed out of the yard.

As the train rattled across a set of points dozens of soldiers appeared from the trees and climbed aboard. The journey lasted three hours. At 2210, they sighted lights close to the line. They stopped and learnt they were on the Gulf of Corinth. The lights they had seen were beacons for ships offshore, waiting to evacuate troops. An hour later the escapees were packed into a landing barge buffetting its way through a choppy sea to the Australian ships *Perth* and *Stuart*.

Clift and Cochrane's escape demonstrated the need for escapees to keep moving. Opportunity is where you find it and seldom does it come to the escaper.

Commanding officers rarely make successful escapes. An exception to the rule was Squadron Leader Edward Howell, who, against the most impossible odds, escaped from the officers' compound at Salonika prison camp in February 1942 and arrived in Turkey three months later. However, his amazing saga started in Crete almost a year earlier, when Howell commanded a squadron of Hurricane fighters based at Maleme. The squadron arrived from Malta in early May with twelve aircraft but by the 13th of the month this number had been reduced to three. Maleme and nearby Suda Bay were the target for the German air fleet based on Athens, Kythera and Scarpanto.

On the morning of 13 May, thirty Me 109 fighters dived on the airfield in a continual strafing attack. Two Hurricanes took off to intercept but the pilot of the third could not be found and Howell, who had not previously flown Hurricanes, took the plane up. The unequal dogfight lasted thirty minutes. Hurricanes and Messerschmitts weaved and climbed in the cloudless skies until only one Hurricane remained. It was Howell's.

When his ammunition was exhausted he flew low out to sea, waited until the air above the tarmac was clear and then touched down. His aircraft was hit and burst into flames only seconds after he climbed from the cockpit. The three Hurricanes shot down six Messerschmitts.

This dogfight was the last fought in the Battle of Crete and Howell and his ground staff now turned to the ground defence of the airfield. The mixed band of grounded pilots, fitters and some Fleet Air Arm personnel were formed into two infantry companies and dug in around the field. They were armed with a few machine-guns, rifles and pistols. An hour after dawn on 20 May, the first German paratroops to land in Crete fell within Howell's perimeter. Despite their lack of experience, the airmen attacked and destroyed this group. More German drops during the day forced the airmen to fall back on the infantry positions.

Howell was wounded while resisting the first of these attacks. A burst of machine-gun fire smashed his left arm and reduced his shoulder to shredded pulp. The fighting moved away and he lay where he had fallen for three days. He was delirious and conscious only for short periods. The sun baked him during the day and he froze at night from the bitter cold. He was tormented by clouds of vicious flies which smothered his clotted wounds.

On the morning of the third day he was found by a German patrol which carried him to a captured British casualty clearing station, where the medical officer in charge was his squadron medical officer, Flying Officer T. Cullen, RAF. Cullen saved Howell's life. He cleaned the shocking wounds, and performed an emergency operation and then convinced the German doctors his squadron leader would die unless he received further surgery in a fully equipped hospital. That evening, despite the many German wounded awaiting evacuation, Howell was flown to Athens in a Junkers transport.

Kokina Military Hospital, in the suburbs of Athens, became Howell's home for six pain-wrecked months. Here, he underwent a series of major operations and at times fears were held for his life. Recovery was slow and when it came, his arm was paralysed, bent at right angles in front of his body like the antenna of a praying mantis.

While he lay in his hospital bed, Howell's mind was never far from plans for escape. He made his first attempt while still a patient at Kokina, hiding in the back of a laundry van and covering himself with dirty linen. It was unfortunate that the sentry at the hospital gates was conscientious and searched the van. Howell spent the next week in solitary confinement.

Permanently handicapped by his useless arm, Howell was transferred to the transit prisoner of war camp at Salonika in November 1941. The camp was the former Greek army barracks, surrounded by high stone walls topped with coils or barbed wire. Tall watchtowers at every corner looked down on the camp and its surroundings. Sentries patrolled the walls at all times and searchlights swept the compounds at night.

The officers' compound demoralised the most ardent escapers. Howell failed to find a weakness in its security in three months of ceaseless searching, but he planned dozens of madcap escapes. In the end, he decided meticulously planned schemes could not succeed, but one so simple that only a fool would attempt it might work.

He waited for the first moonless night, lowered himself one-handed out of a window on the second floor of the barracks and then dropped several feet to teeter on the top

A German Heinkel He 177 bomber operating in the Aegean, 1943. *(U.S. Air Force)*

German Stuka dive-bomber attacking a British cruiser in the Aegean, 1943.

Hurricane long-range fighters flew from Gambut, Egypt to provide cover over the Aegean.

The Beaufighter was the most successful Allied anti-shipping aircraft in the eastern Mediterranean.

The U.S. Air Force P-38 Lightning fighter-bomber was the only effective Allied long-range fighter in the Aegean.

The Hunt Class destroyer *Hursley* participated in the battles of Cos and Leros in 1943 and was later transferred to the Royal Hellenic Navy and renamed *Kriti*.

The corvette, HMAS *Ipswich* was the only Australian warship to participate in the battles of Cos and Leros in 1943.

The light cruiser *Penelope* was heavily damaged in the Aegean.

HMS *Eclipse*, Fleet Class destroyer, sunk by a mine in the Aegean. *(Imperial War Museum)*

The Hunt Class destroyer *Aldenham*, sunk by a mine in the Adriatic in 1944. *(Imperial War Museum)*

Coastal Forces' MLs were strongly armed for their size and proved more than a match for German small craft in the Aegean.

HDMLs were a larger craft than the ML and carried a heavier armament.

German transport under attack by a RAF bomber in the central Aegean, November 1943.

German HS-293 controllable glide bombs were responsible for the sinking of two Royal Navy ships in the Aegean. *(U.S. Air Force)*

of an eleven-inch wide brick wall. Groping like a blind man, he shuffled thirty feet to the roof of a storehouse which adjoined the perimeter wall. Dense coils of barbed wire were secured to the roof, but he squeezed and crawled through them. Bleeding from dozens of painful scratches and cuts, he at last reached the final obstacle to freedom.

For ten minutes Howell stood on the wall like some grotesque witch, his ears tuned for the slightest noise which would reveal the presence of a sentry below him. At last, his frozen arm stretched in front of his body, he stepped out into the blackness below. He plunged seventeen feet to the ground and, miraculously, landed squarely on his feet. When he was sure he had not been discovered, he stumbled over the open ground to a road and ten minutes later was walking warily through a sleeping suburb.

By first light, Howell was clear of the city and climbing the foothills which rose behind Salonika. He walked all that day, avoiding well-used paths and villages, but late in the afternoon he entered the village of Kissos, 4,000 feet up in the Khortiate Mountains. Here he found friendly farmers eager to help him.

The squadron leader wandered for eight long weeks through north-eastern Greece. His strange deformity proved an asset in winning over the religious people whose beliefs encouraged them to help the halt and the maimed. They provided him with shepherd's clothing, fed him and guided him. Eventually he reached the small fishing village of Nikita on the Gulf of Kassandra. Here he met a party of English, Australian and New Zealand soldiers, fellow escapees who were now searching for a boat to take them to Turkey.

This was provided by a group of fishermen some days after Howell joined them. They sailed the same night, hugging the rugged coastline of the Salonika Peninsular, and landed at dawn on the small island of Yerokristos. Here, Howell joined a party of young Greek Army officers and civilians who had obtained a larger caique. They remained on Yerokristos for twenty-four hours and sailed at sunset for Mount Athos, crossing the Gulf of Ayiom Oros. An hour before dawn, they arrived on the peninsular and hid the boat under seaweed. Howell was fascinated by the monasteries built high on the crags of the mountains and resolved one day to revisit them.

The number of British escapees and evaders assisted by the monks of the Holy Mountain is not known, but soon after the war ended, an UNRRA and British Economic Mission visited Mount Athos with a gift of food, clothing and money in recognition of the service they rendered to British servicemen. An officer with this mission was an Australian, Major Alex Sheppard, who had served on General Blamey's staff and was responsible for the evacuation from Porto Rafti.

The most dangerous part of the voyage lay ahead of Howell and the others. Their destination was the Turkish island of Imbros, but to reach it they must sail through the open waters of the Aegean Sea. Imbros was the only island in the Cyclades and the Sporades groups which offered freedom to Allied escapees, but the waters which separated it from mainland Greece were patrolled by strong German sea and air forces.

They set sail after dark in a stiff breeze which quickly carried them clear of the coast. The motion of the boat was violent, and most of the party were seasick. The night passed quickly and daylight found them short of their destination. At 0800 they were sighted by a Junkers 88 aircraft which circled the boat at 500 or 600 feet. Howell could clearly see the features of the crew. Only two men were on the caique's deck, and their waves convinced the Germans it was an innocent fishing vessel.

Soon after the aircraft departed, they sighted land and ran the vessel into a small bay beneath a cluster of fishermen's huts. One of the crew went ashore but returned after a few minutes. They had landed on the heavily garrisoned German island of Lemnos, mistaking it for Imbros. To leave the island in daylight would attract unwanted attention, so the boat was warped under some low cliffs and covered with fishing nets.

They set sail again early in the evening and three hours later reached Imbros. On the next morning Howell, now dressed in a civilian suit, met the British Consul General and a former Prime Minister of Australia, Mr Billy Hughes, who was visiting the island with a commission.

Squadron Leader Howell recovered sufficiently from his ordeal to serve the last year of the war behind a desk in RAF Command. After demobilisation, he entered the church, his experiences having brought him close to God.

The escape of Australian Private S.L. Carroll may have lacked the bizarre circumstances surrounding Howell's epic, but it stands out as one of the finest single-handed escapes in the annals of war. Carroll escaped capture when German parachutists overwhelmed the courageous defenders of Rethymnon. He crossed the island to Ayia Galini and joined a group of around 500 troops from Heraklion and Rethymnon. Half of this mixed group were of the Argyll and Sutherland Regiment.

At Aya Galini, three small A-lighters, abandoned after the evacuation, were being prepared to sail to Egypt, but Carroll realised his chances of being included in the crews were slim. He sought other means of escape and, after a few days of searching along the coast, he found it in an old, abandoned fishing boat. The open craft had seen better days. In places the sun shone through the splintered and rotten planks and the vessel had no oars, rowlocks, mast, boom, sail, rigging or rudder. Undaunted, Carroll set out to make good the deficiencies.

He ranged miles into the mountainous interior and along the rugged coast seeking materials to repair and outfit his vessel. His peacetime experience as a telegraph linesman, truck driver and gold-miner had taught him to improvise, and improvise he did. A piece of a disused well cover provided timber to nail over the split and rotten planks. He caulked the gaps with dry grass. A six-foot length of bamboo became his mast. The boom was a broken fish spear abandoned in a fisherman's hut and the sail a length of sieving material he purloined from a village flour mill. Carroll cut the sail to shape with his pocket knife and sewed it with thread plucked from the material. His needle was a rusted nail. He fashioned a rudder from the end of a small wine cask.

Provisioning the boat for a 380-mile ocean voyage, which could take anything from a week to a month, posed its own peculiar problems. Any food remaining in the abandoned villages had long been pillaged by the large number of hungry soldiers in the area. The flour mill provided a small bag of iron-hard crusts which had fallen behind the machinery. Two green lemons were washed up on the tide and his emergency rations, a two-ounce slab of unsweetened chocolate sealed in a tin, completed his rations for the voyage.

WX593, Private S.L. Carroll, embarked on his great odyssey an hour after sunset on 11 June. He launched the boat without ceremony and paddled through the small surf using a floorboard. Once clear of the undertow, he tackled the problem of setting sail. It was more difficult than he anticipated. The crude rig and his guesswork sail were not designed to draw the wind readily. The boat clawed through the water like a drunken sailor, but the lone voyager persevered. When daylight came, the mountains of Crete were still tantalisingly close. Carroll estimated he logged ten miles on his first night at sea.

The Western Australian had no navigation instruments. The course to bring him to the North African coast was rudimentary. There was no chance of sailing past and missing it, but it was necessary to keep the boat's bow pointing in the right direction. The wind was favourable, and by trial and error he succeeded in maintaining a steady course.

A greater problem was food and water. If he failed to reach land in seven days he would either starve to death or die of thirst. He rationed himself severely. A few crusts of bread and a half-inch square of chocolate washed down by a mouthful of water barely touched the lining of his stomach.

The wind continued favourably and the days passed with excruciating slowness. Carroll knew by the sun and the North Star that he was on course. He sighted neither ship nor aircraft throughout the voyage and only one bird. If there were fish in the sea, they were deep down below. On the morning of the seventh day after leaving Crete, Carroll saw a slight smudge low on the horizon to the south. He knew it was land, and his landfall is best told in the official account he prepared on returning to Egypt:

'At dawn on the seventh morning a strong north-wester blew up and by 1000 had developed into a gale. I was obliged to alter my southerly course and run before the wind. Up till then I had used [for a compass] a pen knife mounted on a piece of board. When the blade cast a fine shadow I knew I was heading south. Sailing by night I used the North Star as a guide. For more than twenty-four hours I ran before the wind, surfing the waves which must have been twenty or thirty feet high. My eyes were giving me a lot of trouble, the left being badly affected, gave me a blind side and made it difficult to judge the waves.

'A little after sunrise on the eighth day I could see a haze in the sky away to the south. Taking a chance, I pushed the boat across the waves, it was quite a battle holding her against them; they were striking me broadside on. The mast, being a misfit, began to kick from side to side. Twice I took a risk and left the tiller to brace it with floorboards but was nearly swamped. Hoping the planks would hold out long enough, I kept on and sighted land about 0800. I gave her every bit of canvas she had, not caring a hang what may happen now. About 1000 she began to leak badly, forward on the port side. With still a good distance to go, the water commenced to beat me; trying to bail and steer at the same time was impossible, I could not keep my feet. Land appeared to be only a few miles off—but it must have been nearer ten.

'When the boat filled and overturned and the mast smashed a hole in the bottom, my dreams of sailing into Alexandria went with it. I fixed the water tin, almost empty now, across my shoulders and struck out for the shore. It took me seven hours to reach land, swimming, floating and surfing. From the crest of waves I could see the breakers pounding on the rocks and dashing spray into the air. This was the closest call I had up to date and I had a terrific struggle to try and keep from being carried on to the rocks and still retain my hold on the tin. If I couldn't find a place to go in, I thought it might serve to take the impact, giving me the chance to scramble clear before the next wave hit me. Fortunately, I was able to work along to a small patch of sand and came ashore, the breakers spinning me around in all directions. I had to crawl on my hands and knees, feeling too giddy to walk.

'I drank most of the water I had left, wrung out my trousers, the only article of clothing I had left, and started inland. I knew the road ran close to the coast. After walking for about an hour I came across an Air Force listening post. Next morning I was taken to Mersa Matruh.'

Luck favoured Carroll all the way. Had the summer squall struck an hour earlier, he most certainly would have foundered in the open sea. As a result of this epic voyage he joined the Royal Australian Navy later in the war.

One of the earliest escapes in the Aegean was made by Trooper L. Addicott of No. 50 Middle East Commando in February 1941. The commandos were landed on Casteloriso early on the morning of the 25th and seized the island. However, reinforcements failed to arrive and the commandos were overcome by a strong force of Italians. Addicott and his comrades were taken prisoner and shipped to Rhodes.

On 3 March, he and nine companions slipped away from a working party on the east coast of the island and hid in a cave close to a beach. From this hideout, the escapees could see a blur low on the horizon which they knew was Turkey. The ten men entered the water soon after dark and started to swim to freedom. They soon became separated but kept swimming. Four were drowned, but six reached the Turkish shore. Addicott lapsed into unconsciousness within sight of the land but was picked up by a Turkish patrol boat.

All six men were well treated by the Turkish soldiers, who allowed them two days to recuperate before taking them to their headquarters at Ankara. The journey was made on horseback and took them over the Taurus Mountains. On arrival at Ankara they were handed over to British Embassy staff who arranged their train journey to the small port of Mersin. Here they were placed on board a ship packed with Polish refugees, which took them to Famagusta in Cyprus. Trooper Addicott and his companions later rejoined their unit in Egypt.

The fastest escape voyage from Crete to Egypt was made by a party of two New Zealanders and an Australian who had been left behind at Sfakia when the evacuation ended. Privates B.B. Carter, D.N. McQuarrie and the Australian, N.R. Buchecher, sought refuge in a mountain village for four weeks after leaving Sfakia. However, at the end of this period they realised the Cretans had little food themselves, so they returned to the coast. They found a fishing boat in a shed some distance from a village and decided to steal it. Unlike the craft used by Carroll a month earlier, this boat was in good condition and complete with sails and oars.

Gathering a small quantity of food from nearby villages, the three men set sail on the evening of 15 July and by dawn on the next day they were out of sight of land. The wind was right and the boat almost sailed itself. On the morning of the 19th they sighted land and three hours later beached the boat several miles east of Sidi Barrani. On the four-day voyage they had seen neither ship nor aircraft. All three were awarded the Military Medal for their exploit.

Persistence and determination were two of the essentials required for a successful escape. Lance Corporal I.D. Welsh displayed these qualities in three escapes attempts, and was finally rewarded for his efforts.

Welsh and another Australian escaped from Skines prison camp, south of Canea, and crossed the mountains of Crete in June 1941. In the vicinity of Souya, they stole a small rowing boat and set out for Cyprus, a most unlikely destination as it led them through the heavily patrolled waters to the south of Kasos, Scarpanto and Rhodes. However, the choice of destination had little bearing on the attempt because, 500 yards offshore they were sighted by two enemy aircraft which strafed the craft until it was reduced to matchwood. Depressed by their stillborn attempt, the escapees retraced their steps over the White Mountains and broke back into the prison camp at Skines.

In late June Welsh was transferred to the transit prisoner of war camp at Salonika. On 13 July he joined a mass breakout from this camp which almost cost him his life. Early on that day, a 24-inch diameter sewerage pipe was discovered which passed under the perimeter wire of the camp and emptied into a large septic tank in a field beyond. He joined some fifty prisoners who squeezed into the pipe and commenced worming their way to freedom.

He reached the halfway point, where the pipe changed direction, and was stopped by the man ahead who had become jammed. Welsh could not go forward or back. Behind him were twenty other prisoners similarly trapped. Eventually, the man nearest the entry point crawled out and informed a sentry. The guards carried machine-guns to both ends of the pipe and opened fire. Welsh was lucky, the bend in the pipe saved him from being hit, but twenty prisoners were killed.

This experience had a traumatic effect on the young prisoner and he became determined to escape at any price. Three weeks later he slipped away from a working party, stripped off his uniform and, walking away in civilian clothes he had donned under his tunic and slacks, he made his way to a working-class suburb. Friendly Greeks hid and fed him before passing him down a chain of villages which led him to the Holy Monastery of Mount Athos.

The monks cared for Welsh until a boat was arranged to carry him and six British escapees to Imbros. This voyage was not without hazards. They set out from Mount Athos in a long, open boat rowed by six tall black-clad monks. Five times, savage storms forced them back to their starting point, but on the sixth they succeeded.

Welsh and the other escapers were transferred from Imbros to Adana in Turkey, where the German Consul lodged a complaint to the Turkish government on the legality of their entry. The Turks smiled and reminded the consul of German troops concealed in his consulate. The small party crossed into Syria on 10 October and became free men.

Individual escapes continued throughout the war. Lieutenant C. White and three other soldiers of the Long Range Desert Group evaded capture when Leros fell to the Germans on 16 November 1943. Moving by night, the small party reached Serocampo Bay where they found an abandoned rowing boat which had been holed during the fighting. They dragged the boat ashore, patched it with pieces of canvas cut from their haversacks and set off that night to row to Turkey.

The voyage was thirty miles longer than the fifty they had estimated, and every mile was through waters continuously patrolled by enemy aircraft and ships. They rowed by night and lay up on small islands during the daylight hours. On the third night they landed on a beach close to the Turkish port of Bodrum. A week later they crossed the border into Syria and were free men.

In 1943 the SBS included escaping techniques in their training and a high percentage of their men who were taken by the enemy escaped successfully and returned to their units.

Captain J. Lodwick and Bombadier Nixon were captured in the last raid on Cretan airfields in June 1944, when they were tracked down by dogs soon after laying their demolition charges and seized by guards. Lodwick concealed his rank and the two soldiers were taken to a prisoner of war camp in Yugoslavia. They escaped on the night of their arrival and crossed Yugoslavia and northern Greece in trucks and on freight trains. The last stage of their journey was made on foot to a secret base of the Levant Schooner Flotilla.

The voyage through the Aegean to Haifa was made in a caique, and ten weeks to the day after they were landed in Crete, they returned to their headquarters in Syria.

The total number of Allied personnel to make successful individual escapes in the eastern Mediterranean area in the Second World War is not known, but it is believed to have reached 6,000. In the three-month period, 1 June to 1 September 1941, an estimated 400 Australians, New Zealand and British escaped by their own devices from Crete to Egypt, despite this involving a hazardous sea voyage of 380 miles.

8

The Organised Escapes

In early September 1941 Middle East Command came under pressure from the Australian and New Zealand governments to take active steps in evacuating the large numbers of Dominion troops still free in occupied Greece and Crete. A clearer picture of the concentrations of escapees and evaders in these areas was now available, and the task of organising their evacuation was made the responsibility of Special Operations Executive.

The main concentrations of this lost army were in central and northern Greece and in western Crete. An unofficial escape route was already in existence in Greece which skirted around Salonika to Mount Athos, where the Greek Orthodox Church, in conjunction with the British Ambassador in Turkey, had arranged a ferry service through the northern Aegean to Turkish-held Imbros. In Crete, however, the problem was more difficult. The German Command had placed a ban on all merchant shipping on the southern coast of the island and maintained both air and sea patrols to ensure its effectiveness. Consequently, evacuations from Crete could only be made by submarine and the fast patrol craft of Coastal Command.

Before SOE took over the responsibility, British and Australian officers had arranged a number of organised escapes from Crete using four small landing barges that had been abandoned when the official evacuation of the island ended.

Major R. Garrett of the Royal Marines salvaged the first of the barges ten miles east of Sfakia on 30 May. The barge was washed up on a beach in a small cove where it was difficult to locate from the air. When the vessel was refloated and repaired, Garrett embarked a party of 138 soldiers and Royal Marines and crossed the eighteen miles of open sea to the small island of Gavdhopoula which had not been occupied by the enemy.

They remained on the island for twenty-four hours, taking aboard water and whatever provisions they could buy from the inhabitants. The fuel tanks of the barge were about a third full and Garrett calculated this would carry them one-third of the way to the nearest point on the North African coast. The major hoped they would be picked up by a Royal Navy ship before their fuel was exhausted.

The barge sailed from Gavdhopoula on 1 June with a light following wind, and they made good progress for the first thirty hours. They drifted for twenty-four hours after the fuel was exhausted. On the evening of the 3rd a soldier shot himself. Realising there was little likelihood of rescue, Garrett set the men to work sewing sails from the blankets they had brought with them. Bootlaces were used to stitch the blankets and the soldiers' webbing belts were joined together for rigging and lines. Flooring boards were unscrewed and joined together for a mast.

On the morning of 5 June the barge was under sail, but the twin rudders and propellers caused it to move crabwise. To correct the course, twelve soldiers went over the side and swam the clumsy vessel back onto line. Garrett estimated they were making two knots. The wind failed on the 6th. The major reduced food and water rations to half a biscuit smeared with bully beef and half a cup of water per day. On the 7th, while still in the doldrums, a soldier died of exposure and his body was committed to the sea. By the 8th, all the men were weak and despondency was setting in. Garrett held a church service 'to raise the spirits of the company'.

A favourable wind rose during the night and at 0230 on 9 June they sighted land. Their landfall was nineteen miles north-west of Sidi Barrani. The major conned the barge for the run in to shore and soon after dawn they landed on an open beach 200 yards west of a British outpost.

Garrett's voyage was an epic. The LCM was designed to carry 100 men and was grossly overloaded. It was not designed for open-sea voyaging and its flat, keel-less hull, shaped like a shoebox, made it difficult to both sail and steer.

There was no communication between Garrett and Lieutenant G.M. Day of the 1st Welch Regiment, who was the senior officer of the group of soldiers who found the second barge. It had been abandoned on the open beach at Sfakia, exposed to the view of enemy coastal defence posts and the regular Luftwaffe air patrol. Day and three of his men reconnoitred the beach after dark and found the side of the barge exposed to the sea had built up a bank of sand and gravel. The task of freeing it was too great for his small party to undertake, so he withdrew to the mountains to recruit more men.

On the night of 31 May, Day returned to the beach with a party of forty-four men, the majority from the Welch Regiment. Two men were posted as sentries and the rest feverishly dug the barge from the bank of sand. They launched the craft and pushed and swam it out to deep water before starting the engine. Their run that night was about twenty-five miles to the island of Gavdhos, where they remained twenty-four hours while they filled the water tanks and obtained some provisions from the inhabitants.

Before they sailed from Gavdhos on the night of 1 June, Day decided to send a party of nine men ahead in a longboat which was found beached on the island. It was thought the smaller craft would make a faster passage and could arrange a boat from Africa to meet the barge.

The barge sailed after dark with an Australian, Private I. Hansen, who had some experience of sailing and navigation, in command. A light breeze was blowing and the sea was calm. They made good progress for fourteen hours until the fuel was exhausted. No attempt was made to improvise sails. The following wind was pushing the barge through the water at about two knots and Hansen believed they were in a south-flowing current.

The last of their food was eaten on the morning of 5 June and water was rationed to four teaspoons per man, morning and evening. Despite his lack of rank, Hansen proved a capable commander. He threatened and cajoled and brought the best out of his men in difficult circumstances. When some of the commandos were discovered drinking sea water, Hansen cocked the Tommy gun he was carrying and threatened to shoot them if they continued.

On the morning of 10 June the barge grounded on a beach close to Sidi Barrani, where they were found an hour later by a patrol from the garrison. The party was too weak to pull themselves out of the barge, having survived after five days without food and two days without water.

The third barge was found by a West Australian, Private H. Richards, twenty miles to the east of Sfakia. Richards and some companions manhandled it into the water and concealed it in a cave until they could find water and food for the voyage south. In the meantime, Richards selected a party of fifty men to accompany him on the voyage. The young West Australian assumed command of the vessel, which he named MV *Leaving*.

They sailed on the night of 1 June, an exceptionally clear night, and were sighted by a German post when only 200 yards offshore. Two machine-guns opened fire on them, but luckily the enemy was aiming too high and the barge was not hit. Like Hansen, Richards put into Gavdhos Island to top up his water tanks and obtain provisions. The poor inhabitants of the island could provide little food, but they were blessed by a Greek priest who was making his monthly call. Two of the barge's complement remained on the island, preferring the risk of meeting German patrols to the hazards of the sea.

They sailed from the island before dawn on the next day. There were eighty gallons of fuel in the vessel's tanks, which Richards estimated would carry them half the distance to Egypt. With this thought in mind, he set the men to work cutting and sewing sails from the blankets which had been brought aboard.

On the afternoon of 3 June another barge was sighted sailing south and signals were exchanged. Hansen, who it most certainly was, made no reference to the sighting in his report on the voyage. Later in the day, MV *Leaving*'s fuel was exhausted and the sail was rigged. The wind held fair and they were soon under way. Richards commented on the strange characteristics of the barge under sail. The blanket sail had much less area than the high freeboard of the vessel, which resulted in it sailing almost 30 degrees off course. To change tack, it was necessary for all passengers to go over the side and swim the barge around to the required course, as Garrett had found.

Richards' log showed the barge made 'fair speed' on the 4th and 5th and 'the wind held good'. The food supply was now almost exhausted. All that remained was several tins of cocoa and a container of margarine. This was mixed into a warm drink which was issued morning and evening.

The entry for 8 June in MV *Leaving*'s rough log read: 'All hands very weak and conditions become worse hourly'. Later on that day Richards recorded: 'I have called all members together and we held a [church] service conducted by an English sergeant. I might mention here, that every man in the boat put his heart and soul into this service.' At 1030 on that day they sighted land. However, the wind had fallen and they drifted for another eighteen hours before running ashore several miles west of Sidi Barrani.

Private Richards demonstrated a rare ability to command under extremely difficult conditions. The passengers in MV *Leaving* included two officers and ten NCOs but all responded to his leadership. One escapee later wrote: 'He exercised his command in a most masterly manner and inspired everyone of us to keep our spirits up'. Richards was awarded the DSM.

A fourth barge in serviceable condition was found beached near Ayia Galini, thirty-five miles to the east of the others on 1 June. This vessel was driven high up onto the beach and a wide sand bar separated it from the sea. It required two days of digging by a large squad of men and considerable hauling to refloat it. Command of the barge was taken by Captain J.B. Fitzhardinge, an Australian artillery officer with considerable experience in sailing. The immediate problem before undertaking a voyage was obtaining rations for a large number of men.

Fitzhardinge, with three men, set out in a small fishing boat to obtain food from the town of Timbaki, fifteen miles to the east. This expedition almost ended in disaster. While in the town collecting food, the party was surprised by a German motor cycle patrol and came under heavy machine-gun fire. The four men reached their boat in a hail of bullets but the boat was holed. Fitzhardinge and Private Mortimer later retrieved the boat and swam it into the shore. Lieutenant T.C. Beddells was wounded in three places but, together with the fourth man in the party, succeeded in reaching the boat. The party arrived back at Ayia Galini later in the day.

Fitzhardinge selected ten officers and sixty-six other ranks for the voyage. One of these was a South African Air Force engineer, Sergeant McWilliam, who was to prove a valuable addition to the undertaking. The barge sailed at 2030 on 2 June and at 0300 next morning, when well off the coast, was stopped by an Italian submarine. The submarine closed the barge and all officers were ordered aboard. Two, however, concealed their rank and remained on the barge. The submarine commander ordered the barge to reverse its course and return to Crete.

Command was now taken by Sergeant McWilliam, who steered for Crete until the submarine was out of sight and then returned to the original course. Fortunately, the fuel tanks were full and they made good progress. McWilliam was a strict disciplinarian and did not experience the problems which plagued Hansen in his barge.

Land was sighted on 5 June and the barge was beached near Mersa Matruh, close to the position occupied by the Australian 2/7th Australian Field Regiment in which the brothers of Captain Fitzhardinge and Lieutenant J. Morish, who had been taken prisoners by the submarine, were serving.

The four self-organised voyages saved 370 Allied soldiers from certain imprisonment. From information supplied by these parties, SOE obtained an accurate estimate of the number of troops still free on the island and plans were initiated to bring them out.

On the suggestion of the Commander-in-Chief, Mediterranean, SOE selected Lieutenant Commander Francis Pool, an intelligence officer who had served in Crete some years earlier, to be landed on the island. Pool was one of those officers whose origins were, and still are, veiled in mystery. It is known he was the representative of Imperial Airways at Heraklion in 1938 and an acquaintance of Colonel Pendlebury, the renowned archaeologist and officer in charge of British intelligence on the island. Many Greeks who were closely associated with Pool during the Second World War also believed he was one of a number of Englishmen who were ordained as priests in the Greek Orthodox Church at Mount Athos in the early 1930s.

During his period in Crete Pool adopted the dress of a Greek Orthodox priest. The author met him in the village of Mythros in August. He spoke Greek fluently and with his fine black hair and beard he certainly played the role of a priest effectively.

Pool was landed at Limni on the south coast of Crete in early July 1941 by the submarine HMS *Thrasher* and held discussions with the abbot of nearby Prevelli Monastery, Agathangelos Lagouvardous, soon after. An outcome of this discussion was the use of Greek priests to direct and muster British evaders and escapees in the villages around Limni.

The choice of Limni as the evacuation point was not accidental. Captain T.A.B. Brattan, RN, commanding the 595-ton survey sloop *Spitfire*, had surveyed the southern coast of Crete in 1851 and, in his report to the Admiralty, emphasised Limni as the only anchorage on the coast affording protection for ships from summer storms. And so, ninety years later the Admiralty made use of Brattan's report.

Pool sought out the head man of the nearby village of Fratti, a former petty officer who had served in the Royal Navy in the First World War and was on the commander's short list. His code-name in Intelligence records was 'The Fat Man'.

By 2 August, a total of more than 100 British escapees and evaders were in hiding in the precincts of Limni. Two nights later the submarine *Thrasher* surfaced in the bay and the party was mustered on the beach close to the cave where the Apostle Paul is said to have sought refuge in his voyage to Rome in AD 61. Signals were exchanged by shaded torches and a Royal Marine swimmer swam into the beach with a line. Before they entered the water, the soldiers stripped off their clothing and boots, which were in short supply on the island. The submarine reached Alexandria on 6 August and the evacuees were whisked away by SOE staff to the Citadel in Cairo. There, in SOE's headquarters, they were interrogated and later returned to their units.

The second submarine evacuation was made by HMS *Torbay* on the night of 24 August. On this occasion, the swimmer was Royal Marine Bremmer who was to be the first member of this exclusive unit to be decorated. Ninety-two soldiers and seven members of the Greek government were taken off. Lieutenant and Commander Pool and the author were in this number.

There is no record of Pool returning to Crete. His activities from this date until 1946 are unknown, but it is almost certain he operated later in Greece and the Aegean. He died in Athens in 1947—some Greek sources believe he was murdered by the ELAS during the Civil War—but as with many other facets of his career, this remains unconfirmed. Royal Navy records show he was awarded the DSO for unspecified duties in Crete in 1941 and the DSC later in the war. Such is the enigma of Lieutenant Commander Francis Pool.

Lieutenant G.J. Greenway, MC, was the only Australian to return to the island on special operations. The Australian Army early in the war issued an order that no Australian soldier could serve in a force outside its command, but Greenway was the exception. Information supplied by this officer to SOE resulted in his being landed on the island in September 1941 to arrange further evacuations. He returned in one of the small ships which had been gathered in by Lieutenant J. Campbell, DSO, RN, for clandestine operations in the Aegean. Greenway made four return voyages to Crete and was responsible for the evacuation of 210 British soldiers and Greek officials. His most important coup was spiriting Abbot Lagouvardous from under the noses of the Germans to Egypt.

Within weeks of the second submarine evacuation in *Torbay*, German Intelligence learnt of the involvement of the monks of Prevelli Monastery in the operations. A strong force of enemy soldiers occupied the monastery in September and the monks were imprisoned. Abbot Lagouvardous was held in custody at Prevelli, and it was from here that Greenway rescued him.

Initially, Campbell used requisitioned caiques in his flotilla but this became too dangerous when the Germans banned the south coast of Crete to all merchant shipping. A number of diesel-engined fishing trawlers were pressed into service and these arrived off the coast in the hours of darkness.

The first of the trawlers to be commissioned was HMS *Hedgehog,* which made her first voyage to occupied Crete in late July 1942, when she landed one of Colonel Pendlebury's replacements, Captain Paddy Leigh-Fermor, close to Mount Ida. In her short life she carried out dozens of clandestine operations in the Aegean and the eastern Mediterranean. The sturdy little ship was finally lost off Levitha near Leros on 15 October 1943, sunk by enemy shore batteries when she put into the island to rectify an engine defect. Her crew was taken prisoner. Two more trawlers were commissioned in late 1941. These were HMS *Porcupine* and HMS *Escampador.* The flotilla was initially based at Bardia, a convenient port for Cretan operations, but later transferred to Mersa Matruh.

The fifth and last evacuation by Campbell's flotilla was made on the night of 14–15 February 1943 from the village of Treis Ekklies (Three Churches) in western Crete. For this operation Campbell used an ML which he commanded himself. The ML took off a party of forty which included SOE agents, RAF aircrew shot down in raids over the island and New Zealand escapees.

Operating conjointly with Campbell's flotilla was the Greek submarine *Papanikolis,* which picked up a large party of SOE, Greeks and Australian and New Zealand escapees in August 1942. Amongst this group was Gunner Dudley Perkins, who returned to Crete in 1943 and became the leader of a successful resistance group. He is still venerated on the island as 'The Lion of Crete'. *Papanikolis* made many trips to Crete and the number of passengers she carried to freedom exceeded 300. She was based on Haifa.

The Levant Schooner Flotilla assumed responsibility for the landing and recovery of personnel in enemy-occupied islands in the Aegean from mid-1943. *LS 2,* a 20-ton caique commanded by Lieutenant Alex McLeod, was particularly successful in these dangerous operations. The caique was no larger than a harbour yacht and the smallest vessel in the flotilla.

When Cos fell, McLeod was ordered to pick up groups of soldiers and airmen known to be hiding in caves on the south coast of the island. He arrived at a rendezvous on the night of 18–19 October to pick up a party believed to number thirty, but when his coxswain rowed ashore in a rubber dinghy he found eighty men waiting.

McLeod embarked thirty men and even this number took the vessel down below her marks. Fortunately, the sea was calm and the passage to Bodrum on the Turkish coast was made without incident. He ran the caique in close to the shore and the passengers went over the side and waded ashore in four feet of water. On the next two nights *LS 2* returned to the rendezvous and took off the remainder of the party under the noses of a German post which had been established on a ridge overlooking the beach. In the last two evacuations, McLeod secured a rope to the shore and the evacuees dragged themselves along it to reach the caique.

From the last of the party McLeod learnt that another group of soldiers had reached the island of Kalymnos and on the night of 21–22 October he rescued another thirty-one troops. In four nights the tiny vessel carried 111 men to safety.

The last organised rescue of evaders and escapees from enemy-occupied territory in the eastern Mediterranean was carried out by the SBS and the LRDG in the weeks following the fall of Leros on 16 November 1943. Small parties of raiding forces were landed on the island on the 18th to seek out Allied troops and concentrate them close to evacuation points. Doing this, particularly in the hours of darkness, proved more difficult than expected. The best cover was some distance from the beaches in rough terrain which was pocked by many caves. However, by the first week in December, 250 soldiers and airmen had been taken off in caiques and landed at the base of Casteloriso.

While this rescue operation was being carried out, patrols of the Greek Sacred Squadron were infiltrated into Samos, which had been occupied by the enemy on 22 October. Within five days the squadron had assembled 220 British and 200 Greek troops and 2,800 Italian soldiers and officials who were loyal to the Allies. To evacuate such a large number, Lieutenant Commander Seligman used every available vessel in the Levant Schooner Flotilla. Six nights were required before the last man was taken off. The embarkation of over 3,000 men from exposed beaches within a few miles of enemy garrisons was an epic comparable to any achieved in the Second World War.

The traffic of small groups of escapees through the Aegean to Turkey continued until German forces withdrew in late 1944. Some senior officers criticised the diversion of resources required for other purposes to assist these groups. However, such criticism failed to appreciate that the large numbers of enemy troops, ships and aircraft which were used in enemy territory to put down resistance from local populations created a further drain on enemy resources.

9

The Italian Naval Successes

Time and two enemies limited the success of the Italian Navy in the Second World War. Its naval building program was based on a war against Great Britain starting in 1942 and the commencement of hostilities in 1940 found this program far from complete. The main enemy was the British, but the fear of German domination was always present.

In June 1940, when Mussolini found himself bemused by the collapse of France and the sweeping victories of the German war machine, Italy had only two operational battleships. The remaining four would not be in service before August 1942. Her cruiser and destroyer strength was 25 per cent below the planned level. Only in the submarine arm was the Italian Navy on a total war footing. However, despite these deficiencies, the Italian Navy in 1940 boasted the most technologically advanced of all the combatant fleets. Her cruisers, destroyers and submarines were faster and better armed than her enemies.

Her Achille's heel, as the British were soon to discover, was in the offensive spirit of her leaders. They entered battle fearing losses and in the two major fleet actions in the Mediterranean, Calabria and Matapan, their failure to concentrate their forces and close the enemy cost them possible victory.

Despite this failing, in 1941 the Italian Navy went close to crippling Cunningham's Mediterranean Fleet. In two operations, employing fewer than 20 men, they succeeded in sinking two battleships and a heavy cruiser. The weapons they used had been dismissed as toys by the British in the First World War.

The first blow was struck by the MTM, Motoscafi da Tourismo Modificati or modified tourist boat. This 17-foot craft was adapted from a popular tourist speedboat designed for Italian tourist resorts in peacetime. It was powered by a 96-bhp Alfa Romeo 2,500 inboard-outboard engine which gave it a respectable speed of 34 knots. Its effective range was sixty-nine nautical miles in a smooth sea. It was crewed by one man who sat at the stern, protected by a detachable life raft. An explosive head was mounted in the bows.

The MTM was intended to make a silent approach to within 300 yards of its victim, increase speed to its maximum and strike its target amidships. The pilot steered the craft to within 100 yards, jettisoned the stern life raft and locked the controls. He wore a diving suit to enable him to swim underwater while escaping. In theory, the unarmed boat was broken into two sections by a series of small charges which were activated on impact. Water entering the bow section caused it to sink to a predetermined depth, where hydrostatic pressure set off the main charge.

Italian naval authorities claim the MTM was not a suicide weapon. The pilot was trained to eject at a safe distance from the target and the life raft served the dual purpose of keeping him afloat and protecting him from the shock wave of the main charge. A patrol boat remained in the target area to pick him up.

The MTMs were operated by the 10th Light Flotilla, which was commanded by Commander Vittoria Moccagatta. A clever and resolute leader, Moccagatta was an early exponent of the use of surprise weapons.

Orders for the attack on major British warships at anchor in Suda Bay were issued early in December 1940 and the 10th Light Flotilla sailed in the mother ships *Francesco Crispi* and *Quintino Sella*, modified Sella Class destroyers, to Parteni Bay in Leros. Missions were mounted in January and February 1941 but were aborted when last-minute reconnaissance revealed no major warships in the bay.

On 25 March the two mother ships, with six MTMs mounted on stern launching cradles, were laying in a bay at Astypalaia Island when the order was received to attack. Aircraft reconnaissance had found the 8-inch cruiser HMS *York*, two destroyers and a large tanker anchored in the outer harbour at Suda Bay.

The expedition almost failed before the mother ship weighed anchor. A British bomber swooped low over the bay and dropped three bombs between the two ships. *Francesco Crispi* was slightly damaged by bomb fragments, but both vessels were able to proceed. They arrived at the rendezvous, four miles off the entrance to Suda Bay, at 2330 and launched all six MTMs which soon vanished into the loom of the high cliffs which flanked the entrance. There was no sign of enemy patrol vessels.

At 0300 on the 26th, the MTMs lay undetected off the three anti-submarine nets which protected the inner harbour. The darkened silhouettes of the cruiser and the tanker were visible. The six craft slipped over the nets close to shore where they dipped some four feet below the surface. Safe in the target area, they lay stopped and silent, feasting their eyes on the sleeping enemy amada. According to the report made by Sub-Lieutenant Angelo Cabrini and Chief Petty Officer Tullio Tedeschi who piloted the first two MTMs to attack, reveille was sounding in HMS *York* when they revved their engines to the maximum and roared across the glass-smooth water to their unsuspecting targets.

Cabrini locked his steering as the superstructure of *York* soared above him. He ejected eighty yards short of the ship and surfaced as a great sheet of orange-tinged flame shot high above the truck of the cruiser's mast. The lieutenant glanced at his watch. It was 0501, and he began to swim silently away. A searchlight swept over him, but he was not sighted and lay on his back for half a minute, savouring the sight of the cruiser listing and then slowly sinking to the shallow bottom of the bay.

At that moment, Cabrini was thrown backwards by a great shock wave as the MTM piloted by Chief Petty Officer Lino Becatti exploded into the side of the 8,324-ton tanker *Pericles*. She, too, listed and several minutes later settled on the bottom.

Tedeschi failed to find a target and found himself deep into the bay when *York* and *Pericles* were hit. The harbour came alive with searchlights and tracer. He turned and roared down harbour, keeping close to the shadows of the shore. At 0530 he scuttled his craft, close to the anti-submarine net, and shortly afterwards was picked up by a boat from *Francesco Crispi*. He was the only pilot not taken prisoner.

The MTMs piloted by Lieutenant Faggioni, Master Gunner Alessio De Vito and Sargeant Gunner Emilio Barberi all missed their targets, but it was a masterfully planned and skilfully mounted operation, deserving of the success it won.

When Admiral Cunningham heard *York* had been sunk, he immediately despatched his Fleet Salvage Officer, Commander G.J. Wheeler, by air to report on the situation. Wheeler arrived at Suda Bay in a Sunderland flying boat, and as he circled over the bay he had difficulty in finding a sunken cruiser. *York* was sitting on an even keel with her anchor down, carrying out normal harbour routine.

An hour later, as he approached the cruiser in a boat, he saw the quarterdeck was only four feet above water. Below deck, he discovered both boiler rooms and engine-rooms were flooded and water was entering the ship's hull through a great 25 × 12 foot hole in her port side. Later, he was to find another great gash in her bottom, below keel level.

Wheeler delivered his report by signal. He could raise the ship within five days, subject to the work not being interrupted by enemy action and a prodigious list of salvage equipment, plus the salvage ship *Protector* and a submarine to provide power all being available.

Admiral Cunningham was somewhat sceptical of the five-day estimate but he knew Wheeler's mettle. There was no more efficient salvage expert in the Royal Navy and the Commander-in-Chief gave him his full support. Four days after he received Wheeler's signal, the battleships *Warspite* and *Valiant*, with salvage equipment piled high on their decks, steamed into Suda Bay. On the fifth day, the submarine *Rover* secured alongside York.

Cunningham was soon to discover the salvage operation was not all plain sailing. On 16 April, a savage gale lashed Suda Bay and ships, both large and small, were driven aground. The same wind played havoc with port facilities and the salvage crew was taken off *York* to refloat the boarding ship HMS *Chakla*, which was now required in Greek waters.

The Luftwaffe arrived on the 17th and the helpless cruiser and the brood of salvage craft were straddled by a stick of bombs. Luckily, damage was small, but from the first warning to the all-clear, divers left the water and no work was done. In a second raid three days later the bombs fell clear of *York* but scored a direct hit on a Greek supply ship nearby. The ship was soon ablaze from stem to stern and a second ship sank after being near-missed. Commander Wheeler's team was transferred to raising and repairing the supply ship.

The salvage officer was determined to save *York* and the air raids and interruptions only strengthened his resolve. Work continued night and day, but further disaster was close at hand. On the 22nd, a bomb fell between the cruiser and the salvage craft. His whole diving crew, who had been brought up when the raid commenced, were either killed or seriously wounded. The same bomb also caused serious damage to *Protector*, and Wheeler's team was diverted to repair her damage. A second bomb intended for *York* sank a tanker anchored nearby.

However, all was not lost. The bomb failed to dislodge the temporary patches attached to *York*'s hull. Work was resumed within two days, this time using Greek civilian divers recruited ashore. Unfortunately this stroke of good fortune was negated later in the afternoon when a bomb struck the floating power station, the submarine HMS *Rover*. She was beached, but a quick survey showed her batteries had been destroyed by the explosion.

Lesser men than Wheeler would have been justified in admitting defeat and abandoning the salvage. He was determined to raise the ship, and by hell and high water he would.

On the morning of the 27th, as the first troops from Greece were landing nearby, the last patch was fixed in place. All that now remained to be done was testing the patches for leaks and pumping out the hull. With a modicum of luck, *York* would be afloat and ready for towing to Alexandria on the 30th.

However, there were more delays and pumping did not commence until dawn on 1 May, but at 0800 a priority signal was received from Cunningham. Salvage of *York* was to cease and all salvage crews and equipment were to be loaded in *Protector* and returned to Alexandria immediately. *Rover* was to be temporarily patched and towed by the salvage ship. Wheeler stared at the slip of paper in disbelief. *York*'s fate was sealed. With victory in sight, it had been snatched from his grasp.

Early the next morning, the small convoy sailed from Suda Bay. Their last view of the cruiser showed her free of the web of lines, hoses and scaffolding, sitting serenely on the sandy bottom.

Abandoning *York* was a bitter pill for Cunningham to swallow, but the decision was dictated by an ULTRA decrypt outlining the enemy's plan to seize Crete by an airborne invasion in early May. The Commander-in-Chief knew that to continue the salvage would cost him not only the cruiser, but the only salvage equipment in the Mediterranean. In the grim year that lay ahead, Cunningham often thought of the cruiser sitting in Suda Bay.

Commander Wheeler did not sail in *Protector*. He was instructed to survey the damage to the many other sunken ships in the bay and salve those which could be raised within ten days. Another duty, before he left, was a meeting with an SOE agent known only as Byron, who was of Greek birth and had a background of shipbuilding. The two men twice visited *York* and held secret meetings with the Greek divers who had worked on the attempt to raise her. Wheeler knew attempts would be made to raise *York* if the island was captured by the enemy and local divers would be employed in the attempt.

In the meantime, Cunningham was confident Crete would be held and salvage resumed, so the cruiser was not damaged in any way. But Crete was lost and on 31 May 1941 the Germans became the owners of a fine British heavy cruiser ready to salvage. The capture of HMS *York* was hailed as a great victory in the German press. Salvage engineers were flown out from Germany to inspect the ship and reported she could be raised within a week when the necessary equipment and personnel reached the island. The Italian Navy, which had excellent salvage facilities, was not consulted. German soldiers captured the cruiser and German salvage experts would raise her. However, six months passed and no salvage team arrived.

German naval officers, using the Greek divers who had assisted the British, then undertook the salvage. Soon after the work commenced, a former British salvage expert recruited by SOE arrived at Suda Bay. He was known as Lieutenant Cane. The mysterious Byron introduced him to the Greek divers, and from that time things went wrong with the German salvage operation.

The divers succeeded in making the hull watertight, but irritating failures of the pumping equipment foiled every attempt to refloat the 8,250-ton vessel, which remained on the sandy bottom of Suda Bay until the end of the war. In late 1951, more than ten years after *York* was sunk by the Italian MTM-boat, Italian salvage teams raised her and towed the weathered hull to Bari where it was broken up.

The second operation by Italian Special Forces was one of the great naval successes of the Second World War. On the night of 18–19 December 1941, three Italian chariots sunk the battleships *Valiant* and *Queen Elizabeth* in Alexandria Harbour. It was the Mediterranean Fleet's greatest single loss.

This vindication of the Italian charioteers was due to the perseverance of a single officer, Captain Prince Giulio Valerio Borghese, the commanding officer of the submarine *Scire*. Borghese made the chariot—also known as Maiale (Italian for pig)—an effective weapon. He contributed to the development of the weapon, and to the training of the officers and men who manned them.

The scion of an historic Sienese family, Borghese was one of a group of young officers who urged the revival of the famous Mignatta manned torpedo which, on the night of 31 October 1918, entered the Austrian Adriatic harbour of Pola and sunk the 20,300-ton battleship, *Viribus Unitis*.

In 1935, two young officers of the group, Sub-Lieutenants Teseo Tesei and Elios Toschi, submitted plans for an improved manned torpedo to the Italian Navy's High Command. Successful tests of a prototype torpedo were carried out in January 1936. Four years later, Captain Borghese, then commanding the submarine *Ametista*, made a mock chariot attack on shipping in the port of La Spezia. The success of this attack won Commander-in-Chief's approval and plans were prepared for attacks on the British bases at Gilbraltar and Alexandria when hostilities commenced.

The final operational model of the Maiale was 22-feet long, 1.8 feet in diameter and armed with a 600-pound detachable charge. It was powered by a battery-driven 1.1 hp electric motor which gave it a maximum speed of 4.5 knots. Maximum range was 15 nautical miles. Its two-man crew rode the chariot bicycle fashion.

Borghese launched the first two attacks on Alexandria. Bad luck dogged both and a submarine was lost in each. Three chariots and their crews were embarked in the submarine *Iride* for an assault on British warships in the Allied base on the night of 25–26 August 1940. A final rehearsal was held in the Gulf of Bomba and, while launching the chariots for the exercise, *Iride* was caught on the surface and sunk by aircraft from HMS *Eagle*. The three survivors were the pioneers Tesei and Toschi and the commanding officer of the submarine, Lieutenant Brunetti.

Disappointed, but undeterred by this first failure, a second attack was planned for the night of 29–30 September 1940. The two submarines used in the operation, *Gondar* and *Scire*, were in position off the entrance of Alexandria when the attack was aborted. Late aerial reconnaissance had revealed there were no suitable targets in the harbour. As the submarines were withdrawing, they were detected by the destroyers HMAS *Stuart* and HMS *Diamond*. *Gondar* was sunk in the subsequent action.

Captain Borghese launched the chariots from the *Scire* for the first attack on Gilbraltar on the night of 29–30 October. The submarine penetrated Algeciras Bay undetected and launched three chariots to attack the battleship *Barham* and three cruisers reported in the anchorage. The charioteers soon experienced difficulties with their breathing equipment and two of the three craft were abandoned before they reached the target area. However, the third chariot, Lieutenant Gino Birindelli and Petty Officer Diver Alcide Paccagnini, fought its way over the anti-submarine net and had reached a point less than eighty yards from the unsuspecting battleship when the chariot's motor stalled. Paccagnini's breathing set failed at this point and Birindelli dragged the 600-pound charge to within fifty yards of the ship before he too was overcome by carbon dioxide poisoning. The charge exploded an hour later but failed to damage *Barham*.

Scire's second attack on Gibraltar also failed. It was launched on the night of 26–27 May 1941. One chariot sank on launching and the other two failed to reach the convoy of merchant ships because of mechanical problems.

Despite these disappointing failures, the Italians did not lose confidence in the weapon. On the night of 19–20 September Borghese again penetrated Algeciras Bay, and at 0100 sent three chariots on their way to the anchorage. Success smiled on the charioteers on this occasion. Three merchant ships, the 10,000-ton motorship *Durham*, the 2,444-ton tanker *Fiona Shell* and the 8,145-ton fleet auxiliary *Denbydale*, were sunk.

Captain Borghese was now given the most ambitious target of all—Cunningham's two battleships *Valiant* and *Queen Elizabeth*. Destruction of the two would open the Mediterranean to the Italian battle fleet.

Rehearsals for the attack were carried out at Leros in early December. The chariot crews were thoroughly briefed on the defences of Alexandria, which at this period were regarded as the strongest of any port in the world. The offshore approaches were patrolled by a flotilla of anti-submarine vessels. Closer inshore, patrol boats crisscrossed the main channels dropping depth charge at irregular intervals and shore batteries were ranged on the harbour entrance. A heavy anti-submarine net reached to the sea bed and other steel nets protected the boom gates.

Borghese knew the odds were stacked against the charioteers, but he was determined the attack would succeed and *Scire* sailed from Leros early on 14 December. On the 17th, 100 miles north of Alexandria, Borghese received the last aerial reconnaissance report. The two battleships and an aircraft carrier were in the harbour.

The submarine surfaced a mile to seaward of Alexandria at 2100 on 18 December. She was trimmed down two feet below the surface and the three chariots were left rocking on the smooth sea when *Scire* submerged minutes later.

Conditions were perfect for the attack. It was a dark night and the pale moon threw little light on the sea. Visibility was no more than 100 feet and the lights of Alexandria touched the southern horizon with a faint glow. The three chariots approached the entrance partially submerged, with only the heads of the crew above the surface. A patrol boat dropping small grenades in the water passed fifty feet to seaward but did not sight them.

Ten minutes later, they saw four faint lights on the boom gate and soon after a destroyer loomed out of the darkness. The three chariots closed the stern of the ship and followed in her wake as she passed into the harbour. Forcing the boom had been unbelievably easy.

Once clear of the defences, the three chariots separated. Lieutenant Luigi de la Penne and Petty Officer Diver Emilio Bianci soon found their target, HMS *Valiant*, moored close to the French battleship *Lorraine*.

De la Penne dived and cruised alongside the torpedo net protecting the ship. The heavy net was draped in folds on the harbour bed and was too heavy to shift. However, he found a gap in one corner where two sections were joined and he squeezed the chariot through. While he unscrewed the 600-pound charge from the chariot, he sent Bianci to swim along the great ship's keel to find a suitable place to clamp it.

Minutes passed but Bianci did not return. De la Penne endeavoured to start the chariot and drag the charge below the keel, but it refused to budge. The diving line was wrapped tightly around the propellers. He commenced dragging the charge and had covered half the distance when he felt water rising in his wetsuit. A quick inspection revealed a three-inch gash below his armpit.

There was no longer a question of securing the charge to the keel. It required two men simply to lift it and de la Penne was on his own and racing against the water rising in his wetsuit. When it reached his face he would drown. He mustered his last reserves of strength, and at last the charge was dragged into position.

Feverishly de la Penne tied his lanyard around his neck to stop the water rising further in his wetsuit and swam for the surface. He passed out before he reached the surface, but came round to find he was alongside the battleship's buoy and that Bianci was clinging to it. Ten minues later they were sighted and taken on board *Valiant*, where they remained until the charge detonated.

Engineer Captain Antinio Marceglia and Chief Petty Officer Spartaco Schergat quickly found their target, the *Queen Elizabeth*, and dived. Like La Penne, they soon found a way through the torpedo net and brought their chariot to rest immediately below the battleship. The charge was quickly secured to the ship's keel and Marceglia swam to the surface to check the position. On his return, he found Schergat almost unconscious from oxygen sickness. He lashed the diver to the chariot and set out for the recovery rendezvous at Rosetta.

Meanwhile, the third chariot, Engineer Captain Vincenzo Martellotta and Chief Petty Officer Diver Mario Marino, hunted unsuccessfully for the aircraft carrier. When an hour had passed, Martellotta found the large tanker *Sagona* and secured his charge to her keel. To make doubly sure of his victim, he scattered incendiary bombs on the surface close to the ship. The two men swam to a nearby jetty, where they were arrested by Egyptian police.

At 0605 on 19 December, Admiral Cunningham witnessed his two battleships sink after the charges detonated. In seventy seconds, the powerful Mediterranean Fleet ceased to be a battle fleet. Cunningham praised the Italian charioteers for their outstanding bravery and enterprise, which had also sunk the *Sagona*. At the same time he ordered them to be held incommunicado for six months.

The magnitude of the disasters was starkly evident to the British leaders, but Cunningham immediately set in motion a plan to ensure the Axis powers would not learn of their success. By a stroke of luck, both battleships had sunk in shallow water with their decks above water, but somewhat lower than they had been before the attack. Barges were brought alongside to pump out fuel and lighten the ships, ammunition was offloaded and water was pumped into various compartments to correct the trim. Five hours after they were sunk, the battleships appeared to be undamaged at their moorings.

The deception did not end there. The Commander-in-Chief's headquarters remained in *Queen Elizabeth* and both ships continued normal harbour routine. The wily admiral, on the very afternoon of the disaster, donned his golf togs and proceeded ashore for his normal round. Meanwhile, fighter protection was increased over the harbour to keep enemy snoopers at a distance and all suspected enemy agents in the port were quietly taken into custody. Short-wave transmissions from Egypt were closely monitored.

The plan succeeded. Italian and German sources remained ignorant of their greatest naval success in the Second World War until after the Italian surrender in 1943. By that time, the Mediterranean Fleet had been greatly increased.

Admiral Cunningham again summoned his Fleet Salvage Officer, Commander Wheeler, and ordered him to concentrate all his staff and equipment at Alexandria. *Valiant* had a great 38 × 17 foot gash below the waterline on the port side. *Queen Elizabeth* had two similar-sized holes in her hull. On this occasion Wheeler did not give his Admiral a time estimate for raising the ships, but within twenty-four hours his crews were on board both battleships, working below in complete secrecy. *Valiant* was raised on 21 December and moved into drydock. She passed through the Suez Canal under her own steam on 5 April 1942. Permanent repairs were carried out at Simonstown Dockyard in South Africa.

Queen Elizabeth was sitting deep in the mud of the harbour floor for four days before Wheeler found the main hole, roughly the area of three tennis courts, in her bottom. She was successfully raised, placed in drydock and followed *Valiant* south two months later.

Lieutenant Luigi de la Penne joined the Allied underwater teams after the Italian surrender and served with them to the end of the war. He was recommended for a high Allied award, which could not be awarded to a former enemy. However, in early 1945, at an investiture by Prince Umberto of Italy, he was awarded the prestigious Italian Medaglia d'Oro al Valor for sinking the *Valiant*. The medal was pinned to his chest by Admiral Miles Morgan, who had commanded the battleship when she was sunk.

10

The Oil Wars

The two years following the bloodbath of Crete were years of survival for the Mediterranean Fleet. Despite the heavy losses of ships and crews, Cunningham was asked to provide squadrons to meet crises from Gibraltar to the Persian Gulf. The evacuation of Greece had not commenced when Axis agents engineered a coup in Iraq and the pro-British government was overthrown. Italy and Germany immediately assured the rebel leaders they would provide troops and air cover to prevent British forces entering the gulf.

Britain, with her commitments in Greece and the Aegean, and supplying Malta and the Western Desert, was totally unprepared to meet the undertaking. The only Royal Navy ship in the Persian Gulf area was the old 635-ton First World War river gunboat, *Cockchafer*. It was armed with two obsolete 6-inch guns and a few machine-guns. Cunningham immediately dispatched the old veteran to Iraq, where, on the night of 12 April 1941, she rescued the Iraqui Regent, Amir Abdul Illah, from Basra. Luckily the rebels possessed no vessel which could oppose *Cockchafer*.

Despite Churchill's promise of naval aid, every ship in the Mediterranean Fleet was needed for the coming evacuation of Greece and supporting the Desert Army which was being driven out of Libya by Rommel's forces. Cunningham appealed for assistance to the Commander-in-Chief, East Indies, Vice-Admiral Leatham, who immediately despatched the Australian sloop *Yarra*, Lieutenant Commander Harrington, which was completing her refit in Bombay before rejoining the Mediterranean Fleet. His only available cruisers, *Falmouth, Leander* and *Emerald*, were ordered to embark British and Indian troops at Singapore and Bombay and proceed direct to the gulf. They arrived at Basra on 28 April.

In the meantime, Harrington had arrived in the trouble area in *Yarra* and was assembling a strange fleet of armed tugs and native fishing vessels. This odd flotilla, with Australian sailors in each crew, fought its way up the Shatt el Arab to Basra. Iraqui forces surrendered to *Yarra* on 31 May, the day resistance ended in Crete.

Success in Iraq turned Churchill's thoughts to Syria, which had cooperated with the Axis in allowing war stores to Iraq to pass through Vichy French territory. On 22 May General Wavell signalled the Prime Minister: 'German air forces established in Syria are closer to the [Suez] Canal than they would be at Mersa Matruh. The whole position in Middle East is at present governed by air power and air bases. The object of the Army must be to try and keep him from establishing himself in Syria and to hang on to Crete and Cyprus.'

The British War Cabinet decided to take steps to occupy Syria and to do so before the Luftwaffe could regroup its forces after Greece and Crete. Orders were signalled to the three Chiefs of Staff in the Mediterranean to make immediate preparations to advance

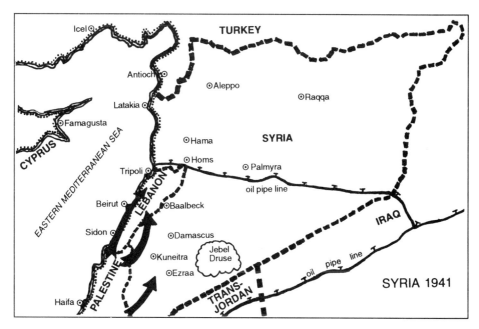

into Syria in the first weeks of June. However, on 1 June, what remained of Cunningham's fleet was licking its wounds in Alexandria. Almost every ship which survived the holocaust of Greece and Crete was in need of urgent repairs and dockyard facilities at the base were inadequate for the task. If a force was despatched to Syria, it would go with its defects unattended.

Unlike Iraq, Syria possessed a fleet. It consisted of four modern destroyers, the equivalent of British light cruisers and much faster, three large submarines and a variety of smaller vessels including a flotilla of torpedo boats. The fleet was supported by well-equipped bases to service it, and a relatively strong air force. Cunningham was also aware that, thirty hours steaming to the west, the French had a strong fleet of cruisers and destroyers which could well be sent to reinforce Syria. More ominous still was the Luftwaffe. The Germans already had one base in Syria and this could be quickly reinforced by enemy air fleets now established in Greece. The coasts of Syria were within hours of the string of operational airfields in the Aegean.

Syria is the narrow coastal link between Palestine and Turkey and the Middle Eastern flank of the Aegean Sea. Through it passed the vital oil pipeline from Transjordan and Iraq to Tripoli. A branch line ran to Haifa in Palestine. To Winston Churchill and his War Cabinet, it was the lifeline for the Mediterranean Fleet and a buffer to any German move to pass an army south from the Black Sea to link up with Rommel's Desert Army, should the latter reach the Suez Canal.

As early as November 1940, the British Prime Minister realised Syria in Vichy French hands was a threat to the canal and to the whole British strategy in the Middle East. In a memo to Lord Halifax, the British Foreign Secretary, he wrote: 'We shall most certainly have to obtain control of Syria by one means or another in the next few months. The best way would be a Weygand or de Gaullist movement, but this cannot be counted on, and until we have dealt with the Italians in Libya we have no troops to spare for a northern venture.'

In early 1941 Churchill learnt through his excellent intelligence network details of a meeting between Pétain and Hitler at which plans to prevent the British seizing Syria were discussed. The two leaders agreed to reinforcing the Vichy French Army in Syria by the transfer of 10,000 Moroccan troops. Hitler agreed to supply additional armaments, which were already in Syria, waiting for transfer to Iraq should a coup displace the Shah, and Pétain responded by offering Syrian airfields for the use of Axis aircraft operating in the eastern Mediterranean. Pétain also agreed to the Axis use of the ports of Bizerta and Dakar in North Africa.

The first German aircraft began using Syrian airfields on 9 May, and in the following week 120 aircraft were reported to have landed and refuelled at these fields. Transport aircraft delivered eight field guns and 354 machine-guns to the Vichy forces.

Churchill realised the time had come to act. On 31 May he informed the Australian Prime Minister, R.G. Menzies, that Syria would be occupied by British forces as soon as possible, and although no record exists, he no doubt requested the use of Australian troops for the planned operation. It was a courageous decision. The backbone of the Middle East army was then in German prison camps in Greece and Crete, Admiral Cunningham was still counting his fleet losses and the RAF was desperately mustering sufficient aircraft to defend the fleet base at Alexandria and the Suez Canal.

General Wavell decided to use the Australian 7th Division as the spearhead for the proposed operation and the 5th and 21st Indian Brigade, part of the British 6th Division, the Free French Brigade and two brigades of British cavalry—one was still equipped with horses—as support. On the border between Syria and Transjordan was Brigadier Glubb's Arab Legion. None of these units was fully equipped and feverish efforts were made to supply their deficiencies.

The Vichy French Army in Syria was estimated at 53,000 men, of whom 28,000 were French regular and colonial troops and 25,000 irregulars. This latter group included many famous units, amongst them the French Foreign Legion, Chasseurs d' Afrique, Algerians, Senegalese, the Afrique Cavalry and the Spahis. The army was well supported with artillery, tanks and armoured cars.

At the outbreak of hostilities the French Air Force was stronger than the British. However, the RAF and the RAAF aircraft were superior in speed and armament and as the campaign progressed reinforcements were received from other areas. French operations deteriorated into sneak raids and strikes against opportunity targets. The German promise was only partly fulfilled and at no time threatened British superiority.

By one of those whims of chance, many of the Australian troops selected to spearhead the attack had come under the influence of P.C. Wren's novels on the French Foreign Legion and, to a lesser degree, the writings of Rudyard Kipling in the early 1930s—and the movie versions of these works in the years before the war. At an impressionable age they were inculcated with the code of the gallant legionnaires, and the crafty desert tribesmen's religious fervour. Gary Cooper, Errol Flynn and Douglas Fairbanks Junior exemplified the virtues of the true fighting man in their impressionable minds. Every unit in the Australian Imperial Force had its own Beau Sabruers and Gungha Dins, although the latter were inevitably cooks.

The German Do 17 bomber used to carry the HS-293 controllable glide bomb. *(U.S. Air Force)*

The later model Do 217K bomber used in the Aegean.

The escort carrier HMS *Attacker* participated in the Royal Navy sweeps in the Aegean in 1944. The ship, renamed *Fairsky*, was an immigrant carrier on the Australian run in the 1950s.

Admiral of the Fleet, Viscount Cunningham of Hyndhope, KT, GCB, OM, DSO.

The Joint Allied Committee signing the surrender of the German Military Command in the Dodecanese on the island of Simi, 8 May 1945. Colonel Tzigantes is on the right. *(Greek Staff College)*

The desert areas in which the Australians were based differed little from the backgrounds so well described in Wren's novels. An even greater impression was made when the soldiers found themselves in the transit camp at Ikingi Marut in Egypt where, just outside the camp limits, a yellow-walled 'Foreign Legion' fort rose out of the desert like a forgotten Egyptian temple. The fort had been built by MGM four years earlier for use in a series of adventure films.

By an equally odd coincidence, Errol Flynn's closest friend served in the author's unit. This handsome South Australian was the equal of Flynn in looks and physique. In the early 1930s he shared with Flynn a windjammer voyage from the Baltic to Australia, visited wild areas of New Guinea and captured the hearts of many of Australia's socialites of the time. This soldier could climb a tree in true Tarzan fashion, hurl an eighteen-inch bayonet twenty feet to quiver in the trunk of a tree and sing magnificently. He soon captured the imagination of many of his younger comrades. He died as a hero in Crete when the volunteer-manned 'I' tank in which he was gunner was disabled in a strongly held German redoubt. Although wounded and surrounded by flames, he kept his gun firing until his comrades leapt clear.

Now, in the hot summer of 1941, the untried young soldiers of the 7th Division were answering the discordant notes of the legionnaire's bugle, not as an ally against the crafty Riffs but as an enemy. The former desert enemies, the Moroccans, Algerians and Tunisians, perversely, were not fighting against the Foreign Legion, but with it.

General Wavell was opposed to the operation. The troops he was committing against a well-trained enemy in strongly fortified lines in rugged mountain terrain and desert were unblooded, and in many cases not fully equipped. An intelligence report from one senior officer described the south-west of Syria as similar to the worst mountain country of Afghanistan. Because of the inexperience of the troops available for assault, Wavell hastily re-equipped some Australian battalions as they returned from Crete. These units found themselves stiffening the line in Syria only ten to fourteen days after stepping ashore at Alexandria.

The 7th Division crossed the Palestine–Syrian border early on the morning of 8 June and soon met strong resistance from Foreign Legion and Senegalese troops. The British attack was three-pronged. The Australians and some attached troops were in the coastal area; the 5th Indian and the Free French Brigades were in the middle; and the 21st Indian Brigade, Royal Fusiliers and a brigade of British cavalry were entrusted with the area to the east of Lake Tiberias.

Facing them was the largely mercenary Vichy French Army. It was dug in behind well-fortified positions and immediately offered strong resistance. The Australians soon found themselves in tangled and rugged country which divided their forces. At sunset on this first day they found themselves close to the Litani River, where the enemy's first main line was established.

Wavell at his headquarters in Cairo realised the French intended to fight for every yard and ordered his staff to prepare more of the Australian troops returning from Crete to reinforce the army in Syria. His great weakness, with an army fighting in the Western Desert, was the lack of reserves.

The advancing troops were surprised at the presence of enemy horsed cavalry on their flanks. Vichy French sappers had demolished all bridges and culverts as they fell back and in several places giant cliff faces had been blown and carried away long stretches of the roads. These demolitions delayed all wheeled transport and, in particular, the vital artillery.

Cunningham's ships were lying off the coast ready to provide gun support for the troops ashore. The first Royal Navy ship to engage the enemy was the destroyer *Kimberley*, a survivor of Captain Mountbatten's flotilla. She closed the coast at 0700 on the 9th and bombarded French positions overlooking the Litani River near Iskandaroun. The fire was accurate and the enemy was forced to retire.

The admiral had allocated the 15th Cruiser Squadron, *Ajax, Phoebe, Coventry* and the Australian *Perth*, supported by the destroyers *Kandahar, Kimberley, Janus,* and *Jackal* as close support. A detached force consisting of the destroyers *Isis* and *Hotspur* and the infantry landing ship, *Glengyle*, joined on the 9th. The whole force was commanded by Vice-Admiral King. *Glengyle* was carrying a force of Middle East Commandos, led by Lieutenant Colonel Geoffrey Keyes, who were to have landed at the mouth of the Litani River on the night of 8–9 June, but heavy seas caused this operation to be aborted.

The British Cheshire Cavalry was in action on the morning of the 9th, clearing the enemy from the precipitous country overlooking Tibrine and Kafr Sir in the coastal sector. It was the first occasion in the Second World War that horsed cavalry saw action.

Despite the strong resistance, the ancient port of Tyre was captured by the Royal Fusiliers, who were with the central force, and Fiq, east of Lake Tiberias and Ezraa, at the foot of the Jebel Druse, fell to the Indian Brigade operating with the eastern forces. On the coast, the Australians swung north-east from Tyre and captured the town of Khirbe, five miles south of the important junction of Merjayoun.

Brigadier Stevens, commanding the Australians on the coast, had prepared plans for the crossing of the Litani River. This was the first combined operation of the campaign and involved the landing of the commandos at the river mouth while the Australians crossed the river in canvas boats. Two smaller commando landings were planned north of the river mouth to confuse the French. These diversionary operations were led by Captains More and Pedder. The well-drawn-up plan went askew when *Glengyle* failed to find the river mouth in the dark and Keyes' force was landed some miles south. On realising the error, the commando leader mustered his men and set off over rough terrain for the river. However, they were stopped by heavy fire from the sea before they made contact with the Australians.

During the day, the French commander of the river defences had called for naval support, and at 0200 on the 10th the large French destroyers *Guerpard* and *Valmy* positioned themselves off the river mouth. They soon opened fire on the Australian positions. Admiral King, who had been standing to sea with the British squadron, ordered the destroyers *Janus, Jackal, Hotspur* and *Isis* to close and engage the enemy ships, which withdrew, although they were larger and more heavily armed than the British. In the running battle which followed *Janus* was hit but was able to remain in action.

Keyes' commando came under enemy fire from the French dug in on the ridges which overlooked the crossing before they reached the Australian positions. The commandos returned the fire and fought their way to the bank, crossing the river with the Australians. On reaching the opposite bank, they were pinned down by heavy fire from the French on the high ground. Pedder's force joined Keyes and, together with the Australians, launched a frontal attack which succeeded in overcoming the enemy. The commandos withdrew after this action and returned to their base in Egypt. Keyes was killed in his next operation, an attack on Rommel's Headquarters, and was later awarded a posthumous Victoria Cross.

Both navies received reinforcements during the short campaign. The cruiser *Naiad*, Captain Vian, and the destroyers *Stuart, Nizam* and *Parthian*, the first two, Australian ships, joined King's squadron on the 10th, while the large French destroyers *Le Chevalier Paul* and *Cassard* joined the French squadron. British Intelligence warned Cunningham of the departure of the destroyers from Marseilles and, as they neared Beirut at the end of their hazardous voyage, they came under attack from Fleet Air Arm aircraft. *Le Chevalier Paul* was torpedoed and sunk.

To the troops in the field, the Syrian Campaign was far from a walkover. The port of Sidon was not taken until the 15 June and to the east, in the important junction town of Merjayoun, French resistance bordered on the fanatic.

During the first week of fighting the French enjoyed air superiority on all three fronts, but thereafter the RAF was able to exert pressure on the enemy airfields. No 3 Squadron, RAAF, flying American Tomahawk fighters and commanded by Squadron Leader P. Jeffrey, provided close support for the Australian ground forces. The Australian airmen fought a savage dogfight with a squadron of German Ju 88 fighter-bombers on 14 June and shot down three enemy aircraft. It was one of the rare occasions the Luftwaffe attacked ground troops in the campaign.

Admiral Cunningham's fears of German air attacks were realised on the next day when a flight of Stukas dived on the destroyers *Isis* and *Ilex* on passage from Beirut to Haifa. *Isis* was near-missed and seriously damaged in the attack. As the two ships were limping away after this attack they were bombed by French aircraft and *Ilex* was also damaged. Fortunately, this was the only attack launched on ships of the fleet by German aircraft, but with large numbers of aircraft based in the islands of the Aegean, the threat remained.

On 15 June the Vichy French launched a strong counter-attack on Kiswe and penetrated the defences of the 3/1 Punjab Battalion. Confused fighting followed, in which the guns of the 1st Field Regiment engaged the enemy over open sights. Fortunately, the Royal Fusiliers and the Rajput Battalion outflanked the French positions and the counter-attack lost its impetus.

A second enemy counter-attack, spearheaded by the Tunisian Regiment, recaptured the vital railhead at Ezraa and routed two companies of the Transjordan Frontier Force. Kuneitra was retaken by the enemy early on the same day when a squadron of armoured cars, supported by infantry, drove out the garrison of Royal Fusiliers.

The position was now serious and there was a real danger of the enemy driving a wedge between the British forces. The Free French Brigade was hurried north of Kuneitra, where they joined Indian troops to form a line across the Damascus Road. This force was supported by the Australian Tomahawks of No 3 Squadron which stopped the enemy advance.

In the meantime, a strong Australian force consisting of an infantry battalion, the cavalry regiment and an artillery battery closed on Kuneitra and forced the enemy to withdraw. On this same afternoon, a Vichy French group which included ten armoured cars, fifty horsed cavalry and infantry attacked the Australian 2/33 Battalion to the north of Merjayoun. The Australians were forced to withdraw before stabilising their position.

These attacks, unleashed over such a wide area, placed the whole campaign in jeopardy for twenty-four hours. The communications of all units east of Lebanon were threatened and there were no reserves available to meet the counter-attacks. Early on the morning of the 16th, charges were placed under bridges and culverts along the main road leading back to Palestine.

On the same day, the town of Kuneitra was entered by a force of 1,500 Vichy French supported by armoured cars, tanks and artillery. The town was held by 570 men of the Royal Fusiliers supported by a single 20-mm Italian gun. A ferocious hand-to-hand battle developed with the enemy tanks and artillery firing a point-blank range. By 1130 the Fusiliers were reduced to 13 officers and 164 other ranks. This force withdrew to three stone houses on the edge of the town and held out until 1830, when a French officer approached under a white flag and demanded their surrender. The Royal Fusiliers, short of ammunition and with three-quarters of their number either dead or wounded, surrendered. Two days later a strong British force of two battalions of infantry, with artillery and armoured cars, attacked the town and took it with the loss of one man.

This proved to be the turning point of the campaign. Wavell resisted the temptation of withdrawing and strengthening his rear areas. On the 18th, Jezzine to the north was taken and the town of Ezraa recaptured. Australian troops entered Damascus on 21 June.

The loss of the capital was a blow to French morale. A month was to pass before Syria was subdued but the British knew they were now winning. On 20 June Major General Clark's force, which had been advancing along the pipeline from Transjordan, had bypassed Damascus and was heading for the coast. This force consisted of the 4th Cavalry Brigade, Glubb's Arab Legion and the 1/Essex Battalion.

On the night of 22–23 June, British bombers attacked the French naval base at Beirut and the destroyer *Vauquelin* was hit and heavily damaged. *Guerpard*, the other warship in the port, put to sea early next morning and was immediately engaged by the cruiser, *HMS Leander*. The destroyer was hit by a 6-inch shell and suffered heavy damage. She returned to port and took no further part in the campaign. Two days later, the destroyer *Parthian* detected a submarine off Beirut and attacked with depth charges. It was later learnt the French submarine *Souffler* had been destroyed in the action.

The opening feints of the battle for Damour decided the Vichy French commander, General Dentz, to capitulate. Although his troops were still fighting strongly, he knew Syria was lost. Feelers to end the conflict had been extended on 22 June and on the 26th, two senior officers were sent to Vichy France to inform Marshall Pétain and Admiral Darlan that further resistance was futile. The two Vichy leaders had already reached this decision and on the 28th it was confirmed. Unfortunately, General Dentz did not receive confirmation for another ten days.

On 27 June the cruisers *Naiad* and *Perth*, with the destroyers of the 14th Flotilla, carried out a daylight bombardment of French positions in the neighbourhood of Damour. The main targets were a strong coastal battery and a wireless station at Khalda. Both were destroyed by *Perth*'s 6-inch guns and the force commander, Captain Vian, gave the credit to the flotilla gunnery officer, Australian Lieutenant Commander A.S. Storey. Vian considered Storey the finest gunnery officer in the Commonwealth navies and took him with him when he assumed command of Malta convoys early in 1942. The two officers were serving in the cruiser HMS *Cleopatra* when she embarked the author C.S. Forrester to obtain colour for a novel on Mediterranean convoys. The captain and gunnery officer in Forrester's bestselling work, *The Ship*, were based on Vian and Storey.

The operation against Damour was repeated on 2 July and mobile batteries brought in to replace the coastal battery were destroyed in what was the last naval action in the campaign. More than thirty ships of the Mediterranean Fleet had served in the short campaign.

The surrender took place on 11 July. Losses in killed and wounded during the campaign were heavy. French losses were 1,092 killed and 2,200 wounded. Australian casualties were 416 killed and 2,133 wounded.

There were many unusual aspects to the campaign. The Australian and the Foreign Legion won mutual respect for their fighting qualities. Perhaps the Australians lost some of their illusions gained from P.C. Wren's novels, but war is basic and has no room for romance. However, the conglomeration of nations in the ranks of the legion came as a surprise to the Australians. Not the least surprising was the discovery of two Australian legionnaires.

The Syrian Campaign was also unusual from a legal point of view. When the fighting ended a number of Australians were charged with the unusual offence of 'unlawfully firing on the King's enemies'. These charges arose from Australian troops stationed in Palestine absenting themselves from their units and crossing into Syria to fight in other Australian units. These soldiers pleaded guilty as charged and lost all pay and allowance for the period of their absence. NCOs were reduced to the ranks.

Lieutenant Hodgkinson of HMS *Hotspur* summed up the feelings of the navy personnel who served in the campaign: 'In a way it is a pity to leave the Syrian coast. After Greece and Crete it was an excellent tonic to do something aggressive again. It is always pleasant to work with an independent squadron rather than to work with the Battle Fleet. At least we had a real squadron of fighters overhead.'

The winning of Syria achieved all the objectives Churchill had sought and one which had not come to his fertile mind. Syria provided the bases and ports for the campaigns in the Aegean islands which lay ahead.

11

Years of Attrition

While the Syrian Campaign was in progress, Cunningham despatched those ships which had been too heavily damaged for repair in Mediterranean dockyards. Among these was the flagship *Warspite*, which sailed on 24 June for a United States' shipyard. *Barham* was repaired at Simonstown in South Africa and the cruelly damaged cruiser *Orion* returned to the United Kingdom to be rebuilt.

Cunningham was reluctant to accept the large 'T' Class submarines for operation in the shallow and translucent waters of the Mediterranean which exposed them to air attack. However, there were no others available in 1941 and in the first two months after their arrival the 1,805-ton submarines sank eight enemy supply ships and tankers, damaged two more and accounted for two enemy submarines. In addition, the 'T'-boats carried out five operations landing agents and retrieving Allied personnel from enemy-occupied territory.

Two minelaying submarines, *Cachalot* and *Rorqual*, were also made available to the Mediterranean. In addition to laying minefields, these vessels, with their large cargo-carrying capacity, were used in the second half of 1941 to carry urgent supplies and fuel to besieged Malta.

Although their plans to obtain air bases in Syria and Iraq had been thwarted, the Luftwaffe had extended its bombing range greatly by the use of Italian bases in the Aegean and the recently captured airfields in Crete. The Western Desert, Egypt, Suez Canal and several hundred miles of the Red Sea were soon to receive Luftwaffe attention.

From the beginning of June 1941, the main operational area of the Mediterranean Fleet moved westward. The eastern Mediterranean was now completely dominated by the Axis but, more specifically, the Germans, and almost became a closed area for the Royal Navy. Malta was the epicentre and the ever-changing fortunes in the Western Desert were on the fringe. The concentration of the German airforce on the Suez Canal and the Red Sea was to be short-lived.

Minelaying operations in the canal commenced on 11 July, and three days later Suez was attacked by a fleet of German dive-bombers. The laying of mines in the canal was not unexpected and an efficient minesweeping force disposed of these without loss. The heavy raid on Suez resulted in the 27,759-ton transport *Georgic* being badly hit and set on fire. She was beached, but the flames reduced her to a burnt-out shell. Later in the war she was salvaged, and when peace returned she became a well-known migrant ship on the Australian run. The landing ship *Gleneam* was also hit in the raid, and run aground. She was soon refloated by the Australian cruiser *Hobart* and towed clear for repair.

German long-range bombers made several unsuccessful attacks on shipping to the south of the canal but were soon withdrawn for other operations.

During the second half of 1941 the supplying of besieged Tobruk made heavy demands on Cunningham's resources. In June, the destroyer *Waterhen* and the sloops *Grimsby* and *Auckland*, all veterans of Greece and Crete, were sunk. In the two months which followed, the cruiser *Phoebe*, destroyer *Hero*, gunboat *Gnat*, sloop *Parramatta* and the fast transport *Latona* were also lost on the 'Tobruk Ferry'. This name is believed to have been coined by Australian sailors. In the early days of the service the old V and W destroyers of the Royal Australian Navy were employed. *Gnat* was later raised and towed to Alexandria, where she served as an anti-aircraft platform until the end of the war.

Concurrent with these demands to hold Tobruk, the Malta convoys were exacting their toll. The aircraft carrier *Ark Royal*, returning to Gibraltar after escorting her convoy, was torpedoed and sunk by the German submarine *U 81* when only thirty miles from port.

Three British submarine flotillas were now operating in the Mediterranean. The medium size 'S' Class boats were based on Gibraltar and were responsible for the western Mediterranean, the small 'U' class based on Malta for the central Mediterranean and the large 'T' class for the eastern Mediterranean. This formidable underwater fleet was soon to make its presence felt.

In early November, *Upholder*, Lieutenant M.D. Wanklyn, VC, DSO, made a patrol into the western Aegean and, in a week-long sweep, sank a medium-size tanker, two schooners and seven caiques. The smaller vessels were disposed of with *Upholder*'s deck gun. The submarine was lost on her last patrol before returning to England and Wanklyn was awarded a bar to the Victoria Cross. Her loss was revenged when *Torbay* sunk the Italian *Jantina* off Mykros soon after.

In December, *Urge* torpedoed and severely damaged the Italian battleship *Vittoria Veneto* and sank two merchant ships. Two others in the same convoy collided and were heavily damaged.

However, the last months of 1941 and the early months of 1942 were the 'happy time' for the German submarines operating from their base at Salamis on the east coast of Greece. At this period, twenty German and fifty Italian submarines were ranged against the British in the Mediterranean.

The Mediterranean Fleet lost its first battleship on 25 November, south of Crete. Admiral Cunningham had taken the battle fleet to sea on the 24th to intercept two enemy convoys reported to be closing Benghazi. The enemy was not sighted and the fleet turned back for Alexandria. At 1630 on the 25th, in full view of the fleet, the 27,000-ton battleship *Barham* was torpedoed by *U 331*, Lieutenant von Tiesenhausen. She sunk within minutes, taking 55 officers and 806 men with her.

Her sinking was reported by the diarist of the Australian destroyer *Nizam*, one of the battleship's screen. Petty Officer S. McAndrew wrote:

'1630: *Barham* hit by two torpedoes—heels over, guns firing at sub astern. *Barham* still signalling "sub astern". Two more torpedoes hit her. *Napier, Nizam, Jackal, Kipling, Jervis* rushing in. Battleship and destroyers going for their life—enemy planes approaching—my God, she's exploded—she's disappeared except for a huge ball of smoke and debris in the air, a 15-inch gun barrel has just shot up about 1,500 feet into the air. Doesn't look if any will come out alive. Debris and bodies falling everywhere. Another minute we'd have been alongside—dropping depth charges on sub. Another air attack. *Nizam* and *Jackal* picked up survivors, being bombed at the same time.'

McAndrew's fine reporting of the disaster remains one of the most graphic eyewitness reports of a ship sinking in the Second World War.

U 331 was sunk almost a year later by Allied aircraft in the eastern Mediterranean. The only survivor was Leutnant von Tiesenhausen.

On 13 December the new cruiser *Galatea* was sunk by *U 557* off the entrance to Alexandria Harbour. The Commander-in-Chief received the news of her loss while reading a signal reporting the sinking of two Italian light cruisers and two destroyers by the destroyers *Sikh, Maori, Legion* and the Dutch Navy's *Isaac Sweers* off Cape Bon. Six days later the Mediterranean Fleet suffered its greatest defeat when its two remaining battleships, *Queen Elizabeth* and *Valiant*, were sunk at their moorings in Alexandria Harbour in an attack described in Chapter 9. The fleet tanker *Sagona* was sunk by the oil wharf and the destroyer *Jervis*, moored alongside, was seriously damaged. In less than one month, the Mediterranean Fleet had lost all three of its battleships.

Cunningham was still recovering from the shock of this loss when he received a signal reporting the sinking of the cruiser *Neptune* and the destroyer *Kandahar* while operating with Rear Admiral Vian's squadron off Tripoli. Both vessels were sunk by enemy mines. The cruiser *Aurora* was damaged in the same minefield.

The Commander-in-Chief's fleet remaining at Alexandria consisted of the anti-aircraft cruiser *Penelope* and the much reduced destroyer and submarine flotillas. Three light cruisers joined soon after, but the new year brought little relief to the Mediterranean Fleet. Malta was reeling and close to the end of her tether with the never-ending raids of the Luftwaffe and the task of supplying the island was growing increasingly difficult. Vice-Admiral Ford, the island's naval commander, wrote on 3 January: 'I've given up counting the number of raids we are getting. The enemy is definitely trying to neutralise Malta's effort. Something must be done at once.'

During this darkest period of Cunningham's command, Churchill signalled messages designed to lift the spirits of the fleet, but not all achieved their purpose. At regular intervals Cunningham was reminded not to forget the Aegean.

However, the Aegean was far from his mind on 21 January, when Rommel went on the offensive in the Western Desert. The admiral's thoughts turned immediately to finding the ships which would be needed to supply the retreating army. At this period, General Alan Cunningham was commanding the Eighth Army and the two brothers shared one of the most difficult periods in the Mediterranean together.

Despite the destruction wrought on the submarine facilities at Malta, the small 'U' Class boats were still hitting the enemy. On 12 January, *Unbeaten* torpedoed and sank the German submarine *U 374* off Cape Spartivento. However, only days later, the large 'T' Class boat *Triumph* struck a mine north of Rhodes and was lost.

In January the Italian Fleet gained its greatest superiority over the Royal Navy in the Mediterranean. It now had 4 battleships, 9 cruisers, 55 destroyers and torpedo boat destroyers and 50 submarines in service. The Germans also had air superiority.

The hard-working destroyer *Gurkha*, named after the famous British Indian regiment, was the third of her name to be lost by enemy action. By an odd coincidence, the first two were incorrectly named *Ghurka*. The error was discovered soon after the second was launched, and she was renamed in 1936. This vessel was sunk by German bombers at Stavanger in Norway on 9 April 1940.

HMS *Gurkha*, the third of the line, was launched as HMS *Larne* and renamed in June 1940. She was torpedoed and sunk by the German submarine *U 133* in the Eastern Mediterranean on 17 January 1942, while escorting the fast transport *Breconshire* to Malta. The cost of this ship was met by the men of the Gurkha Regiment, who voluntarily contributed a proportion of their pay for this purpose.

With Rommel again on the rampage in the Western Desert, new problems faced the Malta convoys. Derna fell, and Tobruk was again under seige. The advanced airfields in Cyrenaica placed the convoys entirely at the mercy of enemy air forces and there were good reasons for naming their route 'Bomb Alley'. Rommel's desert bases, and the increased number of German aircraft using Italian airfields, made Malta almost untenable. On 12 February, another of Cunningham's fleet destroyers, *Maori*, fell victim to the Luftwaffe in Grand Harbour. She caught fire and was reduced to a burnt-out shell. In the same raid, the submarine base in Lazaretto Creek was seriously damaged and thought was given to transferring the flotilla of 'U' Class submarines to Alexandria, a move which would greatly reduce their effectiveness.

Despite these crippling losses, Cunningham was under pressure from the Admiralty to transfer destroyers and submarines to the Indian Ocean and the Far East. In early February he lost the destroyers *Napier, Nizam, Isaac Sweers, Griffin* and *Decoy* and the submarines *Trusty, Truant* and *Rover* to the Eastern Fleet. Within days of the departure of these ships, *Farndale* was hit by a large aircraft bomb which passed through her engine-room but failed to sink her. The destroyer reached Alexandria under her own steam without suffering a single casualty.

The hard-working submarines of Cunningham's submarine flotilla were honoured in February–March by the award of three Victorious Crosses.

Thrasher won two by following a large enemy convoy into heavily defended Suda Bay in broad daylight and sinking a transport. The submarine immediately came under heavy attack from aircraft and patrol vessels which dropped thirty-three depth charges in her vicinity. *Thrasher* lay on the harbour bed until after dark, and on surfacing found two 100-pound depth charges wedged in her forward casing. Although enemy vessels were anchored all around the submarine, Lieutenant P.S.W. Roberts and Petty Officer T.W. Gould volunteered to remove the charges.

The two men climbed out on the casing and the submarine was trimmed down until the deck was at water level. Working in complete darkness, they removed the first charge, which was jammed in the outer casing, and rolled it into the sea. The second charge, however, had penetrated the casing and was firmly wedged against the inner casing. To work it free, the two men were partly submerged. It took fifty-five minutes to free the lethal charge and drag it the length of the vessel before it could be rolled overboard. During the last ten minutes of the delicate operation, an enemy patrol boat passed within thirty yards of the submarine.

Throughout the period of disposing of the two charges, Roberts and Gould were fully aware they would be drowned if *Thrasher* was forced to dive. The award of the Victoria Cross to both men was well deserved.

In the early days of March, *Torbay*, Commander A.C.C. Miers, was operating off Corfu searching for two large transports reported to be bound for the island. Despite the presence of anti-submarine nets and an active flotilla of patrol boats, Miers took *Torbay* into the harbour in daylight. There was no sign of the two transports, but three supply ships were sighted anchored close inshore. Miers closed to short range and torpedoed all three vessels. Two were seen to sink immediately and the third remained afloat, although listing heavily. It was later beached.

The roar of the torpedoes exploding aroused the patrol and anti-submarine vessels which closed the area where *Torbay* submerged and saturated the area with depth charges. Miers worked the submarine close inshore, and lay in deep water in the shadow of a cliff for seventeen hours before escaping to sea. He too was rewarded for his cool courage with the award of the Victoria Cross.

These awards, when added to those won by Lieutenant Wanklyn earlier, brought the total of Victoria Crosses won by Mediterranean submarines to five—a tribute to the courage of the men of the two flotillas.

German submarines were stepping up their successes in the same period. On 13 March, less than 100 miles south of where *Torbay* carried out her daring attack, *U 565* torpedoed and sank the modern cruiser *Naiad*. Eighty-two of the crew went down with their ship.

Ten days after this sad loss the Italian battleship *Littoria*, accompanied by four heavy cruisers, attacked a Malta convoy escorted by a force of cruisers and destroyers commanded by Rear Admiral Vian. The Italian squadron was supported by a strong force of German bombers which attacked the convoy when the two surface forces sighted each other.

Vian ordered the convoy to turn back and launched his cruisers and destroyers against *Littoria* and her escorts. His 8-inch cruisers fired on the battleship at extreme range and registered at least one hit before *Littoria* turned away. Minutes later, in perfect line, the British destroyers launched their torpedoes which ran down her length. The persistence of the German bombers forced Vian to break off what was the only action in the war in which an Italian battleship could claim a victory.

Malta was beaten to her knees in the last week of March. The heaviest air attack in the siege was launched on the 26th. It completely devastated the area between Marsaxlokk and Grand Harbour. The destroyer *Legion* was sunk and the submarines *Talybont* and *Pampas* were seriously damaged. *Talybont* was later scuttled. Cunningham knew the cost of holding Malta was extraordinarily high. For every two supply ships to reach the island, the fleet lost one of its ships, yet the Mediterranean would be lost when the fleet became too weak to defend it. However, he kept his fears to himself and signalled the island: 'Cheer up, Summer is coming. A swallow has been seen in Egypt.'

Three German submarines were operating off the Egyptian coast in the last week of March. *U 652* was responsible for the sinking of the destroyer *Heythorp* and is thought to have sunk *Jaguar* and the Royal Fleet Auxiliary tanker *Slavol* a few days earlier. Another veteran of the Norwegian Campaign, the destroyer *Havock* was lost soon after. It ran aground at high speed when operating off Cape Bon and was destroyed by her crew, who were taken prisoner by the French. To add to the Commander-in-Chief's gloom, *Kingston* was destroyed by German aircraft while in dock at Malta.

In early March Churchill raised the question of further operations in the Aegean with Admiral Pound and Cunningham was directed to carry out a bombardment of enemy airfields on Rhodes. A task force of two cruisers, *Dido* and *Euryalus*, and six destroyers under Pridham-Wippell carried out the operation on the night of 15–16 March. Air cover was provided by fighters based on Cyprus which also dropped flares to illuminate the targets. Heavy damage was done to aircraft hangars, workshops and a large flour mill close to the airfield perimeter.

Admiral Cunningham was called back to England to represent the First Sea Lord at the forthcoming Chiefs of Staff Committee and command of the Mediterranean Fleet was temporarily passed over to Vice Admiral Pridham-Wippell. ABC flew out of Alexandria in a flying boat on the night of 3 April.

On 11 April the Germans commenced laying mine barrages in the lanes used by British convoys and naval formations. The German 3rd MTB Flotilla lay a barrage of 130 mines east of Malta while the Italian destroyers *Vivaldi* and *Malocello* laid another of 360 mines to the west. Two nights later the submarines *U 81, U 331, U 561* and *U 563* laid similar barrages off Cyprus, Beirut, Haifa and Port Said. Within days these fields paid handsome dividends. A 11,754-ton supply ship was sunk and a 4,043-ton tanker was damaged off Port Said. Six small vessels were lost to this cause in the other barrages. The first naval loss was the destroyer *Southwold*.

However, the losses were not all one-sided. On 2 May the two old First World War destroyers *Wishart* and *Wrestler* sank *U 74* and Hudson aircraft accounted for *U 573* in the eastern Mediterranean. A week later the corvette *Hyacinth* detected and destroyed the Italian submarine *Perla* off Haifa. The two smallest war vessels in the Mediterranean Fleet, the South African whale-catchers/anti-submarine vessels, *Protea* and *Southern Maid*, closed another Italian account, the *Ondina*. On 28 May the destroyers *Eridge, Hero* and *Hurworth* sank *U 652* east of Rhodes.

Admiral Pridham-Wippell was highly satisfied with the score, but his elation was to be short-lived. The Fleet Class destroyers *Lively, Kipling* and *Jackal* were sunk by a force of Ju 88s south of Crete on the night of 10–11 May. The destroyers were part of Captain Poland's flotilla despatched to intercept an Italian convoy reported off Benghazi. The only ship of the flotilla to survive was *Jervis*, which picked up 630 survivors.

Acting Admiral Sir Henry Harwood, the hero of the sinking of the German pocket battleship *Graf Spee* in December 1939, was appointed to succeed Cunningham and hoisted his flag in the battleship *Queen Elizabeth* at Alexandria on 20 May. His command had been extended to include the Red Sea.

The change of command had little influence on the fleet's losses. In June, they were to amount to one cruiser, a submarine depot ship and six destroyers. The destroyer *Grove* fell victim to *U 77* and sank off Sidi Barrani on the 12th. *Hasty*, one of the veterans of home waters was sunk by an Italian E-boat on the following night. *Airedale* was providing distant cover for a Malta convoy on 15 May when she was found and sunk by a flight of German bombers south of Crete. She had been in service three months and had survived Russian Convoy PQ 11.

The submarines were the only ships of the fleet to bring the new admiral relief in this black period. *Turbulent*, Commander Linton, on a fourteen-day patrol between 14 and 29 May, sank three supply ships and the Italian destroyer *Pessagno* in a running battle off Benghazi. In the same period, *Thrasher* accounted for one and *Proteus* two more, a total of 11,000 tons and one escort from the same convoy.

Meanwhile, there were more losses from Malta convoys. On 16 May, the cruiser *Hermione* and the Australian destroyer *Nestor* were torpedoed and sunk by *U 205* off Crete. On the same day, the Polish destroyer *Kujawiak*, which had been despatched to meet the convoy, struck a mine in the barrage laid by the Italians and was lost.

Rommel's star was in the ascendant at this period, with his army near El Alamein preparing for the last dash to Cairo. On 30 July Admiral Harwood ordered the fleet to move to new bases at Port Said and Haifa. A new base for the 1st Submarine Flotilla was already established at Beirut.

The German Command foresaw the move and the 14,650-ton submarine depot ship *Medway* was torpedoed and sunk by *U 372* soon after leaving Alexandria. The fleet lost its only submarine depot ship and most of the torpedoes and spares for the 1st Submarine Flotilla. *U 372*'s luck was short-lived; five days later she was sunk by the destroyers *Zulu, Sikh, Croome* and *Tetcott* south of Haifa. On the next night, the small anti-submarine trawler *Islay* surprised the Italian submarine *Scire* on the surface, launching chariots off Haifa, and sank her with depth charges.

Twenty-four hours later, the veteran aircraft carrier *Eagle* was torpedoed and sunk by *U 73*. The carrier had just flown off her cargo of fighters for Malta and was returning to Gibraltar. The delivery of fighters to Malta was part of a dual operation, code-named Operation Pedestal. The running of a heavily escorted convoy to the island was the other. At the time *Eagle* was sunk, the Pedestal convoy was approaching Skerki Channel. Fifteen minutes before sunset the long line of ships was sighted by a flight of enemy torpedo bombers and the destroyer *Foresight* was torpedoed. The ship was seriously damaged and was later sunk by her crew.

More disasters were in hand for the hard-pressed convoy in the next twenty-four hours. Two hours after the loss of *Foresight* the Italian submarine *Axum* surfaced in the track of the column of ships. When the convoy was broadside on, she fired all her tubes. The flagship *Nigeria*, the cruiser *Cairo* and the tanker *Ohio* were hit almost simultaneously. *Nigeria* and *Cairo* were seriously damaged, but the flagship and the tanker were still able to steam. *Cairo* was scuttled early next morning and her crew was picked up by destroyers. The captain and two officers were later court-martialled for prematurely sinking the ship.

A second Italian submarine, *Alagi*, found the convoy early on 13 August and scored hits on the cruiser *Kenya* and the transport *Clan Ferguson*. Both ships fell out of the convoy and turned back. One hour later, the survivors of the convoy were sighted by a squadron of enemy torpedo boats which launched attacks in the next four hours of darkness. The 9,400-ton cruiser *Manchester* was torpedoed by *MS 16* and *MS 22*. She was later sunk by destroyers detached to tow her back to Gibraltar. Five transports were also sunk. This was the first success of the Italian MS-boats which, at ninety feet overall, were almost twice as large as the MAS-boats. They were more heavily armed than their predecessor, carrying 21.1-inch torpedoes and twenty depth charges. The first flotilla was commissioned only weeks before they attacked the Pedestal convoy.

The only success scored by the Royal Navy on that night was the torpedoing of the Italian cruisers *Bolzano* and *Muzio Attendolo* by the submarine *Unbroken*, Lieutenant Alastair Mars. Both cruisers reached port but were out of service for many months.

One of the most ill-conceived operations undertaken in the Mediterranean was the amphibious raid on Tobruk on the night of 14–15 September 1942. The plan was to land a force of 500 Royal Marines from the destroyers *Sikh* and *Zulu* in the port area of the fortress while a land column of the LRDG struck from the landward side. The two destroyers were escorted by the anti-aircraft cruiser *Coventry*, eighteen MTBs and three MLs.

The destroyers, MTBs and MLs made a high-speed run into the harbour under cover of RAF attacks but were immediately met by intense and accurate shore fire. *Sikh* and *Zulu* closed the shore to silence the batteries, but the former was hit and grounded on the beach.

Coventry, and a group of Hunt Class destroyers which had been patrolling offshore closed the beach to provide covering fire while *Zulu* attempted to pass a tow to free *Sikh*. It was now daylight and enemy aircraft arrived overhead. *Coventry* was hit by a bomb and caught fire. The crew were taken off by MLs and the cruiser drifted ashore. At 1615 *Zulu*, accompanied by two MTBs, re-entered the harbour to attempt to tow her sister ship clear, but as she closed *Sikh* she was hit by a large bomb and sank soon after.

The loss of a cruiser, two Fleet Class destroyers, six MTBs and an ML, together with the majority of the marines, was bitterly criticised in the House of Commons some weeks later. The Leader of the Opposition called it 'ill-conceived, wasteful and avoidable'.

During the period of Admiral Harwood's tenure of the post of Commander-in-Chief, Mediterranean, few signals were received from the Prime Minister. The presence of Cunningham in London may have been responsible for this. However, orders for the Mediterranean certainly contained the same Churchillian flavour.

Successes in 1942 were few and far between, but fortunes improved with the new year. The Battle of Alamein was the turning point. On 29 January 1943 Rommel's army was pushed west of the Tripoli–Tunis border and Luftwaffe pressure in the eastern Mediterranean was greatly reduced. The RAF, operating from desert airfields, gained control of the skies north to Crete.

On 1 February the fast minelayer *Welshman*, which with the *Breconshire* had kept Malta alive when all else failed, was torpedoed and sunk by *U 617* south of Crete. This sinking was one of the last successes of the U-boats in the Mediterranean. Twenty-three of their number had been lost in 1942, and these losses were not replaced.

In 1943 the Luftwaffe introduced a new weapon. This was the circling torpedo which had been used in the Atlantic at the end of 1942. The first success was the sinking of two transports on 19 March. Royal Navy countermeasures soon reduced its usefulness and it had been withdrawn from service by the time the glider bomb came into use in October.

Admiral A.B. Cunningham resumed his old post of Commander-in-Chief, Mediterranean on 20 February, to supervise the naval component of the invasion of Sicily. The command was divided into two shortly after, Commander-in-Chief, Mediterranean being responsible for the waters between Cape Spartivento on the toe of Italy to the Tunis–Tripoli border, and Commander-in-Chief, Levant, responsible for all waters east of this line, including the Red Sea. Admiral Harwood assumed this latter command.

Enemy resistance ended in North Africa on 13 April, and the southern shores of the Mediterranean from Gibraltar to the Suez Canal were in Allied hands. In May, the forgotten French battle squadron in Alexandria Harbour stirred. Admiral Godfroy reactivated his ships and at the end of the month sailed for Free French ports in Algeria. Admiral Harwood provided the escort, the cruiser *Carlisle* and four destroyers. Godfroy received a cold welcome on his arrival and, after turning over his fleet to the Free French Commander-in-Chief, was banished to an early retirement.

The eastern Mediterranean was now a backwater. Ships were transferred to other commands and the fleet became a shadow of its former glory. The only units involved in operations against the enemy were the submarines.

Admiral Harwood relinquished command of the Levant Fleet on 5 June and his place as Commander-in-Chief was taken by Admiral Sir John Cunningham, no relation of Sir Andrew, who had commanded the 1st Cruiser Squadron during the Norwegian Campaign in 1940.

Three months of comparative calm passed following this change of command. However, events were already shaping up in Italy which would set the eastern Mediterranean, and the Aegean, ablaze.

12

The Middle East Raiding Forces

The use of raiding forces had been perfected by the British in the Napoleonic Wars, so it was not surprising plans were made for the training of commando-style units in the first weeks of the Second World War. However, it was not until the collapse of France that Section MO9 of the War Office was established for the purpose of recruiting, training and directing in operations the special force which became known as the commandos. Command of the section was given to Brigadier Otto Lund, the Deputy Director of Military Operations. By the end of July 1940, nine commandos, or independant companies, as they were known at the time, had been formed. The first commando raid was launched against the island of Guernsey on the night of 14–15 July of that year.

However, quite distinct from these forces, a Middle East Commando was formed in the Middle East in 1940 by Major George Young, Operations Officer of Military Intelligence. This force was modelled on the irregular force raised by Captain Fox-Davies in Palestine during the unrest of 1936. Fox-Davies joined Major Young and was given the task of recruiting former members of his force for the proposed Middle East Commando. The first recruits were formed into No. 50 ME Commando which, at the time, had not been approved by MO9. Major H.J. Cator, MC, who had commanded 401 Palestinian Company, described the new recruits at this time: 'Three-quarters of them are Jews. The rest are Arabs, Germans and Spaniards and even some Portuguese, Latvians, Sudanese, Egyptians, Iraqui, Sinaites and Palestinians.'

The Middle East Commando was approved early in 1940 with Young, now promoted to lieutenant colonel, as commanding officer and Fox-Davies, with the rank of major, as second-in-command. Their total strength was 370, all ranks. They assembled at Geneifa in Egypt, where they were soon joined by a small force of Spaniards who had served in the French Foreign Legion. Their uniforms were as odd as the composition of the force. They consisted of South African safari jackets, drill slacks, Australian bush hats and rope-soled boots. Later, the uniform was standardised to British regulation dress.

No. 50 ME Commando was shipped to Crete when Greece entered the war in November 1940. They were deployed in the Heraklion area where they came under the direction of Colonel John Pendlebury, an archaeologist and British Consul, who also represented British Intelligence on the island. Nos 51 and 52 ME Commandos were formed on 18th and 29th October 1940 and were trained on the pattern of No. 50.

Before leaving for Crete, No. 50 had embarked on an attack on Italian installations at Bomba on the night of 28–29 October, but it was aborted when the commandos were entering the boats to land. No. 51, commanded by Major Cator, was to have a similar experience on its first raid. They sailed from Alexandria in the destroyer *Hereward* on 9 December, accompanied by the First World War fighter *X-39* carrying weapons and stores. Their target was food and ammunition dumps behind the Italian lines near Sidi Barrani. This operation was also aborted when General Wavell's advance forces overran Sidi Barrani and captured the dumps. A week later, Cator's troops were embarked in the Australian destroyer *Voyager* to carry out a similar operation behind the enemy lines at Sollum. This raid was also abandoned.

The three cancelled operations were not an auspicious beginning for the Middle East Commandos, who were to meet further frustration in their next operations, which took them to the Aegean. No. 50 Commando was alerted and briefed for a raid on an airfield on Cos in December 1940. The operation was aborted when an intelligence report from the island warned the garrison had been reinforced.

Their next operation, a raid on Italian radar and gun installations on the island of Kasos, was abandoned when the boats to land them sank off the target. This raid was repeated on the night of 17–18 February, led by Colonel Pendlebury. They landed on Kasos but the local guides failed to make the rendezvous.

A week later, on 25 February, No. 50 Commando participated in a combined operation to capture the island of Casteloriso, close to the Turkish coast. The commandos, supported by a force of Royal Marines, landed in daylight under a bombardment by the gunboat HMS *Ladybird* and the destroyers *Hereward* and *Decoy* and quickly overcame the Italian garrison. At dusk, the naval commanding officer, Rear Admiral de F. Renouf, decided to withdraw the ships and return on the evening of the 26th with a regular army battalion to garrison the island.

During the night the Italian Air Force carried out heavy bombing raids on Casteloriso and, early in the afternoon of the 26th, a strong enemy army force supported by artillery landed. In the ensuing engagement, the commandos, carrying only light arms, were overwhelmed and the island was recaptured. Admiral Renouf did not return to Casteloriso until 27 February, and only a small number of the commandos and marines were rescued. The island was lost and at a court of inquiry held at Alexandria Renouf was removed from his command.

While No. 50 Commando was being wiped out on Casteloriso, Nos 51 and 52 were joining British forces deployed against the Italians in Abyssinia and Eritrea. No. 52 landed at Port Sudan and joined Brigadier Mann's force defending the Port Sudan-Gedaref Line. Not unexpectedly, the polyglot unit soon run foul of the British commander by being involved in brawls with the local inhabitants in Gedaref and their total lack of discipline. When two of their number were knifed in these brawls, Mann despatched the unit on raiding duties.

However, the blot on their escutcheon was soon erased. In their first two attacks on enemy native troops, they routed two large camel squadrons and took a large number of prisoners. This action gave Colonel Young the opportunity to sort the good from the bad, and twenty-six undesirables and eighteen others who were unfit were returned to base. The remainder of the commandos' service in East Africa was spent as reinforcements for British regular units.

No. 51 Commando arrived at Port Sudan on 30 January 1941 under the command of Major Cator. It soon proved it was superior in every way to its undisciplined sister unit. Under the leadership of officers like Captain Jock Lapraik, who was later to distinguish himself in the SBS, and Lieutenant H. Frost, they soon showed they were tough and disciplined fighters.

Cator's force was soon in action at Beit Gabru, where Lieutenant Frost led 'A' Troop in a fighting reconnaissance of a strong enemy position dug into the crown of a hill overlooking the Italian main positions. Although outnumbered and lacking in heavy weapons, they attacked and seized a forward position, killing ten of the enemy in fierce hand-to-hand combat. No. 51 Commando soon discovered the enemy's black soldiers were far superior to their white compatriots. Three of the commandos were killed in this first action.

Two more actions were fought at Beit Gabru, and again their offensive spirit and aggressive tactics had a decisive effect on the outcome of the battle. With the fall of this strong feature, Keren was taken and the enemy withdrew to Massawa and Asmara. No. 51's last actions were fought in early May, at the Battle of Falaga Pass in Abyssinia. This battle resulted in the surrender of the Duke of d'Aosta's army on 16 May. Major Lapraik was awarded the Military Cross for his outstanding leadership and personal courage in the battle.

In March 1941, the two Commandos were combined to form 'D' Battalion in Layforce. The other battalions in the force were 'A', No. 7 Commando; 'B', No. 8 Commando; and 'C', No. 11 Commando. On completing training, Layforce was shipped to Crete in May 1941 and was lost when committed to the already-lost battle as infantry. It was to take several such disasters before the Army Command learnt commandos were wasted in infantry roles.

The progenitor of the Long Range Desert Group was a little-known unit raised in Egypt in 1915 and given the uninspiring name of the 5th Light Car Patrol. It owed its existence to fears in Whitehall that Senussi tribes in Tripoli were planning an invasion of Egypt through the Western Desert. There was some substance to these fears, as both German and Turkish officers had been infiltrated into Tripoli to train the fierce tribesmen in the use of modern weapons and battle tactics. Arms and money for this purpose reached the Senussi, and by mid-May their camel patrols were sighted deep in the Libyan Desert.

In the closing months of the year, Mersa Matruh fell to a German-led Senussi force and between them and the Nile Delta were only a few small squadrons of mounted yeomanry. The British rear was now under serious threat. Luckily, the British commander remembered a number of light car patrols used to cover the northern approaches to the Suez Canal. No. 5 Light Car Patrol was withdrawn from this area and ordered to the Western Desert front.

The patrol was equipped with light Model T Ford cars which had been stripped of their bodies and fitted with oversize tyres. Condensers were fitted to the radiators and additional water and fuel tanks installed. Armament consisted of two Lewis machine-guns and rifles. Each car was equipped with a sun compass and navy magnetic compasses for navigation. The cars carried several rolls of chain wire for negotiating sand dunes.

No. 5 Patrol was soon operating in the desert 100 miles to the west of the Nile. The horse and camel patrols of the Senussi patrols proved no match for the fast-moving cars and they were driven back from the southern desert and later withdrew from Egypt.

General Wavell remembered No. 5 Car Patrol in 1940 when he was faced with desert warfare on three fronts—Libya, Abyssinia and Eritrea—and ordered his Intelligence Branch to obtain reports on recent expeditions engaged in explorations in the desert areas. He soon learnt of Lieutenant Minshall and Major R.A. Bagnold.

Merlin Minshall, a lieutenant in the Royal Navy Reserve, has already been mentioned in Chapter 3 for his involvement in Operation Iron Gates in 1940. Three years earlier he had undertaken a private expedition to find a route negotiable by motor vehicles from Libya to Lake Chad in Central Africa. This expedition used an air-cooled light vehicle to cross the Western Desert from north to south. Lieutenant Minshall not only discovered a practical route to Central Africa, but met both German and French military officers engaged in a similar task.

Major Bagnold had lived in Egypt for some years, where he took up desert navigation as a hobby. He conducted a number of expeditions into the Western Desert using specially adapted vehicles. Wavell met Bagnold in Cairo and placed him on his staff. Bagnold produced plans for a special desert group, but no action was taken until Italy entered the war. Thirteen days later the Long Range Patrol was formed. Its name was changed to the Long Range Desert Group at the end of 1940.

Major Bagnold decided New Zealanders and Australians were the best troops for desert warfare, and immediately asked both commands for volunteers. To his disappointment, General Blamey, the Australian commander, refused on the grounds the Australian govenment would not agree to their troops serving under another command. This was a legacy of the First World War, when Australians were scattered in special units from Africa to Russia. However, the New Zealand government had no objections, and their troops served in the LRDG throughout its history.

Suitable vehicles for desert operations were difficult to find and Bagnold decided to use the standard British Army thirty-hundredweight truck, modified to his ideas. The vehicles were stripped of doors, windscreens and hoods. Oversize tyres were fitted and condensers installed. Later, GMH in America produced specially built Chevrolet utilities and cars for the group. All vehicles carried steel sand mats and bridges for crossing dunes.

Armament varied throughout the history of the LRDG, but initially it consisted of Lewis and Bren light machine-guns, Boys anti-tank rifles, a 37-mm Bofors gun and the personal arms carried by the crew. Later, twin Browning and Vickers K machine-guns were fitted and the Bofors replaced by .5-inch Vickers and Bredas.

Bagnold worked by trial and error. Patrols in the beginning consisted of two officers and thirty men carried in eleven trucks. A force of this size proved too conspicuous and it was reduced to one officer and fifteen men in five trucks. Initially, three patrols were formed. These were 'R', 'T' and 'W', manned by New Zealanders. As the organisation developed, it was increased to ten, four New Zealand, two Yoemanry, two Guards and two Rhodesian.

The LRDG's first operation was launched in September 1940. At this time the Italian Army was advancing on Sidi Barrani and General Wavell was concerned the enemy may launch a drive through the desert to the south, posing a threat to Cairo. To counter such a move, a strong patrol was sent through the desert to lay an ambush on the Jalo–Kufra road.

Here, the New Zealanders intercepted a small supply column of two trucks. The action was bloodless and the eight Italians manning the trucks were taken prisoner. More important than the prisoners were the 2,500 gallons of petrol, the ammunition and the official mail they carried. The appearance of British troops so far west had a psychological effect on General Graziano and his staff.

From this small beginning, the LRDG launched a series of long-distance raids behind the enemy lines. The Western Desert, which had protected the advancing Italian landward flank, was now a threat, and increased numbers of troops were transferred to guard these vital lines of communications. The range of patrols was increased by laying down secret dumps of fuel and supplies. From the Arabs they learnt of new sources of water and invaluable intelligence on the enemy.

Lessons learnt in these operations were applied to their training. In the beginning, patrols wore normal army service dress but this was gradually changed to shorts and shirts, while a variety of headdress, including that of the Arabs, was adopted. Likewise, Tommy guns were added to their personal arms. From an early stage, air cooperation was used and this was refined with experience.

The LRDG supported the Western Desert Army from the first actions in Egypt in 1940 until the rout of Rommel's Army at Gabes in 1943. Their only failures occurred when they were employed in regular army roles, most particularly in Leros in November 1943.

When first formed in England in 1940, the concept of the Special Boat Section was closer to the Royal Marine role than that of the army. It was a specialised section of the commandos, trained to operate and maintain a wide range of small craft ranging from canoes to landing craft. Their task was to transport raiders to enemy coasts and bring them back again. Action against the enemy was restricted to protecting their craft.

Their first operations were launched in early 1941 against the Atlantic Wall, the long exposed coastline of Occupied Western Europe stretching from Denmark in the north to Spain in the south. The operations were primarily intelligence-gathering missions, but Churchill, chafing under his inability to strike at the enemy, ordered them to spill enemy blood. Soon the commandos were knifing and garrotting enemy sentries and British morale was boosted. The first recruits for the SBS were well equipped for the role. Men like the young Dane, Anders Lassen, who had already participated in the hijacking of a German cargo liner in a West African port, were models for a unit which was to become the elite of all raiding forces.

Three sections of the SBS were transferred to the Mediterranean in late February 1941 and were integrated into already formed commando SAS and LRDG units. A small number, with proven ability in long-distance swimming, were lent to the Royal Navy and became known as Royal Marine Swimmers. Despite the name, they were not carried on the strength of the Royal Marines.

Because of the secret nature of their operations, all specialised clandestine groups, commandos, SAS (Special Air Service), SBS and lesser known organisations such as Popski's Private Army and the Levant Schooner Flotilla, were ultimately brought under Special Operations Executive (SOE) of MO 4. This branch was responsible for infiltrating intelligence agents and sabotage groups into enemy-occupied territory.

Soon after the arrival of the SBS in the Mediterranean, Captain Roger Courtney and Commander Nigel Clostoun-Willmott suggested the units should be employed on individual operations. Both officers were expert canoeists and considered this type of raid should come within SBS responsibility. Clostoun-Willmott's uncle had served with Bernard Freyberg in the Royal Marine reconnaissance group which surveyed and marked the beaches at Gallipoli for the Anzac landings in 1915.

The suggestion was approved and two of the first graduates from the training course, Lieutenant 'Tug' Wilson and Marine Hughes, carried out the first individual SBS operation on 22 June 1941. They landed from a submarine on the west coast of Sicily and successfully blew up an enemy railway line. As they paddled out to the rendezvous with the submarine, they had the satisfaction of witnessing a train being derailed as a result of their night's work. Several days later, intelligence agents reported the derailment of the train and the large casualties caused. The line was put out of service for a week, while damage to a tunnel required some months to repair.

Two more raids were carried out in the next three months, but all failed. The enemy had been alerted.

SBS canoeists operating with submarines landed eight SOE agents in Crete between July and September 1941. The canoeists and their passengers were carried to the island by the submarine HMS *Thunderbolt*, and landing operations were commanded by Sargeant James Sherwood, who was awarded the Distinguished Conduct Medal as a result.

Captain Courtney was invalided home to England in December 1941 and command of the Mediterranean SBS passed to Captain M. Kealy, who had participated in a number of commando operations in the Western Desert. He led a raid on the feature known as Twin Pimples at Tobruk, which opened the way for a breakout by the garrison. Sargeant Dickason, who accompanied Kealy on the raid, later wrote: 'I saw Captain Kealy rush the enemy machine-gun crew and clout them with the butt end of his Tommy gun. The gun was rendered useless, but so were the enemy gunners.'

In December 1941, Captain the Earl Jellicoe was recalled to England where he received a brief from Brigadier Laycock to enlarge the Mediterranean Special Boat Section into a squadron, The strength of the squadron was to be 230 men with a base echelon. Jellicoe was the second son of a British admiral to command a raiding force in the Second World War. The first was Lieutenant Colonel Geoffrey Keyes, who won a posthumous Victoria Cross for his leadership in the raid on Rommel's headquarters.

The SBS reached a high standard of efficiency under Kealy's training and by June 1942 all sections were ready for action. Two weeks later, they were alerted for an operation against the four main airfields in Crete. These were Maleme, Kastelli, Timbaki and Heraklion. Three sections were landed on the south coast of the island by Lieutenant John Campbell's caique flotilla. The fourth section, led by Captain, the Earl Jellicoe, was landed by the submarine HMS *Triton* close to Heraklion. Their exploits are described in Chapter 14. The SBS made two more raids on Crete and on the Italian surrender moved to the Aegean, where their daring operations were legendary.

SOE was responsible for creating the Levant Schooner Flotilla which provided transport for the clandestine forces in the Aegean in 1943 and 1944. After the fall of Greece and Crete, a large number of Greek caiques, schooners and fishing boats carrying escapees and refugees arrived in Allied ports. These vessels were taken to Haifa and Beirut, where they were modified to serve the raiding and intelligence-gathering forces in the Aegean Islands. Initially, the force was called the Blackbeard Flotilla, but in early 1943, on the suggestion of the newly appointed commanding officer, Lieutenant Adrian Seligman, RNR, it was renamed the Levant Schooner Flotilla.

Thirty-eight-year-old Seligman was an excellent choice as flotilla commander. He was born into a sea-loving family and as a young boy accompanied his French brother-in-law, Jean Boureul, on long voyages in an old fishing boat from St Malo south. On completing his education at Cambridge he turned to the sea again. In October 1932 he shipped aboard the Finnish four-masted barque *Olivebank* as an ordinary seaman for a return voyage to Australia. He remained with Gustaf Erikson's fleet and made two more voyages to Australia before transferring to the droghers carrying timber from the Baltic to English ports.

Seligman transferred to steamships in 1934 and in the next two years obtained his second-mate's ticket. A year later, he decided to swallow the anchor and take up a shore profession, but in 1936 England was in the midst of the Great Depression and offered few opportunities for ex-sailors. In early 1937 he purchased the 295-ton barquentine *Cap Pilar* which had been tied up at St Malo for several years. Seligman had the old ship refitted and then advertised for a crew of young men for a round the world voyage. Each crewman was required to find £50 to pay for his provisions. The crew was found, all first voyagers with the exception of Seligman and two others. *Cap Pillar*'s voyage in 1937–38 thrilled the world. She returned to London, and the war clouds which were gathering, in September 1938.

Every man who served in the Levant Schooner Flotilla, whether he be a Greek seaman, an SBS commando or a professional officer of the Royal Navy, respected Seligman. He knew boats, he knew seamen and he knew the sea. Moreover, he never asked of another what he could not do himself.

Seligman selected Haifa as the flotilla base. The facilities were better and caiques and schooners were built in the port. Here the hulls of the motley range of vessels were strengthened, the masts and rigging were refitted and the low-powered oil engines were replaced by diesel ones removed from obsolete Matilda tanks abandoned in depots in Egypt. The first armament of the caiques and schooners was twin Vickers .5-inch and two .303-inch Lewis guns. Later, when they became available, Bofors and 20-mm Oerlikons were added. Two of the guns were fitted in concealed mountings.

It was early June 1943 before the first vessels were ready for service. These were *LS 1* and *LS 2* and they were commanded by Seligman and Lieutenant Andre Londos, Royal Hellenic Navy.

From this humble beginning, the 300 ships of the flotilla grew. All vessels of the Levant Schooner Flotilla flew the British White Ensign and the flotilla pennant, which was changed several times. The crews were usually Royal Navy personnel on special duties, but Greek seamen were embarked to provide local knowledge. Initially, only a small number of army personnel were carried to operate the large guns, but by 1944 the crews were a mixture of both services.

In service, the sea proved more dangerous than the enemy. *LS 5* and *LS 8* were wrecked off the coast of Cyprus and *LS 11* foundered off Samos early in the flotilla's operations. *LS 1* and *LS 4* were lost by enemy action. The former fell victim to a heavily armed German R-boat at Sirina while carrying out an operation. *LS 4* was believed to have been sunk by a German U-boat in Cypriot waters. The last loss of the flotilla was the headquarter ship *MFV 117*, which struck an enemy mine and sunk off Cos. She was the only ship of the flotilla with the necessary draught to strike a mine.

Despite the adoption of modern navigational equipment and new armament, the caiques and schooners retained their age-old lateen rig and tiller steering, which were necessary disguises for penetrating enemy-dominated waters.

In May 1944, with the commissioning of the second flotilla, its name was changed to the Anglo-Hellenic Schooner Flotilla. The first flotilla remained British-manned and the second was Greek-manned. The flotilla base was now firmly established at Port Dereman in the Gulf of Cos on the Turkish mainland. Six months later, in the wake of the German withdrawal from the Aegean, it was transferred to Chios. The Levant Schooner Flotilla was the last Royal Navy flotilla to fight under sail.

The Greek Sacred Squadron, Ieros Lohos, was formed in early September 1942 at Caphriona in Palestine. It was the fifth occasion in Greek history the sacred squadron has been raised. Its forebears fought at Thebes in 371 BC, Lasio in 1821, Thebes in 1877 and North Ipiros in 1913. Command of the Sacred Squadron was invested in Major Christodoulos Tzigantes. The initial strength was 200 men, the majority of whom were drawn from the Greek Officer Corps. It was later increased to 1,100.

Training of the squadron was similar to that of the British special forces and officers from the Long Range Desert Group, Special Boat Squadron and Special Air Services were seconded to the newly formed squadron for this purpose. The Greek volunteers proved good pupils and on 25 January 1943 the squadron departed Palestine to join General Montgomery's army in the Western Desert at El Aghiela. After its defeat at El Alamein, Rommel's army was in retreat and the Sacred Squadron and the largely New Zealand LRDG operated on its flank as they fell back to Tripoli.

In early February 1943 the squadron, under the command of General Le Clerk, participated in the actions which resulted in the capture of the city of Gambes. On 29 March the Sacred Squadron joined General Freyberg's 2nd New Zealand Division. It participated in the capture of Soussa and was honoured when the mayor presented the key of the city to Colonel Tzigantes.

Four days later, the squadron was ordered to return to Egypt to prepare for operations later in the year in the Aegean Islands. The fighting in the desert campaign cost the squadron three killed, eight wounded and two missing—all officers. The Sacred Squadron did not participate in the battles fought in Cos, Leros and Samos between September and November 1943, but during this period its strength was increased to 446 men and the unit underwent intense training.

On 17 February 1944 the squadron was ordered to prepare for operations in the Aegean and, a month later, a patrol was landed at Bromolimano in Asia Minor to block a German withdrawal northward. Shortly afterwards, a second patrol was landed at Agios Georgios for the same purpose. These operations were to prove a pattern for the later use of the squadron. One large operation involving the squadron and British troops was carried out in July 1944. This was the raid on Simi, which cost the Germans heavy casualties.

The crowning success of the Sacred Squadron was the final liberation of the Aegean Islands between September 1944 and May 1945. In these operations, led by the fire-eating Cretan Colonel Travakis, the Ieros Lohos lived up to the motto which is engraved on the squadron badge in the language of Ancient Greece: 'Return victorious or dead'.

The Greek Sacred Squadron and the Special Boat Squadron are today regular units of their countries' armed forces.

13

The Italian Surrender

The eastern Mediterranean had lapsed into a forgotten backwater by the middle of 1943. Admiral Sir John Cunningham's fleet was reduced to one mixed flotilla of destroyers, six Fleets and two Hunt Class; and the 1st Submarine Flotilla, which could muster only six submarines. Coastal Forces' two squadrons, the 24th and 42nd Flotillas, numbered sixteen motor launches. The Levant Schooner Flotilla was in the course of formation, but only four small caiques were ready for service. The flotilla commander, Lieutenant Seligman and his capable second-in-command, Lieutenant Andre Londos, Royal Hellenic Navy, were commandeering suitable craft in all Allied ports.

Air support was on a similarly meagre scale. Two squadrons of Beaufighters, two squadrons of light bombers and a transport squadron equipped with Dakotas were operational. The services of No 680 Reconnaissance Squadron, equipped with long-range Spitfire aircraft, were on call when required.

The SBS was regrouping in their Crusader castle at Azzib, and to the south in Palestine, the Greek Sacred Squadron was being reorganised as a raiding force. Montgomery's Eighth Army was now a thousand miles to the west and the great training camps of Palestine, which had held more than 100,000 troops, were now deserted.

At 1940 on 8 September, the torpor in the eastern Mediterranean was swept away by an electrifying radio announcement by the Italian Chief-of-Staff, General Badoglio: 'Italian forces have agreed to an unconditional surrender'.

Five weeks earlier, on 3 August, Churchill had sent a top-secret minute to the Chiefs of Staff Committee, the first paragraph of which read: 'Here is a business of great consequence, to be thrust forward by every means. Should the Italian troops in Crete and Rhodes resist the Germans and a deadlock ensue, we must help the Italians at the earliest moment, engaging thereby also the support of the populations.'

This minute, when taken in context with a warning sounded by the U.S. Joint Chiefs of Staff in the wake of meetings between Churchill and Roosevelt in June 1943, confirms the surrender of the Italians was not totally unexpected. The warning followed the vetoing of Churchill's plan for an attack through the Aegean on the Rumanian oilfields, and read: 'In any event, if the British insisted on Mediterranean commitments that in American opinion would jeopardise the early defeat of Germany and the ultimate defeat of Japan, the U.S. representatives are to inform the British that the United States might be compelled to revise its basic strategy and extend its operations and commitments in the Pacific'.

News of the surrender was still being digested by the SBS when their commanding officer, the Earl Jellicoe, now a major, was summoned to the headquarters of the Commander-in-Chief, Middle East, General Sir Henry Maitland Wilson. Jellicoe was informed he was to be parachuted into Rhodes to persuade the Italian commander of the island to resist a German takeover until British forces arrived. While these arrangements were being put into hand, Captain Sutherland with fifty men of 'S' Squadron, were landed on the island of Casteloriso, seven miles off the coast of Turkey. Sutherland found the island occupied by 300 Italian troops, who surrendered without offering resistance.

At Rhodes, Jellicoe, Major Dolbey, the official Italian interpreter, and Sargeant Kesterton, a signaller, were dropped by a Halifax bomber over Martiza on the night of 9–10 September. On leaving the plane they were enveloped by a stygian black sky and, tumbled violently by a gale-force wind, the three men landed in widely separated areas. There was no reception committee as the Italians had not been informed they were being dropped.

The Italian airfield guards presumed they were German parachutists, dropped to seize the airfield, and immediately opened fire on them. Fortunately, their aim was wild and all three men landed unhit, although Dolbey struck an obstacle and broke a leg. He was immediately captured by the guards.

Presuming the Italians were hostile, Jellicoe and Kesterton quickly cleared the airfield and hid in some heavy bush. This proved a mistake. Dolbey, with his command of the language, had convinced the guards of the importance of his mission and was immediately carried to Admiral Campioni's headquarters. Before discussions could begin, the other two members of the party had to be found. Jellicoe and Kesterton crept deeper into the clump of brush and were not found by the searching guards. Fearing their reception was hostile, Jellicoe ate the letter he was to present to the admiral.

An hour passed before a second search party located the two missing men. Their bedraggled appearance and absence of the vital letter failed to impress Admiral Campioni. However, he guardedly informed the emissaries that his men were prepared to resist the Germans if they could supply more concrete evidence of the aid promised by the British.

Jellicoe made contact with Cairo on the Italian radio and, after some delay, agreement was reached that the British commander, Brigadier Turnbull, and his staff would be flown to the island of Simi in an Italian flying boat and brought to Rhodes by a MAS-boat.

Three hours after these arrangements had been made, the German commander, General Klemann, delivered an ultimatum to surrender to Campioni. Turnbull and his party were ordered to remain at Simi and Jellicoe and his party, accompanied by Campioni's Chief of Staff, were despatched by MAS-boat to join Turnbull. However, neither party reached Simi. En route they learnt Klemann had attacked the Italians in Rhodes and Campioni had surrendered. The MAS-boat embarked both parties and took them to Cos and then on to Casteloriso.

Cos was captured by a patrol of the SBS on 14 September and Captain Sutherland, who led the assault, negotiated a surrender with Admiral Mascherpa. When Jellicoe arrived later in the day he held talks with the admiral. Three days later Major Lapraik and Captain Lassen led an attack on Simi and the 140-strong Italian garrison surrendered after a short resistance.

While the drama was being enacted on Rhodes, the Prime Minister was bombarding General Maitland Wilson with instructions. He signalled on 13 September: 'The capture of Rhodes by you at this time with Italian aid would be a fine contribution to the general war effort. Let me know what your plans are for this. Can you improvise the necessary

Winston Churchill and United States congressman Harry Hopkins aboard the Australian destroyer, HMAS *Napier*, in late 1941.

The light cruiser HMS *Calypso* was the first ship lost by Admiral Cunningham, sunk by the Italian submarine *Bagnolini* off the coast of Crete in June 1940.

The Italian submarine *Gondar*, forced to the surface off Alexandria, closes HMAS *Stuart* to surrender.

HMAS *Sydney* returns to Sydney following the sinking of the Italian cruiser *Bartolomeo Colleoni* off Cape Spada, Crete, in 1940.

garrison out of the forces in the Middle East? This is the time to think of Clive and Petersborough and of Rooke's men taking Gibraltar.'

No amount of rhetoric could help Maitland Wilson at this time. His thoughts were directed to General Klemann rather than Clive or Rooke. For more than a year his command had been milked of its manpower and its resources to such a degree that it was no longer a field force. The total land force at his disposal was the 234th Brigade, which was retraining after a long period as garrison at Malta. The Middle East raiding forces, which fell short in numbers of a battalion, were already committed piecemeal to seizing the key islands.

Through the excellent intelligence network created in the islands by SOE, the Commander-in-Chief knew the Germans opposing his scratch force were superior in numbers and better trained than the force he had available. Rhodes was the key to the Aegean and a well-balanced army of 7,000 German troops and 35,000 Italians occupied all key positions. Two battalions of German regulars had arrived at Salonika and these were in the process of occupying other important islands in the central and northern Aegean.

Despite these dispositions, the German High Command was divided on whether the islands should be held. Hitler called a meeting of his Chiefs of Staff on 24 September at which Grand Admiral Doenitz and Field Marshal von Weichs expressed doubts on their ability to defend the widely scattered islands which would be required to be supplied by sea. Doenitz warned the meeting that Britain could commit strong carrier forces to the Aegean, which would isolate the many small garrisons. However, Hitler overruled the Chiefs of Staff and issued orders to reinforce the area.

Doenitz was still apprehensive of stretching even further the limited naval forces at his disposal in the Mediterranean and the Black Sea and presented the Führer with a strategical appreciation on the Aegean:

'The bases in the islands, in particular Crete, were established at a time when we were still planning offensive operations in the Eastern Mediterranean area; meanwhile the situation has changed. The Italian armed forces no longer exist and the position in the Balkan Peninsular is in danger for lack of sufficient forces. Maintenance of security in Balkan rear areas has become a difficult task. Advance island bases are of no value in a defensive situation such as this, since the enemy will bypass them and force their surrender sooner or later by cutting their supplies. Thus we shall lose, without a comparable strategic advantage, irreplaceable troops and matériel which could be of decisive importance for the defence of the Continent.'

Von Weichs rallied to Doenitz's support and informed Hitler the Allies were superior both in the air and on the land. However, he wisely omitted to qualify his statement with the fact that these forces were already committed in the western Mediterranean and the Americans had bound Churchill to restrict all operations in the eastern Mediterranean. Hitler replied by charging the grand admiral and the field marshall with pessimism and the German occupation of the key islands of the Aegean continued.

With Rhodes securely in German hands, Major Jellicoe turned his attention to Cos and Leros. He landed on Leros with a small patrol on 17 September and endeavoured to negotiate the surrender of the island and its important naval base. The Italian commander, Admiral Mascherpa, was already under orders from the Germans and refused to be influenced by the SBS leader's promises. Later in the day, Jellicoe landed reinforcements to test the strength of the admiral's forces. He found they were too strong.

Jellicoe met with more success on nearby Cos where he was well received by the Italian commander, Colonel Fanetza, in the Governor's Palace. Fanetza agreed to surrendering the island if the British landed reinforcements. Arrangements were made for a force of British parachutists to be dropped on the island within twenty-four hours.

The second-in-command of SBS, Major Lapraik, had in the meantime decided to test the German strength on Rhodes. Lieutenant Dion Stellin, a New Zealander who had transferred from the LRDG, was landed with a patrol of six men to carry out a reconnaissance. He found the island strongly held by enemy static and mobile forces. The Germans had occupied the former Italian fortifications and a strong mobile force of tanks and armoured cars was patrolling the main roads. The large Italian garrison was cooperating with the German troops. Before he left the island, Stellin laid mines in the narrow channel which gave access to the main port, New Town.

Captain Anders Lassen and his patrol captured the small island of Calchi off Rhodes. The young Dane found the garrison of twelve Italian gendarmes intensely pro-British and supplemented their arms with several machine-guns. This action was later to pay good dividends when the Italians repelled a much stronger force of Germans who attempted to occupy Calchi.

On 23 September the SBS was reinforced by 'A' and 'B' squadrons of the LRDG, who were landed on Leros by the Greek-manned destroyer *Queen Olga*. 'A' Squadron was a predominantly New Zealand unit and 'B' Squadron a mixture of British and Rhodesians. It was a welcome reinforcement to Jellicoe's slender force, and during the next ten days the raiding forces secured footholds on the main islands of the central Aegean. The operations took both Italians and Germans by surprise and they were achieved with surprisingly few casualties, but this was soon to change.

By the end of September, SOE agents reported the enemy had occupied Lemnos, Mytilene, Chios, Kasos, Kythera and Anti-Kythera and many smaller islands. Luftwaffe squadrons were arriving from France and the Russian front.

Italian naval forces in the Aegean at the time of the surrender consisted of six destroyers, thirty MAS-boats and a number of auxiliaries. These vessels were seized by the Germans and manned by Kriegsmarine personnel, and when added to the twenty-six submarines operating from the base at Salamis, were a not inconsiderable force. Several flotillas of UJ auxiliaries and the heavily armed F-lighters were in the course of being transferred to the Aegean from the German Black Sea Fleet.

Churchill was aware of this rapid build-up of enemy forces and, although his hands were tied by the conditions imposed by the Americans at the Quebec Conference not to involve Allied forces in the eastern Mediterranean, applied pressure on the Turks through diplomatic channels to involve their forces in the seizure of the islands lying off their coast. The Prime Minister buttered his proposal with the promise of large supplies of arms and aircraft. The Turks were not tempted. Although they disliked the thought of the Germans so close to their shores, they knew the weak forces available to the British would be no safeguard against German reprisals.

When this ploy failed, Churchill made a personal plea to Roosevelt to temporarily relax the restriction on the eastern Mediterranean so that heavy air attacks could be mounted on the ports in Greece being used by the Germans to ship reinforcements and heavy arms to the Aegean.

On 3 October, Eisenhower informed the Combined Chiefs of Staff Committee: 'Middle East is having some trouble and needs help against increasing hostile air power in Greece. Since this is a threat to our necessary use of the Adriatic ports in Italy, we are immediately throwing entire Strategic Force in quick destructive effort against hostile airfields.' In the six days which followed heavy bombing raids were made on Athens, Salonika, Rhodes and Heraklion in Crete. Although this reduced the flow of reinforcements, it did not stop them and the raids ended on the 10th.

The first LRDG squadron arrived at Casteloriso hard on the heels of the SBS. It was 'B' Squadron, commanded by Captain Lloyd-Owen. The squadron was moved to Leros and a few days later 'A' Squadron arrived and joined the SBS in occupying Kalymnos.

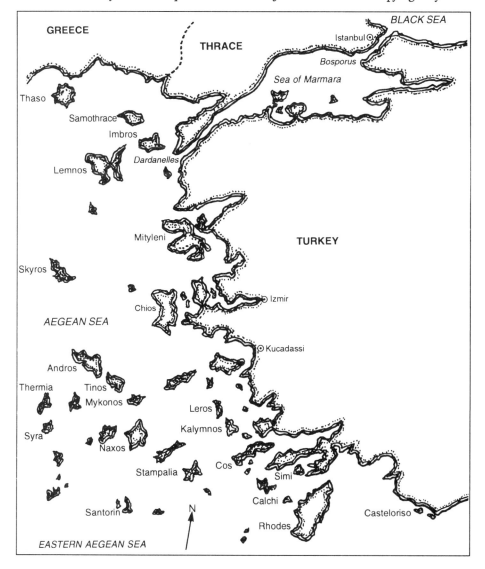

At this time the future operations of the two raider groups was occupying the minds of Major Jellicoe and the LRDG commander, Lieutenant Colonel Guy Prendergast. To clarify the position, a meeting was called by Brigadier Turnbull at Porto Laki and mutual agreement was reached on their respective roles. The LRDG was to be responsible for providing a coastwatcher screen in the Cyclades and Sporades in the northern Aegean and the SBS would carry out harrassing raids and reconnaissance in the islands of the central Aegean and Rhodes. The SBS soon discovered Rhodes was too strongly garrisoned for their style of operations and concentrated on the smaller islands. Rhodes was defended by 7,000 German and 12,000 Italian Fascist troops.

By early October 1943, the LRDG coastwatching groups were established in the north and provided a valuable service by reporting enemy air and shipping movements. 'A' Squadron, which was not required for these duties, was attached to the SBS patrol under Major Lapraik at Simi.

The recently formed Levant Schooner Flotilla's first operation was the transport of the LRDG sections to their coastwatching posts. Not surprisingly, the two caiques employed on this hazardous penetration of the enemy held islands were *LS 1* and *LS 2*, commanded respectively by Lieutenant Seligman and his second-in-command, Lieutenant Londos, of the Royal Hellenic Navy.

Seligman was more than satisfied with the ease of the caiques in passing unchallenged through hostile waters. The vessels moved only at night, laying up during the day under camouflage nets in the shade of cliffs or in reefs. An elaborate system of light steel frames was carried in both caiques, and these were shaped to the contour of rocks and reefs. The caiques were soon put to their first test when aircraft flew over them at 200 feet and a patrol boat approached within 500 feet without sighting the vessels.

Destroyers of Cunningham's fleet spent the last days of September transporting troops from Egypt and Palestine to Famagusta in Cyprus and Casteloriso, where they were transferred to smaller ships for the last leg of the voyage to either Cos or Leros. The 1st Battalion, Durham Light Infantry, was the first regular unit to arrive at Cos and was followed by other units of the 234th Brigade. By the end of September, garrisons had been placed on Cos, Leros, Samos and Casteloriso.

The Germans were also active during this period building up their strength. Reports were being received from the LRDG coastwatchers of enemy troops passing south through the Cyclades and Sporades. On the night of 6 October the post on Kythnos reported a strong convoy steaming south through adjacent waters. An hour later, Wellington and Hudson bombers from Cyprus found the convoy of five ships which were transporting the XI/999 Battalion to Cos. Three of the transports were sunk and the other two were damaged.

At dawn on the 7th, the submarine *Unruly*, Lieutenant Fyfe, RN, made contact with a second convoy consisting of the transport *Olympus* and five Siebel ferries on passage from Piraeus to Cos. Fyfe surfaced within close range of the convoy and engaged the ships with is deck gun. In a five-minute action, *Olympus* was hit nine times and three of the Siebel ferries were sunk. Twelve hours later, the survivors were found by the cruisers *Penelope* and *Sirius* and the destroyers *Faulknor* and *Fury* and only one ship of the convoy escaped. It was estimated that more than 500 troops and all heavy equipment were lost in these two engagements.

Despite these successes, German strength on Cos and Leros continued to increase. Hundreds of schooners and caiques had been requisitioned by the enemy, and these ferried troops from island to island under cover of darkness. In addition, a fleet of Junkers transport aircraft was flying more soldiers from Greece and Rhodes.

A race was now developing between the opposing forces to assemble troops and supplies for the approaching battles. The Royal Navy scoured the ports of Syria, Palestine and Egypt for small ships suitable for use in the small Aegaen ports. The Germans were similarly engaged in Greece and some vessels were brought south from the Black Sea.

One British convoy to sail from Famagusta on 8 October included the Australian corvette HMAS *Ipswich*, the French corvettes *Commandant Domine* and *Commandant Duboc*, the Greek merchant ship *Koritza* and the Italian destroyer escorts *Pola* and *Eola*. The convoy was not molested by the enemy on the passage, but arrived at Casteloriso in the middle of a heavy air raid. On the 13th, *Ipswich* escorted the cargo ship *Galway Bay* to Casteloriso and again arrived in an air raid. On her return passage she carried German prisoners of war. She was the only ship of the Royal Australian Navy to participate in these operations.

Early in October, Hitler ordered air fleets to be withdrawn from the Russian and French fronts to support the battles in the Aegean. These reinforcements began to arrive on 4 October, and by the 11th it was estimated that 90 Messerschmitt 109G fighters, 60 Stuka dive-bombers, 130 Heinkel 111 bombers, 51 Arado floatplanes, 72 Junkers 88s and a squadron of Italian Macchi C.202 fighters were in the Aegean area.

To oppose this formidable air fleet, the British could muster a half-squadron of Spitfire long-range fighters, four squadrons of Wellington light bombers, three squadrons of Baltimore bombers and a reduced squadron of long-range Hurricane fighters.

While this unequal build-up of forces progressed, the powerful British battleships *King George V* and *Howe* were idle in Alexandria. The battleships had arrived from the Eastern Fleet on 16 September but remained in port until 1 October. The diversion of the battleships to bombard and soften up enemy positions in Rhodes at this time may well have turned the scales in British favour.

The sparring period for the Aegean was almost at an end.

14

The Raiders Strike North

Between June 1942 and December 1944 Middle East raiding forces launched 382 raids in the Aegean. The first, launched by the SBS, was directed against German airfields in occupied Crete. It was one of a number of desperate operations undertaken in this period to relieve German pressure on the Desert Army holding Rommel's advance on the Nile. A heavy blow against the Luftwaffe was needed, and the only available force was the SBS.

British Intelligence officers on the island, under the command of Paddy Leigh-Fermor, now a major, reported the main airfields being used for operations against the British front at Alamein were Maleme, Kastelli, Timbaki and Heraklion. Leigh-Fermor suggested that commando-style raids, led by his guides, could neutralise the airfields.

The SBS, which was attached to SAS, and had just arrived from England, was selected for the operation. Command of the raid was given to Major David Sutherland, who had led several successful raids against the Axis forces in the desert. It was a comparatively small force, consisting of five officers and seventeen men. A larger force would be difficult to pass through areas heavily patrolled by the enemy.

Sutherland and his force were embarked in *ML 285*, commanded by Lieutenant Commander R. Campbell, RNR, who had been operating clandestinely on the Cretan south coast for the past year. The crossing was undetected and the party was put ashore at Cape Kochinoxos on the night of 6–7 June. There they were met by Cretan guides provided by Leigh-Fermor, and spent several days in a cave in the mountains while final plans were made for the attacks. Sutherland divided the party into three divisions. The first, led by Captain Mike Kealy, was allocated Maleme; the second, Captain George Duncan, Kastelli; and the third, to Timbaki, he led himself.

Before leaving Egypt, it had been decided to make the fourth airfield at Heraklion a separate operation. Captain, the Earl George Jellicoe, was to be transported in the submarine HMS *Triton*. His group consisted of four Free French commandos.

Kealy's section was the first to set out, having the longest distance to cover. Their route took them through the Idi Mountains and along the spine of the White Mountains before turning north to Maleme. The arduous week-long trek was led by relays of Cretan guides through areas dominated by resistance groups. However, the long march was to be in vain. Kealy found the airfield heavily guarded by German troops with guard dogs. The high wire fence around the perimeter was electrified. The odds against entering undetected were too heavy and the party retraced its steps back to the rendezvous.

Captain Duncan's party was led by an SOE officer provided by Leigh-Fermor. Before launching their attack, they spent a day laying up in a small village overlooking Kastelli.

The airfield was located on the floor of a well-cultivated valley with villages on all sides. However, olive groves provided excellent cover and a watercourse, dry at this time of the year, ran close to the perimeter fence.

The attack was launched three hours after sunset, and entry was gained without raising an alarm. The party split into two sections, one to lay charges in fuel and ammunition dumps and the other to place their charges in hangars and workshops. Duncan withdrew the party to a mountain village from where he saw the charges detonate. Four of the targets were destroyed and seventy Germans and Italians were killed.

Major Sutherland found the airfield at Timbaki abandoned, but local resistance members guided the party to a large ammunition dump which the Germans had left for future use. This they blew up.

The three parties were picked up by Lieutenant Commander Campbell's MLs at Cape Kochinoxos and returned to Mersa Matruh safely.

Meanwhile, the submarine *Triton* had surfaced a mile offshore from Heraklion and landed Captain Jellicoe's party in rubber dinghies. They were met by Lieutenant Costi, a Greek Army officer, who led them to a safe village close to the airfield.

Jellicoe launched his attack on the following night. His party approached the airfield from the landward side and had cut eight of the barbed wire strands when an Italian sentry stopped within feet of them. The French commandos remained calm and provided an excellent impersonation of drunken Italian soldiers returning late from leave. One of the commandos urinated, while another thrust a bottle of wine into the sentry's hands. While this pantomime was being acted out, Jellicoe was standing in the shadows with a cocked Tommy gun aimed at the Italian's head. When the bottle was emptied the sentry resumed his beat, mumbling 'Gracio' and waving the bottle.

After the Italian had passed out of sight the raiding party crawled through the wire and were picking up their weapons and the charges when the sentry and a corporal returned. They ran across the tarmac with the Italians shouting loudly behind them. At that moment, three Stuka dive-bombers roared low over their heads to land. A great cloud of dust blotted out the tarmac and, under this cover, Jellicoe's party raced to a nearby aircraft park and set their charges.

The party was still in the open when a fourth aircraft dived onto the field and dropped a string of four bombs. It was a long-range Blenheim bomber which had followed the Stukas in. Pandemomium broke out among the German and Italian guards and searchlights probed the cloud of dust seeking the attacker. Jellicoe placed his remaining charges in hangars and a fuel dump and then raced to the main gates. They joined a milling group of guards streaming past the sentries and passed through undetected.

Ten enemy aircraft were destroyed and the fuel dump was burnt out. The Germans attributed the damage to the attack by the Blenheim.

The party split up and was hidden in safe villages. Unfortunately, the four French commandos were betrayed by a Greek and were captured. On hearing of this, Jellicoe and Costi withdrew inland. They were taken off the island a week later by *ML 285*.

In early August Captain Duncan led another raid on enemy airfields on Sicily to disrupt German and Italian air attacks on a convoy being passed through to Malta.

Duncan and his party of five were landed close to their target by the submarine HMS *Una* on the night of 11–12 August. The SBS men paddled ashore in canoes which they buried in the sand on landing. They cut through an eighteen-foot entanglement of barbed wire and were moving into the aircraft dispersal area which was packed with Stukas when they blundered into an Italian patrol. They were greatly outnumbered, but Duncan attempted to bluff his way through. He called out 'Camerati Tedeschi', but the Italians were not deceived. Shots were exchanged and the party made a dash for the wire in the dark, but Sargeant Dunbar fell into a concealed weapon pit and was shot.

Dunbar's misfortune enabled the other four to break through the wire and reach the beach, where they launched two of the canoes. By 2300 they were clear of the shore and signalling the submarine to pick them up.

Unfortunately, *Una* did not see their signals. During the night one of the canoes capsized and the other became water-logged with its heavy load. Early next morning, the four survivors were picked up by an Italian fishing boat and were taken prisoners of war. It was later learnt the submarine kept its rendezvous off the beach for three nights.

The next SBS raid was aimed at knocking out the two principle airfields on Rhodes, Maritza and Calato. Command of the operation, which was aimed at reducing the scale of enemy air attacks on the British Army fighting Rommel's advance at Alam Halfa, was entrusted to Captain R.K.B. Allott. His second in command was Lieutenant D.G.R. Sutherland of the Black Watch. Allott was to lead the attack on Maritza and Sutherland that on Calato.

They embarked in the Greek submarine *Papanikolis* at Beirut on the night of 31 August and were put ashore on Rhodes on the night of 4 September. They were met on the beach by a party of local guides and immediately set out to cross the rough mountains which stood between them and the inland plain where the airfields were located.

Loaded with fifty-pound packs and carrying their personal weapons they made slow and painful progress. On the first night they covered only three miles. At first light they hid in a small cave surrounded by razorback ridges devoid of all vegetation. On the second night their progress was five miles. Next morning they looked down on the large flat plain on which their targets were located.

During the day Allott divided the force into two parties of eight with two guides to each. The attacks on the airfields were to be made on the night of 12–13 September and the two parties would rendezvous at the embarkation beach five days later.

Allott's party, which had the greater distance to cover, moved out on the night of the 7th. Their fate was not known until the end of the war. However, they reached Maritza and launched their attack on the night of 12 September. Damage inflicted on the airfield and installations was serious and its use was seriously restricted for two weeks.

The party withdrew without loss and retraced its steps over the mountain range to the embarkation beach. Here, a large Italian search party was waiting for them and they were taken prisoners of war. Postwar research of Italian records verified they were betrayed by one of the local guides who was tortured by Italian police.

Sutherland's group reached the vicinity of Calato early on the 12th. He divided his party, Lieutenant Calambakidis to attack with two Royal Marines from one side of the airfield, and the second party, led by himself with Marine Duggan, to attack from the other.

By luck the night was moonless and heavy with low rain clouds. Rain commenced to fall as Sutherland reached the wire perimeter fence. His first target was a Savio bomber some yards inside the fence. A sentry was sheltering under the aircraft's wing, but he moved away after a few minutes and they placed their first charges. Minutes later they stumbled on a large ammunition dump and laid more charges. They failed to find any other targets on their side of the airfield and retired to a watercourse outside the fence.

Half an hour later, they reaped the reward for their night's work. The bomber erupted with a thunderous explosion. It was bombed up for the next day's operation. Flames from the burning Savio were reflected in the low clouds. The crowning success of Sutherland's efforts was the ammunition dump, which sent flaming bomb pieces in all directions and started subsidiary fires around the field.

The explosions stirred the enemy like an ant's nest. Machine-guns opened fire from both sides of the airfield, causing more damage to their own men than to the raiders. Italian soldiers were running around the flames, unsure whether the enemy was inside or outside the defences.

Of Calambakidis' party there was no sign. However, at 0300, as Sutherland and Duggan were climbing the foothills, they saw a gun fight in progress in the distance and Sutherland believed he heard the bark of a Thompson. He concluded the party was either dead or prisoners of war.

It took the men two days to reach the rendezvous. Enemy patrols were scouring the mountains through which they passed, and several times they narrowly missed walking into enemy lookouts. Then, from a hideout above the embarkation beach, they saw an Italian patrol find the inflatable boats which they had buried in the sand.

On the night of 17–18 September they crept down to the beach, which was still under enemy observation, and flashed the pick-up signal. A flash, far out to sea, replied. They entered the water and commenced swimming. A mile and a half swim lay ahead of them, but by good fortune they had retained their Mae West life jackets. The submarine, HMS *Traveller*, was waiting for them. Twelve hours later they were back at Beirut.

The SAS and the Royal Marine Commando carried out a number of raids in the Western Desert during this period, but all ended in disaster. The Special Boat Section was still a sub-unit of the SAS and was allotted the amphibious operations.

In October 1942 No. 2 SBS was withdrawn from the desert operation of Colonel Stirling's force to carry out a mission which changed the course of the war. SBS canoeists landed General Mark Clark from the submarine HMS *Seraph* at Algiers for the historic meeting with French generals and politicians. The mission almost failed when the canoe carrying the American general capsized in the heavy surf. A quick reaction by Captain Courtney, who was manning the canoe, enabled them both to reach the waiting submarine. The general was re-embarked and landed wet and dishevelled to attend the meeting. It was later discovered the canoe frames were seriously cracked.

When the time came to pick up General Clark, the surf was crashing on the beach. Courtney embarked the general and surfed the canoe through the first two lines of breakers; but on the third, they were thrown into the water. Courtney again re-embarked his charge and swam the general to the submarine, which fortunately was now closer to the beach.

No. 2 SBS also provided the seven canoe teams to act as markers for the invasion of North Africa, Operation Torch. These were Lieutenants Eckhard and Ayton, Sargeant S. Weatherall and Corporals N. Thompson, J. Gilmour, A. Le Salisbury and J. Hutchinson. The canoeists were carried close to the landing beaches by the submarine *Seraph*. At

2215 on 7 November they were all in position, swinging on kedge anchors. Three hours later they illuminated their beacons and the first waves of assault craft swept into the beaches.

After this operation No. 2 SBS returned to England to participate in many more successful and unsuccessful operations, but these are outside the scope of this story.

The Special Boat Squadron came into existence on 3 March 1943 when Earl George Jellicoe returned from England. He was soon joined by Lieutenant Anders Lassen who he had met in England. The Dane had already won some renown for his part in the hijacking of a German cargo liner from Dakar and for his raids on the coast of France and the Channel Islands.

The first operation of the newly formed squadron was a second raid on the airfields of Crete. As with the previous raid, this operation was planned to reduce Luftwaffe raids on convoys, particularly those carrying Allied troops for the invasion of Sicily. Operation Albumen involved a total force of twelve men under Captain Sutherland. It consisted of Lieutenants Lassen and Lamondy and nine non-comissioned men. The force was better equipped than its predecessor and Sutherland was determined that mistakes made on that occasion would not be repeated.

The party was landed again at Cape Kochinoxos and the ship on this occasion was *MTB 361*. It arrived under cover of darkness and was met by guides provided by Major Paddy Leigh-Fermor. Their leader was 'Simon' Ligonfakis.

The guides led the party and carried the stores for the operation to a defended camp some miles inland. On 23 June 1943, the day after their arrival, Sutherland briefed his two lieutenants on their roles. Sutherland's party would attack Timbaki, Lamonby Heraklion and Lassen the most distant, and Kastelli. With each leader would be three non-commissioned officers. All three attacks were coordinated to take place on the night of 4–5 July.

Lassen's party was the first to depart and reached its target area nine days later. The trek was through some of the most mountainous areas of the island. On the last leg of their journey they were met by Gregori Hnarajkis, a resistance fighter who had distinguished himself in several clashes with German forces and would be their main guide. A local guide, Nereanos Georgious, was selected by Leigh-Fermor to guide them to the target area.

Soon after their arrival at Kastelli, Lassen changed into Cretan dress and, in company with Georgious, carried out a reconnaissance of the airfield. He found it heavily guarded. The perimeter was ringed by deep barbed-wire entanglements. Guard posts were spaced every 100 yards and defended by several machine-guns and five men. Roving patrols moved inside the perimeter day and night. Lassen counted eleven aircraft on the tarmac and in the aircraft park. There were five Junkers Ju 87 dive-bombers, five Ju 88 fighter-bombers and one Fiesler-Storch reconnaissance aircraft. Georgious believed there were three more being serviced in the hangar.

The young Dane found a convenient hill close to the airfield and sat down and sketched the installations and security arrangements. Gregorious was concerned at the nearness of the patrols and was afraid of an untrustworthy Cretan reporting them. He told Lassen he was 'stepping on fire'.

Lassen launched the attack at 2230 on the night of 4–5 July. He divided his four-man force into two groups, Sargeant Nicholson and Corporal Greaves to penetrate the eastern perimeter and Corporal Jones and himself the western.

On entering the wire perimeter, Lassen met two sentries. The first he bypassed and the second he shot. The sound of the shot alerted a third guard, who opened fire with a machine-gun. The Dane silenced this man, and two others who joined him, with a well-placed grenade. With the airfield now fully alerted, Lassen and Corporal Jones withdrew to a darkened area and waited until the hue and cry subsided.

Nicholson and Greaves heard the shooting and immediately went into action. They placed thermite charges on four aircraft and in a fuel dump. Searchlights were sweeping the open field and machine-guns were firing on fixed lines. They waited for a few minutes, hoping to locate Lassen and Jones, but after five minutes they crossed the now fully stirred tarmac and slipped through the perimeter fence.

Throwing caution to the wind, Lassen and Jones fought their way through the enemy troops taking up defensive positions. At one stage they stumbled into a camouflaged anti-aircraft emplacement. Never at a loss, Lassen rapped out in fluent German: 'The Tommies have landed on the airfield. Open fire!' The gun crew immediately swivelled around and began firing on their own troops.

Thirty seconds later the two SBS men crashed into a machine-gun nest. Lassen repeated the ruse and the machine-gunners swung their gun around to spray a nearby headquarters tent.

The two fugitives became separated in the dark. Lassen reached the perimeter fence and crawled through. Ahead of him, patrols were scouring the hillside beyond which lay the safe village. He wriggled along the fence for several hundred yards, crossed a road and plunged into a field of cabbages. Realising the whole countryside was alerted, he scooped a hole in the middle of the field and camouflaged it with cabbage leaves.

He lay in this hideout throughout the day. Patrols passed within twenty yards of him but none bothered to search the field. After dark he returned to the village where he found Nicholson, Greaves, Jones and the guide Georgious waiting. They immediately set off for the mountains and, two days later, fell in with Gregori Hnarajkis and his resistance band. Now in safe hands, they made a leisurely return to the base camp near Cape Kochinoxos.

Lassen later learnt the raid on Kastelli was a complete success. All the aircraft on the field and many of the installations were either destroyed or heavily damaged. A not inconsiderable amount of damage had been caused by the enemy's own fire. German personnel losses were estimated at forty-three. However, the cost was too high. In reprisal for the attack, the Germans executed fifty-two Cretan villagers.

Lieutenant Lamondy's party attacked the airfield at Heraklion and also met with success. They took the Germans by surprise, entered the airfield and placed their charges undetected. Several hours later they watched aircraft, fuel dumps and hangars erupt from the safety of a village in the foothills. Their return to the base camp was uneventful although, at a high mountain village, they met a party of eight New Zealand soldiers who had evaded capture for more than two years. They joined Lamondy's party.

Captain Sutherland's party found the airfield at Timbaki still abandoned and also returned to the base to wait for Lassen, who arrived on 9 July. Next morning a German patrol was sighted some miles inland and sentries were placed to cover all approaches to the camp. Strict instructions were given that the enemy was not to be engaged unless he stumbled on the well-concealed camp. Unfortunately, several Cretan resistance fighters opened fire on the enemy party, killing or wounding two or three. In the return of fire which followed, Lieutenant Lamondy was killed. It was the only SBS loss on the successful operation.

MTB 361 returned next night and the party and the eight New Zealanders were taken off and reached Egypt without further incident.

A fine accolade for the success of the raid came from Lieutenant D. Harrison of the SAS who, on the night of 9–10 July, was in the troopship *Ulster Monarch* on passage to Sicily. He wrote:

'As we came within range of Crete with its large German airfields there was a certain air of expectancy. We scanned the skies for the first reconnaissance plane. Once spotted, it would be but a short time before we would be in the thick of it. But, over in Crete, a small force of the Special Boat Squadron—like ourselves descended from the same force, were keeping the German aircraft on the ground.'

15

The Royal Navy's Second Crete

In the second week of September 1943, the Mediterranean Fleet consisted of 6 battleships, 2 fleet carriers, 4 escort carriers, 10 cruisers, 6 anti-aircraft carriers, 2 gun monitors, 110 destroyers, 33 submarines, 2 headquarter ships, 12 landing ships infantry, 4 landing ships tank, 2 fighter direction ships, 90 minesweepers, 80 anti-submarine trawlers, 27 tugs, 5 gunboats, 62 HDMLs, 12 repair and depot ships, 22 boom-defence vessels, 5 ocean-boarding ships, 31 Royal Fleet Auxiliaries, 15 armament-issuing ships, 24 petrol and water carriers, 4 salvage ships, 26 miscellaneous vessels, 112 MLs, 234 MTBs and 24 MGBs. In ships and striking power it equalled the Allies' Atlantic Fleet.

The bulk of this huge armada was stationed in the western Mediterranean to support operations in Italian waters. In the eastern Mediterranean the Levant Fleet, about to meet the full fury of the Luftwaffe and the Wehrmacht, was understrength in every class. It consisted of eleven destroyers, the majority of which were the small weakly armed Hunt Class, twenty auxiliaries ranging from destroyer escorts to trawlers, an understrength Coastal Command Squadron and two submarine flotillas.

When Italy surrendered, the focus returned to the eastern Mediterranean and Admiral Sir John Cunningham despatched signals to the First Sea Lord for immediate reinforcement of the Levant Fleet. Unfortunately these signals were received in London when Admiral of the Fleet, Sir Dudley Pound, was seriously ill and the Prime Minister was considering appointing Admiral A.B. Cunningham to the highest office of the Royal Navy. The request for the Levant Fleet's reinforcement was not acted on immediately.

Churchill had also recently returned from the Quebec Conference, at which he had reluctantly agreed to American demands not to open a major front in the Balkans or the eastern Mediterranean should Italy withdraw from the war. Although the Prime Minister had given his assurance, within weeks he was badgering his Chiefs of Staff to initiate plans to occupy the islands of the Aegean.

Not surprisingly, Cunningham's request for ships received little support. Four cruisers were made available to the Levant Fleet subject to demands from other theatres. In the same communication, he was instructed to provide his only four Fleet Class destroyers to escort the battleships *King George V* and *Howe* from Alexandria to Gibraltar.

The German High Command reacted more vigorously. From their intelligence reports, they knew the Levant Fleet was at its lowest strength and only two of Cunningham's destroyers had the range to intercept their convoys moving south from Salonika. Operation *Polar Bear*, the capture of Cos, was approved by Hitler on 24 September. Field Marshal von Weichs immediately ordered the transfer of troops from as far afield as Bulgaria,

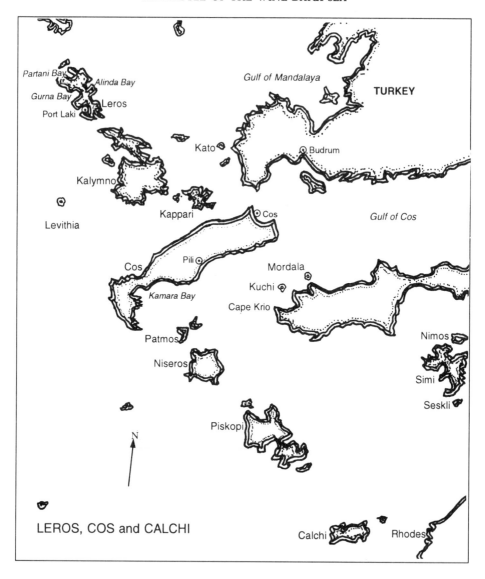

LEROS, COS and CALCHI

northern Greece and Crete. The 22nd Panzer Grenadier Division and the parachute battalion of the Brandenburg Regiment were to provide the spearhead for the assault.

The major problem confronting the Germans was the shortage of sea transport to carry the troops to Cos. At this period, German naval forces in the Mediterranean consisted of a submarine squadron based on Salamis, a mixed squadron of auxiliary vessels and a small number of F-lighters and Siebel ferries. To overcome this shortage, small steamships, landing barges and ferries were sent south from the Black Sea and the Danube. No mention was made in German records of the four Italian destroyers which were seized in the Aegean when Italy surrendered.

Admiral Cunningham launched his first operations in the Aegean on 7 September, when the destroyers *Faulknor*, Captain A.K. Moncrieff, DSO, and *Eclipse*, Commander E. Mack, DSO, and the Greek Navy's *Queen Olga*, Lieutenant G. Blessas, sailed from Alexandria to patrol waters around Stampalia and Rhodes.

Late on the night of 7–8 September, Captain Moncrieff received a signal from a RAF reconnaissance aircraft reporting a convoy of two 4,000-ton transports, the *Pluto* and the *Paula*, escorted by the heavily armed auxiliary *UJ 2104*, heading south from Stampalia for Rhodes. The convoy was sighted at 0300 and Moncrieff worked his ships into a down-moon position before closing at high speed. All three enemy ships were hit by a fusillade of shells. *Paula* was straddled by three salvos from *Faulknor* and *Eclipse*. She stopped dead in the water with flames reaching up to her masthead. Several minutes later a violent explosion tore her apart and she rolled over and sank.

As the destroyers turned away, *UJ 2104* was seen closing rapidly. She was hit by salvos from the two destroyers which tore great holes in her hull and wrecked her superstructure. She stopped 1,000 yards short of her assailants, and lay on her side and sank.

Queen Olga had engaged the other transport, *Pluto*, which was hit repeatedly at close range. The vessel caught fire and the passengers and crew were observed jumping into the sea. *Faulknor* closed and sank the transport with a torpedo. German records recovered after the war revealed 250 troops were lost in the battle.

However, there was to be little time to celebrate the success. On the 26th, *Intrepid* and *Queen Olga* were surprised in Leros Harbour by a squadron of Ju 88 fighter-bombers which dived on the naval base and the ships at anchor. The anti-aircraft defences were caught unprepared and not one gun opened fire. The thirteen bombers divided into two flights and the first demolished the Italian naval barracks. Seconds later, the other flight of seven aircraft struck at *Queen Olga*. Three heavy bombs hit the ship, which split open and sank.

Intrepid's guns immediately opened fire and brought down a low-flying aircraft. Commander Kitcat ordered the ship to get under way, but before she had moved twenty feet another wave of bombers was overhead. A 500-kilogram bomb hit her on the port-side upper deck and penetrated to explode between the boiler and engine-rooms which were soon flooded to a depth of five feet. When the aircraft departed, *Intrepid* was towed to shallow water and beached. Repairs were immediately undertaken, but two hours later she was hit again and her stern structure was destroyed. She capsized and sank at 0200 on the 27th.

Queen Olga lost six officers and sixty-four ratings and *Intrepid* fifteen ratings. Ironically, the destroyers may have been saved if the RAF radio set ashore had not been out of service. A fighting patrol of Spitfires was in the air only ten miles away.

During this period, Allied submarines were also active in the area. *Trespasser*, Lieutenant R.M. Favell, DSC, and the Greek *Katsonis*, Commander Lascos, attacked a small transport and a UJ escort on the night of 11 September. Both boats missed their targets. Favell made three more attacks in the next forty-eight hours without success. One of his targets was a Sauro Class destroyer. *Katsonis* landed a party of SOE agents on Euboea on the night of 12–13 September and vanished soon after. German records later revealed she was surprised on the surface by *UJ 2101* on the night of the 14th and sunk by gunfire. Fourteen of her crew were picked up.

Between 15 and 24 September, Levant Fleet destroyers were employed in transporting troops and stores to Cos. Intelligence reports showed German forces were ready to launch their assault on the island. It was a race against time.

The narrow straits were patrolled by enemy aircraft during the day and the destroyers made their runs after dark. Despite this limitation, they landed 3,400 troops and their equipment on the island by 21 September. However, this was not enough, and in the nine days which remained before the battle, every available vessel was pressed into service. The small Italian destroyer *Euro*, the sloop *Ago*, the minelayer *Legnano* and eight MAS-boats all carried their quotas.

Cunningham's three destroyers, *Faulknor*, *Fury* and *Eclipse* landed 1,200 troops and eight Bofors guns on the night of 22–23 September and then sailed in two divisions to sweep Kaso and Scarpanto Straits for enemy shipping. All three destroyers had operated together some time earlier in the escort of Convoy PQ 18 to Russia.

At 0110, while off Cape Prosoni on the Turkish coast, Captain Mack in *Eclipse* sighted the 2,428-ton enemy transport *Donizetti*, escorted by the destroyer *TA 10* and the former Vichy French ship *La Pomme*. Although outgunned by the enemy, Mack, after making a sighting report, opened fire. By a stroke of luck, *Faulknor* and *Fury* had completed their sweep and were close by. The two destroyers opened fire on the transport and hits were observed. *Donizetti* turned away and beached herself some minutes later.

While her two companions were engaging the transport, Lieutenant Commander Taylor in *Fury* closed the destroyer *TA 10* and scored two hits on her bridge. She escaped into the dark, by which time the battle had drifted well into Turkish waters and the three British ships came under fire from shore batteries.

Admiral Sir John Cunningham, like his predecessor and namesake, was a destroyer man and realised the smaller vessels of the fleet were more suitable for operations in the Aegean. He also realised it was unlikely the Levant would receive cruisers and additional destroyers immediately, and requested a build-up of Coastal Forces.

The MTB flotilla based on Cyprus and operating from Casteloriso was insufficient to cover the many approaches to the central Aegean. Ten days later, *ML 823*, commanded by Australian Lieutenant Commander B. Close, RANR, arrived at Casteloriso. The remaining vessels of the flotilla followed fourteen days later. *ML 823* proved her worth within a week by sinking the heavily armed 1,000-ton cargo ship *Volta* and shooting down a Junkers 88 fighter-bomber which attempted to protect the ship.

Three MTBs were transferred from Malta nine days later, and the submarines *Unsparing* and *Trooper* were deployed in the central Aegean. The submarines patrolled to the south and west of Cos to intercept enemy ships transporting troops and supplies from Greek and Cretan ports.

Unsparing, Lieutenant A.D. Piper, RN, scored the first success on 28 September, when she sunk a large caique packed with troops off Malea. Four days later he sighted a convoy bound for Cos but was unable to close the enemy.

Trooper, Lieutenant J.S. Wraith, RN, sailed from Beirut on 16 September to patrol the area to the east of Leros. Wraith remained in this area until 17 October, but failed to sight a suitable target. The enemy was obviously not transferring troops to Cos from Leros. On the night she left to return to Beirut, the submarine struck a mine and was lost.

Early on the morning of 1 October, an RAF Halifax sighted the German invasion fleet off the island of Naxos. It was reported as seven medium-size transports, three destroyers, a flotilla of R-boats, eight landing craft and ten or more large caiques and schooners. A second convoy consisting of caiques and schooners, motor fishing vessels, tugs towing barges and the auxiliaries *UJ 2101, UJ 2102* and *UJ 2109* was not sighted until it was unloading troops at Kamara Bay.

The three Hunt Class destroyers *Aldenham*, Lieutenant Commander J.L. Jones, DSO, DSC, RN, and the two Greek destroyers *Themistocles*, Lieutenant Commander N. Sarris, RHN, and *Miaoulis*, Lieutenant Commander C. Nikitiases, RHN, had sailed from Alexandria on the morning of 1 October and on that night patrolled Kaso Strait but failed to make contact with enemy vessels. Faulty intelligence received in Alexandria had suggested the armada was heading for Rhodes and not Cos, and this resulted in the destroyers patrolling the wrong area.

The former Italian destroyer, *Euro*, which was patrolling in Partenia Bay, was the first naval loss of the battle. At 1100 on 1 October she was attacked by a mixed force of Stuka dive-bombers and Me 110 fighter-bombers. The small destroyer fought back, but with aircraft diving simultaneously from both sides she had little chance. She was hit by two bombs and sank within minutes. Fortunately, casualties were light and the survivors landed on Leros.

The German advance guard of 1,200 troops landed on Cos at 0500 on 2 October under a powerful umbrella of aircraft. Not one enemy vessel was lost in the landing. Later in the day, another 1,000 men were put ashore. Fighting was sporadic, and German unit diaries for 2 and 3 October refer only to skirmishing. The entry in the OKW Diary for 4 October succinctly sums up the battle: 'Cos occupied. 600 English and 2,500 Italian prisoners. Forty guns and twenty-two partly damaged aircraft captured'.

The loss of the island was attributed by the British to the early loss of the Spitfire fighters on the island, but the reason for the failure went deeper. The German claim 'of a lack of fighting spirit in the defenders' was obvious. Despite the overwhelming superiority in firepower of the defenders, not a single German vessel was sunk and German casualties, dead and wounded, were a mere eighty-five.

Churchill heard of the fall of Cos early next morning. Admiral Sir Philip Vian had been summoned to Chequers to receive his appointment as Deputy Commander-in-Chief of Operation Overlord, the landing at Normandy, when the signal was received. Vian later recalled the Prime Minister was so upset by the debacle in the Aegean that the appointment was forgotten until he was entering his car to depart. Churchill at this period held high hopes that a breakthrough on this front would enable the Allies to link up with the Russians in the Black Sea area and pose a threat to Germany from the south and the east.

While General Maitland Wilson and Admiral Cunningham were being bombarded by signals from London requesting an explanation of the failure, Coastal Command's MTBs and MLs, supported by caiques and schooners of the Levant Schooner Flotilla, were evacuating troops from the island. This evacuation continued for several weeks, with SBS and LRDG patrols guiding evaders to several evacuation points. The last to be taken off Cos were sixteen RAF personnel from Nos 74 and 291 Squadrons. They were rescued by the RAF Rescue Launch *HSL 1602*.

One positive outcome of the debacle of Cos was the Admiralty decision to rescind the ban on the use of cruisers in the Aegean. On 4 October, only hours after the surrender of Cos, the cruisers *Sirius* and *Dido* sailed from Malta to Alexandria. They were followed on the 5th by *Aurora* and *Penelope*. On the same day, Cunningham's destroyer force was reinforced by the three Fleet Class destroyers, *Petard, Penn* and *Panther*—all veterans of Malta convoys.

Aurora and *Dido*, with the destroyers *Tumult* and *Pathfinder*, entered the central Aegean on the night of 5–6 October and carried out a sweep of Kaso Strait. The force was withdrawing through Cos Channel at 2100 when the two cruisers collided. Lieutenant Commander C.W. Malins, RN, *Petard*'s commanding officer, commented on the incident in his Letters of Proceedings: 'There was no air attack on at the time and I must presume it was either an error of judgement in taking up station, or more likely, when both cruisers were zig-zagging, a rudder jammed. In any case the damage was not serious.' Although in no way defamatory, these were strong words from a junior commander.

Malins' report, however, was over-optimistic. Both cruisers sustained serious damage, being holed above the waterline, and some plates and frames were fractured. *Dido* was unable to participate in operations for three weeks and *Aurora* was in dockyard hands until 13 October.

The submarine *Unruly* made contact with a small enemy convoy off the island of Amorgos on 6 October. It consisted of the 852-ton transport *Olympus*, six well-armed Siebel ferries and the armed auxiliary *UJ 2111*. Lieutenant Fyfe made a sighting report before shadowing the enemy. At dawn on the 7th he sighted a mixed force of Wellington bombers from No 38 Squadron and Hudsons from the Australian No 459 Squadron over the convoy.

The aircraft attacked through heavy anti-aircraft fire, but no ships were hit. However, the diversion assisted Fyfe to improve his position, and two hours later he fired a salvo of torpedoes at the ships. All missed their targets. Fyfe immediately surfaced and engaged the surprised enemy with his deck gun. In the short period of three and a half minutes, thirty-five shells fell on the convoy. *Olympus* was hit three times and two of the Siebel ferries were sunk.

The results would have been better had not the armed auxiliary *UJ 2111* attempted to ram *Unruly*. Fyfe crash-dived and settled on the bottom while depth charges exploded on all sides. Two hours later the submarine surfaced, but there was no sign of survivors of the convoy.

Unknown to Fyfe, his sighting report was picked up by the cruiser *Penelope*, Captain G.D. Booking, RN, which was disappearing over the horizon with *Sirius* and the destroyers *Faulknor* and *Fury*. Booking ordered the squadron to increase speed, and forty minutes later sighted the quarry. The engagement lasted less than ten minutes and when the smoke cleared, all enemy vessels, except an F-lighter which had dropped back with engine trouble, were sunk. It was later learnt that 400 enemy troops were lost with the convoy.

Penelope and her victorious consorts steamed east to Kaso Strait, where they joined the destroyers *Rockwood* and the Greek *Miaoulis*, which had patrolled the strait throughout the night, but no enemy sightings were made.

At 1130, *Sirius*' radar showed a formation of aircraft approaching from the south. Identification signals showed them to be United States Air Force Lightnings. The Americans had agreed to provide a limited number of flights by the long-range fighter squadron. Minutes after they vanished over the horizon, a second force of aircraft were picked up by *Sirius*, screaming in from the north—five Ju 88 fighter-bombers with an escort of Me 109 and FW 90 fighters.

The Lightnings were operating near the limit of their range but reappeared over the horizon. They sighted the ships and the enemy aircraft, climbed rapidly and dived out of the sky. One Ju 88 was shot down into the sea and a second, trailing a plume of black smoke, turned away. This was the first occasion that American aircraft supported a Royal Navy operation in the Aegean.

Twenty-five miles to the east, *Penelope* and her destroyers were also under attack. Captain Booking increased speed to join *Sirius* and her consorts, but had covered only two miles when two Stuka dive-bombers plummetted out of the sky and swept over her from bow to stern. A large bomb struck the cruiser on the port side and penetrated through to her lower decks, but failed to explode. *Penelope* slewed off course and rapidly lost speed. Water flooding into the lower decks caused her to list and her main armament was unable to train on her attackers. A minute later she was straddled and near-missed on both the port and starboard and she lay dead in the water.

The ships of the squadron closed to provide a protective screen around *Penelope*. Captain Booking assessed the damage to the ship. Power to the 4-inch anti-aircraft batteries and the 6-inch gun director was cut and her guns were out of action. Sea water had entered her fuel tanks and contaminated the fuel. However, her engine-room crew soon had the engines in operation and the ship was steaming at 16 knots. At 1400, eight more Lightnings arrived overhead and their presence probably saved the cruiser from being sunk.

Throughout the remaining four hours of daylight, the squadron remained in close formation. At 1800, *Rockwood* and *Miaoulis* detached to refuel at Limassol and the remaining four ships increased speed for Alexandria. *Penelope* survived and, after four weeks in dockyard hands, was returned to service. Eighteen months later, the long-serving cruiser was torpedoed and sunk by *U 410* off the beachhead at Anzio.

While *Penelope* and her squadron were limping back to Alexandria, a second squadron, consisting of the anti-aircraft cruiser *Carlisle*, Captain H.F. Nalder, RN, and the destroyers *Petard* and *Panther*, was steaming north to join the destroyers *Aldenham* and *Themistocles* south of Scarpanto Straits. The augmented squadron carried out a sweep of the straits on the night of 7–8 October, but no enemy ships were sighted. *Petard* and *Panther* were detached before dawn to return to Alexandria and their places were taken by *Rockwood* and *Miaoulis*, which had refuelled at Limassol.

In spite of the strong British naval presence in the inner islands, the enemy continued its preparations to seize Leros. The island of Simi was attacked by a small German force on the morning of 7 October. It was landed by a fleet of schooners and caiques escorted by a UJ Class auxiliary and an R-boat at Pedia Bay and soon came under attack from an SBS patrol which had arrived on the previous night to reinforce the small Italian garrison. After early advances, the Germans were severely mauled by the SBS and pushed back to Pedia Bay. The survivors were re-embarked in schooners and caiques and returned to Cos. Sixteen of the enemy were killed and thirteen wounded. The bulk of their stores and heavy weapons were left behind.

Although this operation was unsuccessful, it was an indicator that the Germans were ready to launch their offensive. The island was evacuated by the SBS and the Italians two days later and was occupied by the enemy.

On the morning of 9 October, a Lightning reconnaissance aircraft sighted an enemy convoy near the island of Pserimos. The convoy consisted of four destroyers, the minelayers *Bulgaria* and *Drache* and six landing craft transporting the X/999 Battalion from Piraeus to Cos. Unfortunately, the sighting report was not received by the cruiser *Carlisle* and her destroyers, which on that morning were only 100 miles to the east of the convoy and in an excellent position to intercept. Captain Nalder was withdrawing to the south after a patrol in Kaso Strait. At 0700 he signalled headquarters in Alexandria: 'All quiet so far. Am now withdrawing.' Had Nalder's withdrawal been delayed for two hours, he would have been in a position to sink the convoy.

However, far to the west, Lieutenant Fyfe in the submarine *Unruly* had sighted the convoy. Throughout the day he remained in a position to shadow the vessels. Two hours after dark, Fyfe fired a full salvo of torpedoes at the unsuspecting ships. Luck was on Fyfe's side and, ninety seconds after firing, one of the torpedoes exploded in a great column of flame against the side of the 1,106-ton minelayer *Bulgaria*. The ship sank within a minute, and carried her crew and 195 troops to the bottom, two miles off Amorgas.

At 0830 next morning, the cruisers *Penelope* and *Sirius*, in company with the destroyers *Faulknor* and *Fury*, found the survivors of the convoy—four small transports, two armed trawlers and six F-lighters—and attacked with guns and torpedoes and by ramming. In fifteen minutes all enemy ships were either sunk or burning. There was one survivor from the convoy, an F-lighter which took cover behind two small islands.

Four hundred soldiers of the German X/999 Battalion were lost. Eighty soldiers and seamen reached the island of Stampalia on rafts and in life jackets, where they were taken prisoner of war. Not one member of the 700-strong battalion reached Leros. *Penelope* reported in her Letters of Proceedings: 'Also captured were two field guns and three trucks'. No reference was made as to how these heavy loads were transhipped in the middle of an action.

The force, it was known as 'Nostril Force', now increased speed to work clear of Scarpanto Straits, but it was soon under heavy air attack. An urgent request was made for air cover. *Faulknor*'s W/T operator later recalled: 'We literally screamed for help on the W/T'.

The appeal was picked up by the Americans' 12 Fighter Wing at Gambut and at 1030 eight Lightnings sighted the force, which in the meantime had been joined by *Rockwood* and *Miaoulis*. The force turned south and reached Alexandria on the 8th.

Meanwhile, the anti-aircraft cruiser *Carlisle* and the destroyers *Petard* and *Panther* were at the northern approaches to Scarpanto Straits, where they rendezvoused with *Aldenham* and *Themistocles*. During the morning they had enjoyed partial air cover from the Lightnings. However, at 1155, when the squadron was not protected, a force of enemy Stuka dive-bombers and Ju 88 fighter-bombers from Gruppe I/StG 3 found them.

The ships threw up a heavy anti-aircraft barrage and commenced weaving, but the Stukas pressed their attack regardless. *Panther*, Lieutenant Commander Viscount Jocelyn, vanished in a cloud of smoke and spray. Six bombs, two direct hits and four near-misses reduced the destroyer to a sinking wreck. The first struck abaft the funnel amidships and penetrated to the keel, breaking her back. She broke in two and the halves sunk within a minute, taking most of her crew with her.

A swarm of dive-bombers now concentrated on *Carlisle*. She too was struck by two bombs. Both exploded in the engine and boiler rooms. Two more bombs hit a minute later, blowing off her starboard shaft and propeller and jamming the steering gear. She stopped in the water with fires burning in three places. The twenty-five year-old cruiser would have been sunk had not seven Lightnings dived out of the sky and attacked the still circling Stukas and Ju 88s.

A series of dogfights developed and planes whirled over the squadron. The enemy aircraft were no match for the Lightnings and seven of eight Stukas which had been circling overhead, waiting to attack, were shot down into the sea. Other enemy aircraft were seen trailing black smoke as they skimmed away at wave-top level.

This was the last action fought by Lightnings in the Aegean. The two squadrons were withdrawn on the order of the United States Commander, General Eisenhower. This action was ordered by the United States' Congress. When Italy surrendered and offered her armed forces to fight alongside the Allies, the powerful Italian voting bloc in the United States flexed its political muscles and demanded the Allied forces in the Mediterranean be concentrated on liberating Italy.

Carlisle remained afloat. Captain Nalder made emergency repairs to stop the flooding, and later in the day she was taken in tow by the destroyer *Rockwood* and returned to Alexandria. This was the cruiser's last operation. In the dockyard her damage was surveyed and the ship was declared a constructive loss, beyond economical repair. She was converted into a stationary base vessel and saw out the remainder of the war in a backwater of the harbour. She was hulked at Alexandria in 1948.

16

The Price of Admiralty

In 1943 the German and British Navies received new Commanders-in-Chief. On 30 January Admiral Karl Doenitz replaced Admiral Erich Raeder, and on 17 October Admiral A.B. Cunningham replaced Admiral Sir Dudley Pound. In an indirect manner, there had been an association of the two men since the first days of the First World War. Doenitz was a lieutenant in the cruiser *Breslau* when she, in company with *Goeben*, made a dash from the Austrian port of Pola to Constantinople with the Mediterranean Fleet hot on their heels. Cunningham was commanding the destroyer *Scorpion* which led the British ships. Doenitz was the only senior officer in the German Navy in the Second World War with a knowledge of the Aegean and Black Sea areas.

During his first weeks in his new office, Cunningham held discussions with Churchill on the war in the Aegean and an attack on the 'soft underbelly' of Europe. They were discussions which need never have taken place. At Quebec earlier in the year, the Prime Minister had assured the Americans that Britain would not engage in further military operations in the eastern Mediterranean. Now, despite these assurances, he was suggesting ways to the new First Sea Lord of exploiting the situation in the Aegean.

The operations in the eastern Mediterranean were not immediately affected by the Allied Accord although, on 15 October, command of the Levant was transferred from Admiral Sir John Cunningham to Vice-Admiral A.E.U. Willis. The new Commander-in-Chief was assuming office as the Aegean was about to erupt.

On the day ABC symbolically cut his ties with the Mediterranean, the cruiser *Aurora*, Captain G. Barnard, CBE, DSO, RN, and the destroyers *Jervis*, *Hursley* and the Greek *Miaoulis* scored a minor success off Kalymnos. At 0200 on 19 October, while the squadron was patrolling close inshore, two E-boats were sighted lying in the shadow of the cliffs. Captain Barnard ordered his ships to engage, and the two enemy vessels vanished in a rain of high explosive. When the smoke cleared, there was no sign of the E-boats, but survivors of their crews were seen scrambling ashore.

Hursley and *Miaoulis* were directed to search the other bays and inlets of the island. In the first bay, their searchlights picked up two more E-boats at anchor. These, too, were sunk by gunfire. However, as the destroyers were passing out of the bay a fifth E-boat, which was well camouflaged, opened fire on the destroyers. The turrets were still manned and this vessel suffered the fate of her sister ships. The operation cost the enemy a third of his E-boat fleet.

Not so fortunate was the patrol which relieved Barnard. This squadron consisted of the cruiser *Sirius*, Captain P.W.B. Booking, DSO, RN, and the destroyers *Eclipse*, *Pathfinder* and *Belvoir*. Booking's squadron had ferried troops to Leros before commencing the patrol and was some hours late in effecting the relief.

At 1830 on the 19th, the ships were clearing Scarpanto Straits when they came under attack from a flight of six Stuka dive-bombers. Four Beaufighters which were providing air cover attempted to intercept, but the dive-bombers dived through the formation and dropped their bombs. *Sirius* was hit on the quarterdeck by a large bomb which tore a twenty-foot-diameter hole in the deck. A fire was started in the Oerlikon gun magazines and three guns were put out of action. A minute later, the cruiser was near-missed by a stick of four bombs which damaged her torpedo tubes and carried away her aerials. The ship's radar was put out of action and bomb splinters holed her hull and superstructure.

In this brief attack, fourteen of her crew were killed and more than thirty wounded. The ship's ability to fight was severely impaired and Captain Booking turned back for Alexandria. Arriving on the 20th, she was immediately docked for emergency repairs. Her damage was too great to be made good at the base and six days later she sailed for Massawa for permanent repairs. The cruiser was out of action for three months.

Eclipse, Pathfinder and *Belvoir* continued the patrol and returned to Alexandria.

Diplomatic approaches to the Turkish government at this time brought some relief for the destroyers and smaller ships operating in the central Aegean. Despite their neutrality status, they approved ships laying up in their waters during daylight hours. This increased the duration of the smaller Hunt Class destroyers in the battle zone. Some weeks later, the Turks turned a blind eye to a small tanker being stationed in one of their bays, where it provided a much-needed refuelling facility. These concessions, however, were not restricted to the Royal Navy. German ships, especially small transports, schooners and caiques, also sought the sanctuary of neutral waters.

Support for the navy was given by the aircraft of the RAF whenever they were available. On 16 October a flight of Mitchell bombers severely damaged an E-boat and sank a large caique off Rhodes. Three days later, Beaufighters from 227 Squadron severely damaged an armed trawler, sank three small landing craft and shot down a Dornier flying boat north-east of Crete. A second attack by this squadron on the 19th severely damaged a 2,000-ton transport and an F-lighter entering Port Kalymnos. The next day, Wellington bombers of 38 Squadron torpedoed and sank the 4,750-ton transport *Sinfra* east of the Anti-Kythera Channel. The transport was carrying 300 German and 2,300 Italian troops from Crete to the Piraeus. Enemy records showed more than 500 were lost.

Aurora and the destroyer *Adrias* bombarded the port of Rhodes on the night of 20–21 October, sinking several small ships and damaging installations. While this operation was in progress, the other two destroyers of the squadron, *Fury* and *Beaufort*, landed troops and stores at Alinda Bay on Leros. The squadron rendezvoused in the Gulf of Cos and at dawn located a small fleet of German schooners and caiques landing troops on the island. *Aurora* stood off while her three destroyers illuminated the enemy vessels with their searchlights. Two of the schooners were sunk by gunfire and a large caique was rammed.

Cunningham's Levant Fleet was now operating a shuttle service in the Aegean. While *Aurora*'s squadron was withdrawing, the destroyers *Jervis, Pathfinder, Hurworth* and *Adrias* returned to the Alinda Bay area, where more troops and stores were landed. On departing Alinda Bay, the destroyers separated and searched the shorelines of Cos and Leros for

more enemy small ships, but none was found and they withdrew into Turkish waters
to lay up during the daylight hours.

Soon after sunset, *Hurworth* and *Adrias* steamed south to create a diversion off Leros
and were passing east of Kalymnos when *Adrias* was torn apart by a violent explosion.
A sheet of flame rose high above the destroyer's mast and she broke in two. Following
in her companion's wake, *Hurworth* sheered away and almost immediately a dark object,
thought to be an E-boat, was sighted off her port. Commander Wright ordered full
ahead to ram the enemy vessel but, too late, identified it as the bows of *Adrias*. Before
she could alter course, *Hurworth* struck a second mine. In the space of ninety seconds,
the unmarked minefield claimed two victims.

Hurworth struck the mine amidships and immediately broke in two. A sheet of burning
oil and super-heated steam engulfed her decks. The bow section sank in five minutes
and took thirty men with it. The after section, fortunately, remained afloat for ten minutes
and enabled eighty-five crewmen and her captain to abandon ship. Half of the destroyer's
complement was lost.

Close by, Commander Toumbas was desperately striving to save what remained of
his ship. Twenty-one of the crew had died instantly in the explosion. Burning oil from
the *Hurworth* swirled round the stern of *Adrias* and Toumbas ordered full ahead to pull
clear of the conflagration.

In the hours which followed, desperate efforts were made to salve the Greek ship,
or more accurately, the bowless remains. The forward bulkhead was shored up with
timber and the heavy list was reduced by pumping. While the pumps battled to reduce
the ingress of water, the crew mustered on the port side to prevent her rolling over.
As these desperate measures were being taken, an undamaged boat was lowered and the
survivors of *Hurworth* brought aboard. Two hours after the mine exploded, *Adrias* was
under way. The nearest haven was Turkey—six hours steaming.

Initially, the destroyer crept forward at five knots, but careful pumping of sea water
and the transfer of fuel from one tank to another improved her trim and speed was increased
to nine knots. Four of her crew were stationed forward to watch the bulkhead, but luckily
it held. Forty minutes after commencing her voyage to safety, an aircraft was heard circling
overhead. Speed was reduced to ensure the wash would not give the ship away. Toumbas
thanked his patron saint for a moonless night. The aircraft departed and speed was increased.

At 0130 on the 23rd, the navigator informed Toumbas they had entered neutral waters
and, two hours later, the crippled destroyer was beached in shallow water in Gurvergenik
Bay. *Adrias'* impossible saga was over. Several months were to pass before *Adrias* could
resume her interrupted passage to Alexandria. She set off under tow, but after two hours
of wallowing on the end of a hawser, Toumbas cast off and completed the voyage under
the bowless ship's own steam.

Twenty-four hours after *Hurworth* and *Adrias* sailed into catastrophe, *Eclipse* met a similar
fate. On the night of 23–24 October, the survivor of Russian and Malta convoys, in
company with *Petard*, was carrying 200 troops to Sandamah Bay in Turkey for transhipment
to Leros when she detonated a mine laid in forty-eight fathoms in Karabakla Channel,
east of Kalymnos. The mine exploded under *Eclipse*'s forward boiler room and set the
fuel tanks ablaze. Ready-use ammunition for B gun and the Oerlikons was set on fire
and was soon exploding in all directions. Within three short minutes, the 1,375-ton

The aircraft carrier HMS *Illustrious*.

The only hit on the Sydney by the *Bartolomeo Colleoni*.

A prewar photograph of the 8-inch cruiser HMS *York*, sunk by Italian explosive motor boats in Suda Bay.

Troops of General Ringel's Mountain Regiment embarking on Italian destroyers at Piraeus.

The landing ship *Glenearn* landing troops evacuated from Greece at Suda Bay, Crete, 1941.

The destroyer HMAS *Nizam* arriving at Alexandria with troops evacuated from Crete, 1 June 1941.

HMS *Defender* sinking after an Italian attack south of Crete on 11 July 1941.

A 'T' Class submarine similar to *Torbay* and *Thrasher*.

destroyer took on a heavy list and broke in two. She sank soon after, with the tragic loss of more than 200 passengers and crew.

Aurora and the destroyers *Pathfinder, Exmoor* and *Blencathra* sailed from Alexandria on 27 October and followed a course which took them well to the east of Rhodes. On the 30th, the cruiser was attacked by waves of Stuka dive-bombers and Ju 88 fighter-bombers in the Gulf of Cos. A large bomb struck her on the conning position, just abaft of the after funnel. The explosion knocked out her 4-inch anti-aircraft batteries, damaged the P1 mounting and severely damaged both funnels, the pom-pom batteries and port torpoedo tubes. The ship's vital radar sets were put out of action.

Further devastation followed when the ready-use ammunition on *Aurora*'s 4-inch gundeck caught fire and exploded, putting out her 6-inch guns. The ship's speed fell to 22 knots. Forty-six of the cruiser's crew were killed and twenty wounded. In four short minutes the ship's offensive strength was reduced to nil and she limped back to Alexandria. She was five months in dockyard hands before she put to sea and returned to England. She was not to serve again in the Mediterranean.

While the surface ships were striking at and being struck by, the enemy, Allied submarines were fighting their own silent war in the same waters. At the beginning of October 1943 they numbered eight. These were *Surf, Torbay, Unruly, Unsparing* and the four Greek boats *Katsonis, Papanikolis, Pipinos* and *Triton*.

Fyfe's modus operandi in *Unsparing* has already been mentioned, but on the night of 8–9 October he engaged a large enemy caique close to Turkish waters. The first shots from his deck gun caused the crew to abandon their vessel, but when it remained afloat Fyfe decided to board. It proved a most rewarding decision. Some 1,500 cases of high-class brandy was found in the cargo and transferred to the submarine. This windfall added great laurels to the submarine service in the Aegean.

In the same week, *Katsonis* and *Pipinos* scored successes. The former torpedoed and sank the German heavily armed auxiliary *UJ 2101* south of Rhodes. *Pipinos*' victim was the destroyer *TA 19*, the former Italian ship *Calatfoni*, which was sunk east of Crete. Three days later *Triton* sank another German auxiliary, *UJ 2102*, off Rhodes.

The fourth Greek boat had been used by SOE in 1942 and early 1943, landing agents and rescuing Allied servicemen in Crete and the Greek mainland. On two occasions she carried British commandos on raids in the Aegean. *Papanikolis* was commanded by Commander Spanidi, who was later to rise to the rank of admiral and in the postwar years led Greece's delegation in the United Nation's Organisation.

A desperate race was now developing between British and German forces to decide the fate of Leros. The British were reinforcing their garrison on the island and the Germans were assembling their assault force on nearby Cos. The relaxation of Turkish neutrality was aiding the British and on 21 October a shuttle service of troop trains was established between Syria and the small Turkish port of Kudashi. This concession enabled troops and stores to be landed on Leros within several hours.

In granting this concession, the Turks risked going to war with the Germans.

However, transferring the troops and stores across the narrow waterway in daylight hours was prevented by the Luftwaffe, and recourse was made to running fast convoys of small ships at night. On 21 October the old submarine *Severn* was pressed into service for daylight runs. Experiments were made in carrying large equipment, such as Bofors guns and jeeps, as deck cargo on the submarine. These proved successful and, in addition to all space below decks being crammed with stores and ammunition, six Bofots guns and three jeeps were lashed on the external decks.

The success of *Severn* resulted in a second submarine, *Rorqual*, being used. Later, four captured Italian submarines, *Atropo, Corridoni, Menotti* and *Zoea*, were added to the service. *Rorqual*'s commanding officer, Lieutenant Commander L.W. Napier, recorded in the submarine's Letters of Proceedings: '*Rorqual* came under low-level attack from enemy aircraft. The guns had been removed to provide accommodation for deck cargo and *Rorqual* was forced to manoeuvre at high speed to dodge bombs and cannon fire until an opportunity presented itself for diving.'

While these operations were being carried out, cruiser and destroyer patrols were maintained in the inner Aegean. The cruiser *Phoebe*, Captain C.P. Friend, RN, and the destroyers *Fury, Hursley* and *Beaufort* carried out bombardments of Cos Harbour and Port Kalymnos. Each of the ships fired 150 rounds from their main armament. In this engagement, *Hursley* had the misfortune of being struck by a heavy-clibre shell from a shore battery. One man was killed and three wounded. The ship's fighting ability was not impaired. On their withdrawal, the ships steamed to Casteloriso, where they discharged 500 tons of stores and ammunition. Small ships were now being used to carry these items to Leros.

Phoebe was the last cruiser to operate in the inner waters of the Aegean at this period. Damage inflicted on *Carlisle, Sirius* and *Aurora* by the Luftwaffe caused the Admiralty to instruct Admiral Willis not to operate the valuable ships within range of enemy air bases. Provision was also made for equipping destroyers with radio direction equipment, similar to that fitted in the long-range Beaufighters. Another decision implemented at this time was the provision of large Fleet Class destroyers as flotilla leaders.

The veteran submarine *Torbay*, Lieutenant R.J. Clutterbuck, RN, opened her account on 15 October by torpedoing and sinking the 1,925-ton transport *Kari* east of the island of Naxos. Admiral Cunningham was opposed to the use of 'T' Class submarines in Aegean waters on the grounds that they could be sighted by aircraft in clear waters at depths of fifty fathoms or more. Despite this serious handicap, in 1941 and 1942 *Torbay* and her sister ship *Thrasher* had both won Victoria Crosses for their successes. However, *Surf* did not enjoy the same success as her larger sister ship.

On 16 October Lieutenant Lambert sighted a 3,000-ton transport under heavy escort south-west of Leros. He closed to 1,500 yards of the target but was sighted and driven off by escorts before he could fire his torpedoes. Ten days later Lambert brought *Surf* to the surface to engage a small merchant ship with his deck gun. The enemy replied with a 4-inch gun and a Bofors which forced the submarine to dive and withdraw.

Surf's third attack, four days later, also failed. The target on this occasion was a 3,000-ton transport sighted off Mykonos. Lambert surfaced to close the range and was immediately attacked by escorting aircraft. An hour later the submarine surfaced close to Port Panormos and sighted her intended victim anchored offshore. Lambert closed the coast and fired two torpedoes from the entrance of the harbour. To the submarine commander's chagrin, they ran deep, passed under the target and exploded harmlessly on the shore.

On the same day, Lieutenant Fyfe in *Unsparing* torpedoed and sank the troop-laden transport *Ingerborg* south-west of Anaphi. Fyfe remained in the area of the sinking while the escort *N 101* picked up survivors. Two hours after sinking the 3,500-ton transport he sank *N 101*. More than 100 troops were lost.

Unsparing's third attack almost proved her last. On the 31st, Fyfe surfaced to sink a caique which he sighted close inshore at Cos. The submarine's first round drew rapid and accurate fire from the enemy. All four men in the gun crew were hit and one man died within minutes. A hole, two feet in diameter, was blown in the conning tower. Fyfe withdrew and buried his gunlayer at sea.

Simoon, Lieutenant G.D.N. Milner, RN, arrived in Kaso Strait on 4 November to patrol the waters around Naxos. However, next day she was despatched to the Dardanelles patrol but failed to arrive. She is believed to have struck a mine and sunk with all hands. *Simoon* was the last Allied submarine lost in the Aegean in the Second World War.

The German invasion of Leros was now daily expected by the British command. On the night of 9–10 November, two units of destroyers were patrolling in the Cos–Leros area seeking the invasion convoys which intelligence reported as ready to sail. *Petard, Rockwood* and the newly arrived Polish destroyer *Krakowiak*, Commander Naracewisz, covered the area around Kineros and Levithia while the second unit, *Fury, Exmoor* and *Blencathra*, covered the eastern approaches to Leros and Amorgos. No enemy vessels were sighted and the combined force cleared the area by 0530.

Five hours later, Beaufighters sighted the enemy fleet at sea between Amorgos and Cos. The opportunity to attack, for which the Royal Navy had strained and sacrificed, had come but not one ship was within range of the elusive fleet.

17

The Aegean Lost

Hitler's decision to seize the island of Leros posed serious problems for the Admiral, Eastern Mediterranean. German naval forces in the Aegean were greatly inferior to those available to the Royal Navy and the Straits of Cos, like the English Channel in 1940, could well become a watery grave for them. The vessels available for the transport of the assault forces to Leros were two former Italian destroyers, the minelayer *Drache*, a mixed squadron of R-boats, T-boats and Italian MAS-boats, two UJ-type auxiliaries, a flotilla of F-lighters, Siebel ferries and thirty requisitioned Greek caiques and schooners.

This shortage was aggravated by the need of a second fleet in the Black Sea where the Battle of Kerch Straits was being fought. During the first days of November 1943, Russian troops crossed the straits and made a strong bridgehead in the Crimea. The German High Command knew, if this lodgement was not eliminated, the Crimea was lost and Eastern Europe would be under threat. The German Black Sea Fleet consisted of twenty 120-ton minesweepers of the 3rd Minesweeper Flotilla, a half flotilla of Siebel ferries and five E-boats. This force was reinforced by seven R-boats and six UJ-type auxiliaries withdrawn from the Aegean.

Two factors favoured the Germans. Transport across the straits in daylight was prevented by the Luftwaffe, and two minefields limited the use of the narrow channel by the Russian flotillas. The straits, however, were well within range of the Russian long-range artillery.

The battle commenced on the night of 7–8 November, when the minesweepers, ferries and E-boats drove a wedge into the closely packed mass of Russian vessels in the channel. Darkness allowed the Germans to close the enemy and the actions which followed were reminiscent of sea battles of the eighteenth century. The enemy was grappled and boarding parties shot their way across the narrow gaps separating the vessels. Larger vessels fired salvos of shells into the enemy vessels at point-blank range. The minesweepers sought out the larger enemy ships and dropped depth charges under their sterns. Burning vessels drifted ashore and cast fiery shadows among the combatants.

On that first night, two-thirds of the Russian reinforcements failed to reach Crimea. At dawn, the survivors withdrew and the Luftwaffe reappeared overhead. The battle resumed at nightfall. A line of heavily armed Russian gunboats, supported by two destroyers, was waiting for the Germans. They succeeded in sinking the German advance guard, but more vessels took their place. One by one, the gunboats were boarded and the guns turned on the Russian second line. Heavy casualties were suffered by both sides.

The battle continued until 17 November. When dawn broke on this day, the Kerch Straits were in German hands and the Russian bridgehead in Crimea was under heavy attack. It was the Germans' last offensive.

In his plans for an attack on the soft underbelly of Europe, Churchill had forecast such a battle. However, the Allied army which was to penetrate the Bosphorus never materialised and nine months of bitter fighting were to follow before the Russians could resume their advance through the Crimea.

Willis' Levant Fleet, although reduced in strength, was stronger than the Germans with a squadron of cruisers, a large force of destroyers and several flotillas of MTBs and MLs. In addition, four submarines were deployed in the waters around Leros.

Far away in Bletchley Park on the night of 11 November, an ULTRA intercept revealed full details of the projected invasion of Leros. This information was immediately relayed to the British commanders in the eastern Mediterranean. Unfortunately the decrypt made no reference of the transfer of KG 100, the Luftwaffe Dornier Do 217K Squadron equipped with HS-293 anti-shipping guided missiles, to the Aegean on 10 November. KG 100 had already scored successes with the weapon in the Atlantic and west Mediterranean.

At 0300 on 12 November, the destroyers *Rockwood, Petard* and the Polish *Krakowiak* were retiring from a successful bombardment of an enemy concentration at Kalymnos. A 3,000-ton transport was hit by several salvos from the destroyers and later sank, partly blocking the entrance to the harbour.

As the three ships were passing out of Cos Strait they were sighted by a flight of Junkers Ju 88 fighter-bombers screening a Dornier Do 217K guided-missile bomber. The bombers made two dummy passes over the destroyers and, as they withdrew, *Rockwood* was struck on the afterdeck by a missile which failed to explode. It ricocheted twice, gouging through the deck close to the gearing room, and passed out of the ship's hull below the waterline. In its passage it ruptured the steering gear and jammed the rudders. Lieutenant Lombard-Hobson, *Rockwood*'s commanding officer, attempted to steer using the ship's engines, but the destroyer had already taken a heavy list. Fire broke out in the switchroom and water was flooding the lower compartments. Within minutes, the ship started to settle.

Lombard-Hobson signalled *Petard*, which came alongside and passed a tow. Although the sea was smooth, difficulty was experienced in securing the line. *Rockwood* was under way, but a heavy list caused her to yaw badly. Added to these difficulties, the destroyer's crew were divided between serving the guns and carrying out damage control. *Rockwood* stopped to allow the tow to be secured and for seven long minutes lay motionless with enemy aircraft overhead. *Krakowiak* closed the disabled ship and stationed herself to port to protect the two destroyers from attack by aircraft until she could again proceed.

The coast of Turkey and temporary refuge were six hours steaming to the east, and only four hours of protective darkness remained. *Petard* took the strain and slowly nosed forward. *Rockwood* yawed and twisted heavy with the water which now flooded her lower compartments. Commander Egan in *Petard* led the little convoy south about the island of Niseros and two hours later was clear of the straits. Daylight found them close to Turkish waters. At 0750 *Rockwood* anchored in the Bay of Losta.

Rockwood survived her ordeal and two days later, the gaping holes temporary patched, the thousands of gallons of water pumped from her hull and her dead committed to the sea, she was taken in tow for the long haul to Alexandria. But the gallant destroyer had fought her last battle. Engineers at the base surveyed her as a total constructive loss and she spent the remainder of the war rusting in a backwater of the port.

Admiral Willis did not attribute the loss of *Rockwood* to an anti-shipping guided-missile attack, although accounts of similar attacks in other threatres should have forewarned him. The presence of the Ju 88 fighter-bombers suggested a normal bombing attack. However, the Dornier Do 217 Ks were to strike again, and later losses were attributed to the guided missile.

Admiral Lange disposed his invasion force in two waves supported by a covering force. The first wave of 800 men of the II/16 Grenadier Battalion was embarked in a fleet of requisitioned schooners and caiques which were escorted by the heavily armed auxiliaries *UJ 2102* and *UJ 2120*. The naval commander of this fleet was Oberleutnant zur See Weisenborn. The second wave of 750 troops of II/65 Grenadier Battalion was embarked in schooners and caiques and two small transports and escorted by *UJ 2141* and *UJ 2144*, under the command of Oberleutnant zur See Reserve Kampen.

To provide cover for the combined force, Lange allocated the minelayer *Drache*, flagship, two Italian destroyers and the four torpedo-boat destroyers of the 9th Destroyer Flotilla. In close support was the 21st UJ Flotilla of four anxiliaries, two mixed groups of R-boats, MAS-boats and armed fishing boats. Optimistically, this motley fleet would hold off the Royal Navy's cruisers and destroyers until the troop-laden transports reached shore. Distant cover was entrusted to two U-boats from the German submarine base at Salamis.

To reduce this imbalance of sea forces, the German Navy overlanded twelve R-boats, motor minesweeper-minelayers armed with semi-automatic guns and depth charges, from Genoa to Venice and floated them down the Danube to the Black Sea and then through the Bosphorus to the Aegean. This 2,000-mile journey by land, river and sea involved a road journey on great eighty-four-wheel semi-trailers, three rail transfers and the negotiation of the locks at the Iron Gates. Its success depended on the Turkish government turning a blind eye to ships of war passing through its waterways.

The German trump card, however, was the transfer of the specialised aircraft of the Luftwaffe's Anti-Shipping Air Fleet, I/KG26 and I/KG 30, to the Aegean. These two air groups were equipped with Heinkel 111 twin-engined torpedo bombers and Junkers Ju 87 dive-bombers. Supporting these special assault squadrons was a force of Dornier Do 217Ks of 1/KG 100, armed with anti-shipping guided missiles.

Admiral Lange's preparations were completed on 10 November, twenty-four hours before the attack on Leros was launched. The motley surface armada sailed from several harbours on Cos during the night of the 11th. Its air cover was provided by a squadron of Junkers Ju 88 night-fighter bombers. The convoy was sighted at 0512 on the 12th by a British observation post at Alinda Bay: 'A long line of small vessels creeping across the flat sea under an umbrella of circling aircraft'.

The first attempted landing at Blefuti Bay was repulsed by a hail of accurate artillery and machine-gun fire. The survivors of the several hundred troops to reach the beach were re-embarked and the force turned back to Cos.

A second fleet, carrying 500 troops, entered Palma Bay which was undefended and landed unopposed. This force of Panzer Grenadiers immediately advanced inland, where they were met by the 4th Buffs Battalion who attacked vigorously with bayonet and Mills bombs, driving them back to the beach where they dug in. German casualties were estimated at 50 killed and 125 wounded.

The landing at Gurna Bay was also successful. A mobile force of the King's Own Rifle Regiment surprised the Germans as they were disembarking from a fleet of caiques and schooners. The enemy troops were driven back into the water and suffered heavy losses while attempting to re-embark.

Unfortunately, the troops in the Gurna Bay area were spread along some miles of coastline and later in the day a second enemy landing was effected. The King's Own were sent in again, but immediately came under intense shellfire from a captured Italian battery. They were repulsed with heavy loss. This foothold was strongly reinforced and helped decide the fate of Leros.

The enemy met with no successes at the northern end of the island where the terrain was open and covered by well-sited defence posts. The 4th Buffs captured one enemy group, consisting of three officers and forty-five troops, as they reached the beach. Several large schooners packed with soldiers were engaged by gun batteries and sunk before they reached the beach. These reverses caused the Germans to concentrate their attack in the southern area of the island.

The British commander, Brigadier Tilney, was handicapped from the outset by the failure of his communications. Telephone lines were cut by bombing and shelling and not a few passed through areas held by the enemy. From the beginning, he was forced to resort to the use of runners and this contributed greatly to the loss of the battle. Many hours passed before Tilney could make an accurate assessment of the enemy lodgements. This delayed the concentration of troops to attack. In several instances, enemy counter-attacks overran the troops concentrating for this very purpose.

The German commanders were never in doubt as to their objectives. First and foremost was the capture of the Italian-manned gun batteries which commanded the island on all sides. Ciano Battery, a key position, was taken in the first hours of fighting. Their second objective was to drive a wedge into the British defences, and so divide the defending forces. The main target was the ridge separating Gurna and Alinda Bays. German troops secured a strong lodgement on the ridge in the first hours of fighting.

However, throughout the first day it was touch and go. Fortunes swung like a pendulum. British counter-attacks succeeded in a number of areas, but the vital features remained in German hands. Reinforcement would decide the battle.

At 1600, heavy enemy attacks were made on British positions around the vital ridge to prevent counter-attacks. These attacks had continued uninterrupted for thirty minutes when a large fleet of transport aircraft was observed approaching low over the sea. They were the all-too-familiar Junkers 52 troop carriers.

The aircraft advanced in serried lines beneath a weaving umbrella of Me 109 fighters. They banked and climbed as they crossed the coast and were met by a withering fire of 4.7-inch shells, machine-gun and rifle bullets. Six of the aircraft were hit, staggered and crashed. The others closed their ranks and suddenly a cloud of multi-hued parachutes opened in their slipstreams. The 500-strong 2nd Einheite Hase Parachute Battalion, named after the heroes of a similar attack on Dutch forts in 1940, was joining the battle for Leros.

Estimates of the parachutists' losses vary, but more than 200 reached the ground uninjured. This number was soon reduced by the fire which now sought them out. A section of the SBS was deployed in the area where they fell, and these hardened fighters exacted a grim toll as the parachutists struggled to reach the containers which held their heavy weapons. It was the first use of a large force of parachute troops since the invasion of Crete in 1941.

Once more, the defenders failed to launch an immediate counter-attack to eliminate this new threat. The surviving parachutists, believed to be fewer than 100, reached their lines and Rachi Ridge. The vital feature was even more in the German grasp.

Surprisingly, the Royal Navy was not in position to meet the sea forces as they crossed the narrow strait to Leros. The invasion fleets were sighted by Lieutenant Commander F.R. Monckton in *ML 456* at 0546 and he made an immediate sighting report. The close-packed armada of small vessels filled the straits.

Monckton turned and closed the enemy with his Bofors and Breda guns blazing. A tight line of F-lighters and R-boats was waiting to meet him. *ML 456* came under fire from an estimated 100 guns before she turned away, leaving three of the enemy stopped and burning. Although her deck was a shambles, the ML's engines had not been hit and she reached the Turkish coast where she was beached with her flag still flying. Commander Monckton landed his wounded and immediately set to repairing his damaged ship.

Also in Cos Strait on that morning was *ML 358*, Sub-Lieutenant K.L. Shute, RNVR, who failed to sight the enemy fleet. Shute closed the shore of Cos but was driven off by heavy fire from shore batteries and destroyers. The ML was hit several times and caught fire before she sank.

The destroyers *Faulknor*, Captain A.K. Moncrieff, *Beaufort*, Lieutenant J.R.L. Moore, and the Greek Navy's *Pindos*, Lieutenant Commander D. Fifas, RHN, laid up throughout the 12th in Turkish waters. There was no air cover to protect them in the cauldron between Cos and Leros.

Soon after darkness cloaked the approaches, the three destroyers sailed for the battle zone. Off Leros, they rendezvoused with *MTBs 263, 266* and *315*. The combined force patrolled the straits throughout the night but failed to sight a single enemy vessel. The patrol was unlucky. Postwar examination of enemy records show two small convoys of reinforcements crossed to Leros on that night and landed their troops.

On shore, the night passed quietly. It seemed both sides were recuperating from the violence of the previous day, but with the first glow of sunrise, dive-bombers and fighter-bombers swept in from the sea and heavily strafed and bombed the British positions around Rachi Ridge.

When these squadrons withdrew, another force of Junkers 52 transports was sighted flying low to the sea. This parachute drop was smaller than that of the previous day, consisting of half a battalion of the 2nd Parachute Battalion, estimated at 300 men. This drop lacked the advantage of surprise, and Bofors and machine-guns engaged the aircraft as they rose to clear the coast. During the night, Brigadier Tilney had ordered the New Zealanders of the LRDG forward to join the SBS close to the dropping ground. These hardened raiders stalked the parachutists as they attempted to reach their lines on the ridge, and once more, fewer than 100 joined their comrades.

Numerically, the British were much stronger than the enemy on the ground, but there was a marked difference in their calibre. Many of the Germans had fought in Crete, the Western Desert, Russia and Italy, whereas the majority of the British had not been blooded in action. One brigade had recently been withdrawn from Malta where they had served as passive defence for two years. In both command and men, there was a lack of aggressive spirit.

However, it was the superiority of the Luftwaffe, and the fine liaison between ground and air, which turned the scales.

Local successes were achieved by individual units, particularly in the northern sector, but these were not pursued with the vigour necessary to win the battle. In the vital area of Rachi Ridge, the Buffs, Royal West Kents and the King's Own Royal Rifle Regiment made individual attacks which won initial gains, but each in turn was driven back by the Germans. A concerted assault by all three units at this time would have routed the enemy.

While the army struggled on 13–14 November to eject the enemy from the vital ridge, the navy was hard hit in Cos Strait. At 0310 on the 13th, the cruiser *Phoebe*, Captain C.P. Friend, RN, with the destroyers *Echo, Dulverton* and *Belvoir* entered Cos Strait to search for enemy convoys. German aircraft were overhead but no bombs had been dropped. Suddenly, *Dulverton*, Commander S.A. Buss, MVO, RN, was hit by a large bomb and erupted in flames. The destroyer lost way and fell out of formation. Within minutes, she took a heavy list to port. *Belvoir* closed her sister ship, and took off six officers and 103 other ranks from the sinking ship. Commander Buss, one of the Royal Navy's most distinguished flotilla leaders, and one-third of the crew went down with the destroyer which was later torpedoed and sunk by *Belvoir*.

German records retrieved after the war disclosed *Dulverton* was a victim of an HS-293 guided missile fired by an aicraft of KG 100 Squadron. The British ships were sighted by a Dornier Do 217E anti-shipping guided-missile bomber as they entered the straits. *Dulverton* was hit on the port side, beneath the bridge, and the resulting explosion tore away her bows.

The glider bomb exacted a heavy toll of Allied ships off the landing beaches at Salerno some months later. Cunningham's former flagship *Warspite* was hit twice and towed to Malta and the battleship USS *Philadelphia* was near-missed and withdrawn for repairs. The cruisers HMS *Uganda* and USS *Savannah* were also hit and put out of action.

Phoebe and the remaining destroyers continued the patrol and withdrew to Turkish waters to lay up just before daylight.

Echo and *Belvoir* sailed from these waters soon after dark on the 14th. Once again, they failed to sight any enemy ships. At 0045 on the 15th they commenced a bombardment of enemy positions on the slopes of Mount Appetici in support of an attack by the King's Own Rifles. The fire from the destroyers knocked out several enemy gun batteries but the paratroopers, who held the high ground, threw back the ground attack and inflicted heavy casualties.

Conditions on Leros were reminiscent of Crete in 1941. The terrain was rough and there was little vegetation to provide cover. Every movement in daylight attracted the attention of the dive-bombers and fighters hovering overhead. The soldiers on the ground cursed the RAF, which was operating from distant bases and could only provide limited cover over the battlefield. However, on 12 November a force of six Beaufighters and two Mitchell bombers savagely mauled a convoy of two transports and six heavily armed UJ auxiliaries as they approached Leros. All vessels were heavily damaged and returned to Cos. Casualties among the troops they carried were high.

Churchill was aware of this weak air support and made urgent appeals to President Roosevelt to resume the flights of USAAF long-range Lightning fighters, but the president's hands were tied by Admiral King and General Eisenhower. The two American commanders were adamant that none of the resources would be used for what they termed 'British adventures in the Eastern Mediterranean'.

On the night of 13 November, Brigadier Tilney sent a signal for urgent reinforcements. His battalions were reduced to half-strength and some units were cut off by enemy forces in the north of the island. However, these isolated forces were still in action and tying down enemy troops who could otherwise be brought to bear on Tilney's positions on Rachi Ridge. The request could not immediately be met as there was a shortage of vessels to transport them.

The destroyers *Penn*, *Aldenham* and *Blencathra* provided gun support for the land forces on the night of 14–15 November. Their shells fell on enemy positions on the rocky slopes of Rachi Ridge and in the Alinda–Gurna neck. This bombardment also served to direct enemy attention from a small fleet of minesweepers and other small ships which landed British reinforcements and supplies nearby. As the destroyers withdrew, they were sighted by an enemy reconnaissance aircraft and shortly afterwards *Aldenham* was near-missed by a large bomb. German records claim the attack was launched by a Dornier Do 217E guided-missile bomber.

Other Royal Navy units were active off Leros on that night. *MTB 315*, Lieutenant Newall, *MTB 266*, Lieutenant Broad, and *MTB 307*, Lieutenant Muir, had sailed from their base at Casteloriso soon after dark to attack enemy destroyers reported at sea. They arrived off the island at 0200 and immediately came under fire from the enemy shore batteries.

As the three MTBs were retiring from these unhealthy waters, two enemy R-boats were sighted approaching from Cos. Newall signalled the other two MTBs to attack but, before they could manoeuvre into an attacking position, the R-boats vanished behind a smokescreen. The MTBs followed, and as they broke through the screen sighted twelve F-lighters and landing craft steering for Leros, their decks packed with troops.

MTB 315 curved around to pass down the enemy line and signalled the other two boats to follow. Newall chose the port side of the convoy and Broad and Muir the starboard. Unfortunately, at this moment *MTB 307* lost power and slewed to a stop. Her companions, high on their planing steps and almost obscured by spray, roared down both sides of the convoy with all guns firing.

Newall, a New Zealander, silenced the first F-lighter in the line and left her stopped and burning, with troops leaping from her deck into the sea. Muir engaged the first F-lighter in the starboard line and came under heavy fire from two directions, but pressed the attack firing burst after burst into the enemy's wheelhouse. The lighter lost power and slewed out of line, sinking.

While these two actions were being fought, two heavily armed German minesweepers closed the two MTBs and opened a heavy and accurate fire. Newall spun *MTB 315* in her length, and with *MTB 307* close behind, charged the minesweepers head-on. The four vessels were on a collision course but the minesweepers broke first, and in turning exposed their decks to the guns of the MTBs. The tightly packed troops on their decks crumpled under the concentrated fire.

As he swung clear, Newall sighted a destroyer approaching at high speed with her forward turrets firing over his head. He changed course to bring his torpedoes to bear, and was waiting the 'Ready' signal from his gunner when the destroyer flashed her challenge, to which Newall responded. It was HMS *Echo*.

With shells from the destroyer plunging into the milling convoy, the MTBs pulled clear and engaged an enemy lighter endeavouring to escape in the dark. They poured burst after burst into her and left her burning like a beacon.

Lieutenant R.H.C. Cyld, DSC, *Echo*'s commanding officer, described the encounter in his Letters of Proceedings: 'The F-lighter I could see through my glasses was crammed with vehicles and guns. She was taken completely by surprise, and never attempted to return our fire, perhaps her guns were silenced by the first salvos. Now we were flinging over scores of 4.7-inch shells that erupted all round her in the water until she was lost in smoke and spray. Some of our bricks were plunging into the hull, causing great gouts of flame and then, after a sharp action lasting at the most only five to ten minutes, we left her blazing furiously and helplessly.' It was a destroyer captain's dream.

Meanwhile, the MTBs were attacking two heavily loaded landing barges packed with troops and guns. Newall and Muir circled the enemy vessels and attacked from different angles, in a manner similar to Indian attacks on American waggons a century before.

Tiring of these sallies, Newall signalled Muir to cover him while he swept in close to drop depth charges under the sterns of the trapped barges. The charges detonated prematurely, showering the two boats with a rain of burning fragments.

Enemy shore batteries were now ranging on the three British ships and they broke off the action to retire to nearby Pharos Bay, where they joined HMS *Belvoir*. Newall later found *MTB 307* and covered her while she withdrew at 10 knots. Although unable to join in the action, Broad had taken two prisoners who were floundering in the water alongside the MTB. 'Operation Light Brigade', as Newall called the action, did little to tip the scales on Leros, but it was the MTBs finest action in the Aegean war.

The MTBs were old American-built Elcos which had seen better days and were plagued with defects. Lieutenant Newall reflected their condition in his innumerable reports to the commander of Coastal Forces. On 7 December, while returning to Casteloriso from a repair and refit visit to Alexandria, *MTB 266* lost her starboard rudder. An investigation found the loss was due to negligence in the dockyard. When the boat arrived at Casteloriso her crew plugged up the rudder gland and thereafter *266* operated on only two rudders. Four days later, the boat's centre driveshaft became uncoupled while the craft was under way. This defect was also rectified by the crew but on the 13th, while operating southwest of Rhodes, *MTB 315* burnt out her port vee drive. Newall's report read: '*315* was reduced to two engines and it was necessary to run on the wing engines while on patrol and use the centre only in an emergency'.

Commander R.E. Courage, the commander of Coastal Forces, commented in one of his reports at the time: 'It is remarkable that commanding officers and crews do put so much faith in the work done on their boats by base repair staff, when the latter are often no more skilled than themselves'.

Despite handicaps which would daunt larger ships in the fleet, the 10th Flotilla MTBs filled an important gap in naval defences in the Aegean until the arrival of MLs, MGBs and HDMLs in larger numbers.

The OKW diary entry for 13 November reflected the German High Command's misgivings on the outcome of the battle. 'Enemy warships are attacking off Leros. The fighting is confused and information scarce and [continuing] changes in control by the enemy result in a continuous crisis'. An ULTRA intercept received in London two days later revealed that the German commander saw the situation as critical, but although reinforcements had reached Brigadier Tilney, and more were on the way, the Germans improved their position on the ground. The Luftwaffe and German artillery batteries were methodically knocking out the remaining British guns.

During a day of mixed fortunes, the Buffs and the King's Own made three determined attacks on enemy positions on Rachi Ridge on the 13th. Local gains were made but the enemy still held the key features at the end of the day. Similar stalemates existed in other parts of the island. Heavy attacks on positions held by the parachutists dug in on the slopes of Mount Meraviglia caused heavy casualties and the Grenadier Regiment supporting them made urgent signals for reinforcements, but the enemy held on. Later in the day, the Germans counter-attacked and recaptured most of the ground they had lost.

In what proved to be the last Royal Navy sortie, the destroyers *Penn* and *Aldenham* closed the coast soon after dark on the 15th and patrolled the waters between Cos and Leros but failed to make contact with enemy vessels bringing in reinforcements. They withdrew at 0300 on the 16th. Three hours later, the RAF scored its final success. A flight of Torbeaus of No. 47 Squadron commanded by Wing Commander Giles sighted two F-lighters escorted by a mixed Luftwaffe force in Cos Strait. The Torbeaus dived through the cover of Ju 88 fighter-bombers and Me 109F fighters and sank one lighter and heavily damaged the other, which was left sinking. One Torbeau was lost.

The navy had been reinforced in the battle zone by the Free French destroyers *La Fantasque* and *La Terrible*, the equivalent of British light cruisers, but it was too late to affect the outcome of the battle.

Brigadier Tilney surrendered his force at 1730 on 16 November, much to the surprise of the enemy commanders who were considering a possible evacuation of their surviving forces. Neither army had achieved ascendancy and the British force was still numerically stronger. A total of 3,200 British troops and 5,350 Italians fighting alongside them laid down their arms and became prisoners of war. Fewer than 400 troops and airmen succeeded in escaping. The only British troops to leave the island with their arms were the SBS and the LRDG. For the patriotic Greeks on Leros who had taken up arms to support the Allies, there was no escape. They were hunted relentlessly by the Germans and executed summarily. The number who died is not known.

Traditions and shibboleths, which existed in all three British services, contributed to the defeat on Leros. There was a lack of unity and purpose which was recognised by the enemy from the start.

The Royal Navy did not surrender. All available Coastal Force's MTBs and MLs were ordered back into enemy waters to rescue evaders and escapees. During the night of the 16–17th, eight of these craft were sighted and attacked by Ju 88s and two Dornier

Do 217E8s. Two HS-293 guided missiles were fired but both missed their targets. This was the last action by German guided-missile bombers in the eastern Mediterranean.

Two weeks after the Aegean was lost, General Maitland Wilson received a copy of an exuberant signal from Churchill to Roosevelt. It read: 'Rome in January, Rhodes in February, supplies to the Yugoslavs, the opening of the Aegean subject to the outcome of the approach to Turkey, and all preparations for "Overlord" to go ahead full steam within the framework of the foregoing policy for the Mediterranean'. It was salt in the wound for the long-suffering Commander-in-Chief.

The Prime Minister on this occasion did not draw on his great storehouse of classical quotations to bolster the sagging confidence of his commanders in the eastern Mediterranean. The most appropriate for the Aegean as 1943 drew to a close was written by Confucius two thousand years before: 'In all things success depends upon previous preparation, and without such preparation there is sure to be failure'.

18

The Navy's Last Actions

As November 1943 drew to a close, the Admiralty assessed the cost of the three months of operations in the Aegean. The cruiser *Carlisle* was a constructive loss and *Aurora* was damaged beyond the repair capacity of Mediterranean dockyards; 6 destroyers, 2 submarines and 10 lesser vessels had been sunk; 3 cruisers, 4 destroyers and 11 other ships were seriously damaged. These losses exceeded those of the Greek Campaign of 1941.

Although disappointed at the loss of the islands that had been seized so easily, Churchill now turned his attention to drawing Turkey into the war on the Allied side. Large quantities of British and American arms were shipped to this prospective ally; more than £20,000,000 worth in the last months of 1943. Turkish opinion was now swinging in favour of the Allies, but it still stopped short of entering the conflict. However, the Turks were now turning a blind eye to the numerous instances of Allied breaches of the country's neutrality. By the beginning of 1944, Royal Navy Coastal Forces and the Levant Schooner Flotilla were operating from bases set up on the Turkish coast, and ships of the fleet were withdrawing into Turkish waters to escape attacks by the Luftwaffe. Trainloads of British troops were transported on the Turkish railways.

The rearming of the Turkish forces did not pass unnoticed by the Germans. However, Hitler interpreted this change in Turkish policy as being directed against the advancing Russian armies, rather than against German forces. Indeed, Ankara regarded the eight German divisions and the strong Luftwaffe presence retained in the Aegean as a second line of defence. Churchill was well aware of the Turkish strategy, but needed the bases and particularly the airfields now being used by the Allied air forces to attack Germany. His ploy in supplying arms was also responsible for stopping supplies of chrome from Turkey to German factories. The shipments ceased in April 1944.

The continuing threat of the British bases in the Aegean was tying down considerable numbers of German troops which were desperately needed on other fronts. General Klemann estimated the number as 18,500. It was a cause for reflection then, and still is today, that while the weak land, sea and air forces committed to the battles of Cos and Leros were being destroyed by superior enemy forces, only 500 miles to the west the fleet carriers *Illustrious* and *Formidable*, the light carrier *Unicorn* and the escort carriers *Attacker, Hunter* and *Stalker* were unengaged in Italian waters. This large air support group, or even part of it, could have turned the tables in the Aegean.

Enemy losses in the two battles amounted to 12 small transports and supply ships, 1 destroyer and 20 minor small warships. His air losses were 160 aircraft of all types and personnel losses were 4,800. At both Cos and Leros, enemy commanders reported their position as critical. The margin between victory and defeat was narrow, but the Commander-in-Chief, Mediterranean withdrew all surface forces from the Aegean after the fall of Leros. Coastal Command vessels were transferred to Turkish and Cypriot waters. Within the space of a week all islands of the Aegean were occupied by German forces.

However, the raiding forces did not remain idle for long. Seven days after the loss of Leros, a small force of SBS and the Greek Sacred Squadron landed on the island of Casteloriso. They found the island was held by a garrison of fifty German troops and immediately launched an attack. The garrison was taken by surprise and, after a short but fiercely fought battle, overcome. Forty-one of the enemy were killed and nine taken prisoner. The British and Greeks were back in the Aegean.

While the 10th MTB Flotilla was becoming re-established in the central Aegean, to the south, Egypt-based small ships were conducting a 'milk run' from Mersa Matruh and other small African ports to the south coast of Crete. This service was initiated in 1942 to support cloak-and-dagger operations conducted by SOE on the island and by the time the island surrendered in May 1945 it had chalked up more than fifty return passages. The vessels used in this highly dangerous service were MLs *355, 361, 841, 842, 1011* and *1032*, only one of which was lost to enemy action despite the fact enemy aircraft dominated the 760-mile return passage.

In May 1943, *ML 842*, Lieutenant Brian Coleman, RANR, a former Levant Schooner Flotilla skipper, was responsible for one of the most audacious operations conducted by Coastal Forces in the Second World War when he took off the kidnapped Commandant of Crete, General Kriege, and landed him into captivity in Egypt. The general had been seized by Captain Stanley Moss and SOE's Major Patrick Leigh-Fermor on the outskirts of the island's largest city, Heraklion, and spirited through the mountains under the noses of 10,000 enemy troops searching for their commander. The ML was waiting for the party at the prearranged rendezvous.

The Flag Officer Levant, Admiral Willis, ordered an all-out offensive on enemy shipping in the Aegean in December 1943. For this purpose, Coastal Forces in the area were reinforced by a flotilla of MLs and a flotilla of long-range HDMLs. The heavier ships of the fleet were deployed in the waters of the outer Aegean where they were less susceptible to enemy air attack.

Tenth Flotilla's next action took place on 12–13 December. Intelligence reports showed an enemy 3,000-ton supply vessel was due to pass Cape Krio on the Turkish coast during the night and MTBs *266* and *315* were despatched to intercept it. Newall sighted a vessel answering the description at 2200 on the 12th and shadowed it for six hours. At 0400 on the 13th the vessel left neutral waters and the MTBs converged on her. Newall swept in close, only to discover the ship was the Turkish vessel *Dumpulinar*. Disappointed by his lack of success, he turned west and soon after sighted a small enemy convoy between Simi and Rhodes. He closed and found it consisted of two 100-ton caiques being towed by a tug.

The two MTBs increased speed and roared down on the convoy from both sides, raking their decks with Bofors and machine-gun fire. All three enemy vessels stopped and, as the MTBs turned, engaged them with a concentrated fusillade of fire. Newall closed to observe the enemy and was immediately bracketted by heavy-calibre shells from a shore battery. He realised the advantage had passed to the enemy. *MTB 266* was close at hand and he ordered her to stand off and engage the enemy from his blind side.

While the enemy directed his attention on *266*, Newall raced in under the sterns of the three vessels and dropped a pattern of depth charges. The two caiques received the full blast of the depth charges and were smothered in flames. Five minutes later, both vessels rolled over and sank. The tug, in the meantime, had deserted her consorts and run under the cover of the shore batteries on Simi. *MTB 266* picked up one survivor from the caiques.

With the onset of winter the operations of the 10th Flotilla were restricted by adverse weather and mechanical defects. However, one operation was carried out on the night of 18–19 December. This was a reconnaissance of the Simi Harbour to provide information for a projected raid by the raiding forces.

Two more MLs arrived at Port Vathi in the first days of the new year. These were *ML 357* and *ML 836*. The MLs were larger and of sturdier construction than the MTBs. They were 112-feet long with a beam of 18½ feet and more heavily armed than the MTBs. They carried a 6-pounder cannon, a 20-mm Bofors or Oerlikon, twin .5-inch Vickers machine-guns in a power turret and two depth charges. Although slower than the MTBs at 20 knots, they were more than a match for the German R-boats and the Italian MAS-boats.

MLs were not strangers in the eastern Mediterranean. They had operated in these waters in the First World War and were credited with the sinking of three German submarines and dozens of enemy surface vessels. The Aegean was well known to the first ML skippers, but the enemy in those days was the Turk. Like their Second World War counterparts, they were used for special operations, and on one mission they landed Lawrence of Arabia at El Arish. Of more interest, they were the first light ships of the Royal Navy to be subjected to sustained air attacks in the Mediterranean, an ordeal which became all too familiar to their lineal descendants.

ML 357, Lieutenant A.H. Doughay, and *ML 836*, Lieutenant A.E. Clarke, fought their first action on the night of 10–11 January 1944. The MLs were patrolling between Casteloriso and Piskopi when they sighted two enemy schooners in Lavadi Bay. Clarke led the attack, entering the bay on silent running, and opened fire with his full armament at point-blank range. To Clarke's surprise, he failed to hit either vessel. The schooners were too heavily laden and were low in the water. However, his fusillade was not in vain. It struck a third schooner which was camouflaged under a hanging cliff face. This vessel exploded, rolled over and sank.

The MLs next success was a large caique crammed with troops which they intercepted in the same waters on the night of 8–9 February. Once again the heavy firepower of the MLs proved too much for the enemy vessel. It was hit amidships, and went down in two minutes with a heavy loss of life.

Not surprisingly, the Turks followed the operations off their coasts with more than a little interest. In principle, they showed equal favour to British and Germans, although they considered the former less dangerous to their interests. Germany and Russia posed a threat to their very existence, which may be summed up in the popular Turkish saying at that time: 'The last German soldier should fall upon the last Russian corpse'.

The flotilla commander knew the Turkish authorities were leaning towards the British in the operations in the Aegean and briefed his commanding officers to use Turkish waters when under pressure from enemy air and surface forces. The Luftwaffe respected territorial waters and on many occasions broke off their attacks on British vessels rather than raise protests from the Turks and a possible restriction on the use of the Bosphorus by their ships.

With the recapture of Casteloriso, the 10th Motor Torpedo Boat Flotilla which had arrived in the operational area set up base at the former Italian Navy base at Port Vathi. The flotilla, which consisted of only three boats—*MTB 315*, Lieutenant Leonard Newall, RNZNVR, *MTB 307*, Lieutenant John Muir, RNVR, and *MTB 309*, Lieutenant R. Campbell, RNVR—had been despatched from the Adriatic. Some of the original Italian MAS-boat facilities still remained, and in the space of a few weeks a refuelling depot, ammunition dump and a maintenance workshop were in operation.

The flotilla came under the overall command of Commander R.E. Courage, RNR, Officer in Charge, Coastal Forces, Eastern Mediterranean. A former MTB captain who had seen service in the English Channel in the first year of war and an aggressive leader, he knew from intelligence reports received from agents scattered through the islands to the north that German naval strength in the Aegean had been drastically reduced after the fall of Leros. In the weeks following the fall of the island, four heavily armed UJ auxiliaries, six R-boats and three MAS-boats were transferred to the German Black Sea Fleet. Conditions were now favourable for MTB operations. On receiving Newall's signal reporting the flotilla ready for operations, Courage issued the first combat order. It was only three words long: 'Attack! Attack! Attack!'

Newall's first target was Kalymnos, the main staging area for enemy craft bound for Rhodes. Within twenty-four hours of receiving Courage's terse signal, the three MTBs attacked a small convoy in the narrow channel which separates Cos and Kalymnos. The convoy consisted of a 600-ton coastal steamer, an F-lighter and a small schooner. Newall flashed the flotilla's hunting call and all three boats converged on their prey at full speed. A fan of torpedoes raced towards the surprised enemy.

The steamer was hit amidships and erupted in a cloud of smoke and flame. She lost way and slowly rolled over and sank. The F-lighter had also been hit and was burning, but her guns were still firing. Newall sent *MTB 307* in from the starboard and *MTB 309* from the port, diverting the enemy's attention while he raced in from behind to drop depth charges under the lighter's stern. It was the MTBs' classic manoeuvre. Smothered by gunfire from both beams, the lighter was unprepared for the searing explosions which tore off her stern. The schooner was left afloat to pick up survivors.

Newall next directed his attention to the waters between Simi and Rhodes, but the enemy was licking its wounds and no vessels were sighted.

Realising the Germans would use Turkish waters to evade MTB attacks on the more direct route, Commander Courage ordered the flotilla to set up an advanced base at Port Sertech on the Turkish coast. Although this was a breach of neutrality, the Turks once again turned a blind eye to the incursion. The new base reduced the distance to Cos and Leros by half and placed the boats astride the mainland route. Courage despatched two hulks to the advanced base for refuelling and re-ammunitioning and arranged for caiques of the Levant Schooner Flotilla to deliver supplies.

In February, soon after Port Sertech became operational, Newall received three more MTBs from the Adriatic Squadron. These were MTBs *266, 260* and *305*. The new section was commanded by another New Zealander, Lieutenant J. Breed, RNZVNR. A third ML arrived at the end of the month. This was *ML 1226*, Lieutenant J.E. Hickford, RNVR.

On the night of 6–7 March, Hickford landed an SBS patrol on the island of Niseros and was under orders to pick up the patrol on the following night. However, on returning to the rendezvous, Hickford was informed by a Greek coastwatcher that the patrol had returned to base in a captured caique. Hickford decided to make a sweep of the Turkish coast on his return to base, and when off Cape Krio, stopped and boarded a large schooner which proved to be a Turkish vessel.

As *ML 1226* turned away, a second schooner and three lighters were sighted rounding Kuchi Island. The small convoy offered no resistance when Hickford ran alongside and boarded the schooner. It was crewed by a German officer and eight soldiers, who readily surrendered. Two sailors and a Greek interpreter were placed on board as a prize crew and ordered to follow the ML.

In the meantime, the lighters had drifted close to *ML 1226*, and as Hickford turned to run alongside and board them he was met by heavy bursts of automatic fire. Hickford increased speed and turned away to engage this new threat, and was almost immediately hit by a heavy calibre shell fired from a concealed gun on the schooner, whose prize crew had been overcome by the prisoners on board.

Realising he now had two enemy groups firing on him, Hickford manoeuvred the ML to present the smallest target to the schooner and then silenced the lighters with his automatic weapons. At this point, the 88-mm gun mounted on the stern of the schooner fired again and the shell struck the ML's wheelhouse on the starboard side, killing one sailor and seriously wounding three others. The hit started a fire which quickly spread to the magazine and set off the ready-use ammunition. While the unwounded crewmen were struggling to contain the fire, a third shell from the schooner hit, and put out of action the 3-pounder gun.

With *ML 1266* now in a critical situation, Hickford increased speed and ran for cover behind nearby Mordala Island. The schooner followed at a distance, keeping up a rapid fire with its gun. One of the last rounds fired hit *ML 1226* on the waterline. As the schooner turned to rejoin her consorts, the captured prize crew seized a machine-gun and fired a burst along the deck before diving overboard. As they started swimming for the shore, the Germans opened fire and one sailor and the interpreter were hit and drowned. The second sailor reached the island and was picked up next day by a Greek caique and returned to the base at Port Dereman.

Hickford beached *ML 1226* on the island and carried out temporary repairs, arriving back at his base that night. The young skipper dismissed the engagement in five words: 'It was a tough tussel'.

By early April 1944, the Germans had set up their own coastwatcher network throughout the islands of the northern Aegean. The network was similar to that established in the Pacific by the Royal Australian Navy. Two petty officers operated each post which was equipped with a radio transceiver under the supervision of a junior officer who was responsible for several posts. The network reported all Allied air and surface movements to their Naval Headquarters at Salonika.

This network posed a threat to the raiding forces and the vessels of the Levant Schooner Flotilla, and the SBS was ordered to eliminate the posts. Brigadier Turnbull sent off three patrols, one under Captain Lodwick to deal with the post at Mykonos, a second under Captain Lassen to Santorin and a third, under Lieutenant Clarke, to Ios and Amorgos. Lodwick and Clarke destroyed their targets without difficulty, but Lassen's target on Santorin was fiercely defended. In the fighting, two of his best men, Lieutenant Stefan Castelli and Sargeant Kingston, were killed and two others wounded.

The strength of Coastal Command's MTB, MGB, ML and HDML flotillas increased steadily as 1944 progressed. Most of the new boats came from the Adriatic, where American craft were now operating, and only one was lost in transit. This was an HDML which foundered in rough weather north of Cyprus. Two officers and five ratings were drowned.

The heavily armed MGBs and HDMLs were a particularly welcome addition to Commander Courage's caique and schooner busters. These sturdy craft were gun ships and more than a match for any enemy vessel short of the UJ auxiliaries and the few ex-Italian destroyers still afloat.

The MGBs were seventy-footers, capable of 40 knots and armed with twin 20-mm Oerlikons and four .5-inch Vickers mounted in power turrets. The HDMLs were a much larger vessel, diesel-powered with a range of 2,000 miles. They were armed with 40-mm Bofors forward, a 20-mm Oerlikon aft and twin .5-inch Vickers machine-guns. Unfortunately, the HDMLs were slow and their maximum speed of 12 knots prevented them being used effectively with the speedy MTBs and MGBs.

After the heavy losses of October and November 1943, cruisers and destroyers operated outside the central Aegean. However, in April, the veteran HMS *Ajax* carried out a bombardment of Rhodes. The German sea and air forces were now greatly reduced and the cruiser withdrew without sighting an enemy ship or aircraft.

Allied confidence in their Greek allies, who had fought so valiantly in the desert and the Aegean, was badly shaken in late April when soldiers of the Greek Brigade in Egypt and sailors in the cruiser *Georgios Averoff* mutinied against their officers. The Royal Navy prepared plans to sink the cruiser with limpet charges, but happily, loyal members of the crew regained control of the ship before this plan was implemented. On hearing of the collapse of the mutiny in the *Georgios Averoff*, the army mutineers surrendered. Loss of life was minimal.

The mutiny was politically inspired. SOE agents in mainland Greece had warned Middle East Headquarters of the increasing militancy of the ELAS some weeks before the mutinies. By now, large Communist armies had been established in rural areas and these were closing on Athens to seize power when the Germans withdrew. Control of Greek forces raised in exile was vital to the plans. Fortunately, the Greek Sacred Squadron and sailors serving in Greek vessels operating with Royal Navy flotillas remained loyal.

In June, Coastal Command was preparing for the largest operation mounted by Middle East raiding forces. This was the assault on Simi, now occupied by a strong German garrison. Before the assault could be launched it was necessary to destroy the last two former Italian destroyers in the Aegean. The vessels were based on the former Italian naval base at Portolago on Leros, two hours steaming from Simi. Both destroyers had been damaged in earlier attacks by Allied submarines and aircraft, but SOE agents on Leros reported they had been repaired and were now ready for use.

The Flag Officer Levant made a request to the Admiralty for the use of Royal Marine Commando canoe teams to sink the destroyers. Three teams and their equipment arrived in the Aegean on 14 June. They were commanded by Lieutenant J. Richards. The canoes were *Shark*, *Salmon* and *Shrimp*.

On the night of 17–18 June the teams were landed by *ML 360* close to Portolago. The first canoe, manned by Sargeant King and Marine Ruff, entered the harbour at 2200 on the 18th. They found the small harbour crowded with enemy ships. Two anti-submarine booms protected the entrance, but the shallow-draft canoes passed over them easily. A patrol launch was sighted, but it was at the shoreward end of the net and failed to see them. Despite the reflection of ships' lights, the surface was dark and they passed unseen through the moored vessels.

King experienced no difficulty in finding the destroyers at anchor some distance from the nearest ships in a small bay. The canoeists made a silent approach to the nearest destroyer, drifting into the shadow of her hull. The marines heard two sentries talking in the waist of the ship, but they remained out of sight while Ruff slipped into the water and carefully secured the limpets to the ship's hull, four feet below the waterline. With Ruff clinging to the end of the canoe, King turned away and allowed the outgoing tide to carry them back to the harbour entrance. Ninety minutes after leaving the destroyer's side, they were back at the rendezvous.

Corporal Horner commanded the second canoe which entered the harbour at 2250. It crossed the boom nets and slipped undetected through the now quiet harbour. His primary target was the ammunition ship *Anita*, which was anchored some distance from the main anchorage. As they paddled alongside, they were hailed in Italian and invited aboard. A rope ladder splashed into the water a foot from the canoe. They froze in the shadows, but when nothing more was heard from the hospitable sailor, they placed their charges and left the harbour undetected.

Meanwhile, Lieutenant Richards and Corporal Stevens in the third canoe had secured charges to the second destroyer and were about to withdraw when a dog secured to the ship's rail snarled at them and commenced to bark. Luckily, the German crew paid no attention to the animal and the marines drifted clear on the tide. Richards still had two more charges so he paddled alongside a destroyer escort tied up at a wharf. Stevens was in the water securing the second charge when a sailor walked to the rail and urinated into the canoe. The man looked out across the harbour and walked away.

All three canoes were back at the rendezvous at Kalymnos by dawn. The canoes were slashed and buried in the sand and fourteen hours later the commandos were picked up by *ML 360*.

This was the most successful canoe raid against enemy shipping in the Mediterranean in the Second World War. SOE agents later reported that both destroyers were seriously damaged, while the *Anita* and two destroyer escorts had been sunk. The damaged destroyers were towed to Greek mainland ports for repair, but were destroyed in dock by RAF bombers soon after.

Before they returned to England, the Royal Marines were embarked in the submarine *Unruly* for attacks on enemy shipping in Cretan harbours. They visited seven likely ports but failed to find a single ship worth attacking. The six commandos were decorated by King George VI for their raid on Portolago.

In late June 1944, as it was preparing for the raid on Simi, the Levant Schooner Flotilla was renamed the Anglo-Hellenic Schooner Flotilla. A second Greek-manned squadron, under the command of Commander A. Londos, had joined the original one formed by Lieutenant Commander Adrian Seligman, RNR, in late 1943. In the months that lay ahead, the renamed flotilla would have the honour of liberating the majority of German-occupied islands.

The raid on Simi was launched by Brigadier Turnbull on the night of 13–14 July. His force consisted of 224 men of the Greek Sacred Squadron commanded by Colonel Tzigantes, and 100 men of the SBS under Major Jock Lapraik. The raiding force was put ashore by ten MLs and a large number of caiques and schooners of the Anglo-Hellenic Schooner Flotilla. The German garrison was taken by surprise and their resistance was ragged. Many were captured in their pyjamas. The only spirited opposition came from the strongly defended castle, but this was overcome by a frontal attack from the SBS and a close-range bombardment by guns of the ML flotilla.

Two enemy F-lighters attempted to escape from Simi Harbour, but were met by a line of MLs which drove them back. The two vessels were captured by soldiers of the Greek Sacred Squadron. Nineteen caiques, some of more than 150 tons, were sunk by the troops and the MLs. When demolitions were completed, the raiding forces re-embarked and returned to their bases. They had lost two men, officers of the Sacred Squadron, who were drowned when they attempted to land in deep water. Another six men were wounded. Enemy losses were twenty-one killed and 151 taken prisoner of war.

In late July 1944, the first indications of a German withdrawal from the islands of the Aegean became evidence. SOE agents reported installations being destroyed and heavy equipment being transported north by rail. These activities were later confirmed by ULTRA intercepts.

The German Naval Command realised the hopeless position of their submarines in the eastern Mediterranean in early September. Some officers remembered Grand Admiral Raeder's remark to Hitler in 1941: 'They will be caught like a mouse in trap—there will be no escape'. His premonition was realised on 9 September, when the Submarine Squadron Commander at Salamis received a secret signal ordering him to destroy all remaining submarines in his command. Three U-boats remained, they were *U 19*, *U 20* and *U 23*, all of them veterans commissioned in 1939. On 10 September the three U-boats were sailed into Turkish territorial waters and scuttled by their crews. Ten days later, the last remaining U-boat in the Mediterranean, based in southern France, was sunk off the northern coast of Crete by the destroyers *Terpsichore, Troubridge* and the Polish Navy's *Garland*.

At the beginning of August only three German Navy ships remained in the eastern Mediterranean. These were former Italian destroyers manned by German crews. *TA 14*, the former *Turbine*, was sunk by United States Army Air Force bombers off Salamis on 15 September. *TA 17*, ex-*San Martino*, was one of the ships damaged by the Royal Marine canoeists in June and was destroyed in dock at Piraeus on 19 September.

These losses were replaced at the end of the month by three more former Italian destroyers transferred from the Adriatic. Their service in the Aegean was short lived. *TA 15*, ex-*Gladio*, was torpedoed and sunk by the submarine *Termagent* north of Leros on 4 October. *TA 1* ex-*Tuscan*, was torpedoed and sunk by the British submarine *Turbulent* two days later in the same waters. The third ship, *TA 38*, ex-*Spada*, fell victim to Baltimore bombers flown by South Africans off Volos on 4 October. The last German naval vessel in the Aegean was the minelayer *Zeus*, ex-*Morosini*, and she was sunk off Rhodes by RAF bombers in the last days of October when carrying supplies to the beleagured garrison.

These losses spelt the death knell of the Axis navies in the Mediterranean. The task commenced by Admiral Cunningham almost four years before was brought to a successful conclusion. The last hope of Italian naval aspirations, the aircraft carriers *Sparviero* and *Aquilla*, never put to sea. The former was sunk in Genoa Harbour on 15 October 1944 and the latter, which had been partly disabled by the Germans, was set on fire and destroyed by the destroyers HMS *Lookout* and USS *Woolsly* on 6 January 1945.

The Admiralty had a complete change of mind on its involvement in the eastern Mediterranean during the first days of September 1944. HMS *Ulster Queen*, the Royal Navy's specially equipped fighter direction ship, was ordered to operate in the waters between Crete and the Greek mainland. From this position it would direct the long-range Beaufighter squadrons against transport aircraft evacuating German troops from Crete and in attacks on enemy airfields in the Peloponnese. In the first two weeks of the ship's operations in these waters, twenty-five German aircraft were shot down. However, these successes did not stop the evacuation and German records show 37,000 troops were brought out of Crete in the second half of 1944. Approximately 13,000 were taken prisoner when the island surrendered in May 1945.

Admiral Troubridge's Special Carrier Task Force commenced operations in the Northern Aegean on 20 September. This force consisted of the assault escort carriers *Attacker, Hunter, Emperor, Khedive, Pursuer* and *Searcher* with a strong cruiser and destroyer escort. Its first sweep took it as far north as the Cyclades and the Sporades. On its return south, it carried out heavy air attacks on airfields in Rhodes.

Nor were Commander Courage's flotillas of MTBs, MGBs, MLs and HDMLs idle. The boats were now ranging as far north as the Sporades, hitting the hundreds of caiques and schooners evacuating troops to the mainland. One successful attack was made on shipping off the island of Paros, only seventy miles from the Piraeus. At long last the enemy was experiencing the horrors suffered by British troops and their Greek allies in the early years of the war.

The Anglo-Hellenic Schooner Flotilla carried the Greek Sacred Squadron and the SBS to islands which had not seen British or Greek troops for almost three years. Liberation to these long-suffering islanders was as intoxicating as the long-hoarded ouzo, vino and rakki which now flowed as freely as water.

Kythera was the first island of the Aegean to be occupied by the Allies. The strategically placed island controlled the seaward approach to Greece. On 16 September, the 5th Minesweeping Flotilla from Malta with the 28th ML Flotilla set up a Coastal Command base to harry the small enemy convoys from Crete and the scattered islands of the southern fringe of the Dodecanese. The Royal Navy's thorn in the side for so many years was now its jumping-off base for the liberation of Greece. Admiral Troubridge returned at the end of September with an even larger task force which included two American assault carriers. Attacks were launched on Crete, Scarpanto and Rhodes. The participation of United States' ships reflected a change in Admiral King's policy of 1943 and early 1944. It did not impress the Greeks.

Hitler and his generals now recognised the futility of holding Greece and the islands and on 3 October a Führer Order was issued for the evacuation of all Greek territory

with the exception of Crete, Rhodes, Leros, Cos and Samos. These islands were to fight
to the bitter end.

On 13 October the powerful British battleship *King George V* bombarded Rhodes
and Leros. A little more than a year before, the ship and her powerful consort *Howe*
had lain at Alexandria while the cruisers and destroyers of Cunningham's fleet had fought
against impossible odds in the central Aegean.

A few weeks later the greatly reduced garrison in Crete withdrew to a small stronghold.
Two-thirds of the island was now free.

October was a month of great celebration in mainland Greece. The joyful cry of
'Phetasane i Angli!' (The English have arrived) echoed from Athens to Salonika. Three
and a half years of brutal oppression had ended, but in the 1,300 villages and small towns
destroyed by the Germans, there was little cause for celebration.

Colonel, the Earl George Jellicoe, led the liberation army of SBS, SAS and British
regulars from the Peloponnese to Athens. He swept through the streets of the capital
in a sea of wildly cheering Athenians. One happy Greek woman later recalled the
intoxicating moment of liberation: 'I was dressed up in British flags and emblems. I
ran alongside them and asked them to bend down so that I could kiss them.'

Far away, in the north of Greece, another SBS officer, Major Anders Lassen, led the
force through the streets of liberated Salonika. Lassen's troops, supported by Greek ELAS
irregulars, had seized the city's fire engines, mounted machine-guns on them, and attacked
the last German rearguards on 22 October and liberated the city. The SBS force was
garlanded with flowers by the exuberant population and carried through the main
thoroughfares of the liberated city.

The liberation of Athens was Jellicoe's last action in the Mediterranean. He was
promoted to the rank of brigadier and flew back to England to take command of a brigade
of the raiding forces. His successor was Major Jock Lapraik, the former lawyer who
had served with the commandos from the first actions in Abyssinia in 1940.

While the citizens of Athens were celebrating their newly won freedom, a large naval
task force was converging on Piraeus. This force of cruisers, destroyers and Coastal
Command MTBs, MLs, MGBs and HDMLs, and not a few of Commander Seligman's
Anglo-Hellenic Schooner Flotilla, was commanded by Rear Admiral Mansfield with his
flag in HMS *Orion*. This ship, and HMS *Ajax* which followed next in line, were the
two surviving cruisers of the force which had evacuated Greece in April 1941. The Royal
Navy had kept its promise to the Greeks and returned.

Twenty-four hours later, the Greek government arrived in the cruiser *Georgios Averoff*,
the ship in which, only months before, Greek sailors had mutinied against their officers.

Although mainland Greece and the majority of the islands readily surrendered, Cos,
Leros, Rhodes, Levithia, Piskopi, Scarpanto and the stronghold of Crete remained in
the hands of their obdurate garrisons.

Scarpanto, so long a thorn in the side of A.B. Cunningham, resisted to the end. On
28 September, the three Hunt Class destroyers *Brecon*, *Liddesdale* and *Zetland* entered Pegadia
Bay to bombard the defences and force the surrender, but the enemy guns fought back
vigorously and the destroyers were forced to withdraw. *Liddesdale* was struck by three
heavy-calibre shells and seriously damaged.

The strong German garrison on Aliminia was repeatedly shelled by the destroyer

Kimberley to no avail. As *Kimberley* was withdrawing from one bombardment, she intercepted two landing barges attempting to land reinforcements and forced them to surrender.

Between 24 September and 31 October, ships of the British Aegean Force and RAF aircraft sank forty-two enemy vessels. Thirty-three of these were German naval manned ships. The British submarines *Unswerving, Virtue, Vampire* and *Vigorous* accounted for twelve ships and the French submarine *Curie*, one. The last three enemy vessels remaining in Greek waters, the auxiliary minesweepers *Alulu, Otranto* and *Gallipoli*, were scuttled by their crews on 31 October.

Rhodes and Crete held out until the general surrender in May 1945. The former was repeatedly bombarded from the sea and air. A frontal assault on Rhodes Harbour by the destroyers *Marne, Meteor* and *Musketeer* did little to weaken the garrison's resolve to resist. In this sortie all three destroyers closed their targets at point-blank range.

Piskopi, north-east of Rhodes, was the last island of the Aegean to be taken by force of arms. A force of 500 men of the Greek Sacred Squadron stormed ashore under a strong bombardment on 2 May, but twenty-four hours of fierce hand-to-hand fighting was required before the defiant garrison lay down its arms.

Liberation for Greece, and to a lesser degree the islands, was a bitter-sweet victory. Days after their triumphant entry into Athens, British soldiers were being shot down in the birthplace of democracy. The first shots of the Civil War claimed their first victims within the sight of the Acropolis. ELAS forces were to devastate the unfortunate land for another three years.

The Civil War was a byproduct of the war in which the various resistance armies were formed by the political parties. It was inevitable that when these parties obtained arms they would use them to seek power.

> Ring out a slowly dying cause,
>   And ancient forms of party strife;
>   Ring in the nobler modes of life,
> With sweeter manners, purer laws.

> —Tennyson, *In Memoriam*

HMS *Barham* was the first British battleship lost in the Mediterranean, sunk by the German submarine *U 331* off Crete in November 1941.

German parachutists over Suda Bay, 20 May 1941.

The light cruiser HMS *Ajax* served in the Aegean from 1940 to 1945.

A painting of the Royal Hellenic Navy submarine *Papanikolis* by Germenis. *(Hellenic Navy Museum)*

Troops of General Ringel's Mountain Division advancing on Rethymnon.

19

Crete Redeemed

On 2 November 1944 a priority signal from SOE's headquarters in Crete informed Levant Command in Cairo the German garrison was withdrawing to a defended enclave at the western end of the island. A second signal, five days later, reported the city of Heraklion had been evacuated and the 13,000-strong garrison was now located in an area bounded by Georgioupolis on the east and the bloodsoaked airfield of Maleme on the west, and by the foothills of the White Mountains on the south.

A later report from Major Leigh-Fermor warned that ELAS forces were about to launch a civil war to seize Free Crete. This information was received when the Commander-in-Chief, Levant was endeavouring to muster troops for despatch to Greece, where another ELAS army was advancing on Athens. Northern Greece was already in the hands of the Communists.

The request for additional troops for Crete could not have arrived at a worse time. All available troops in the command were being despatched to Italy to replace units being withdrawn to reinforce General Montgomery's armies in Europe. Not surprisingly, a stopgap decision was made to transfer the SBS mobile force being equipped for service in Italy to Crete.

Like other decisions made in haste, little thought was given to the role of the force or the responsibilities of the commander. Leigh-Fermor's despatches, which had evidently not been studied closely, described the political–military situation on the island as a dangerous triangle. The Communist and Royalist resistance were sparring for full control of Free Crete while the considerable German army had adopted a passive role.

Major Anders Lassen was appointed force commander and Civil Governor of Free Crete, and instructed to obtain a briefing from the senior officer of the Military Liaison Corp in Heraklion on his responsibilities and the current situation. The twenty-four-year-old Dane had distinguished himself as a commando-style leader in the islands of the Aegean and in the capture of Salonika, but was absolutely lacking in civil administration skills or political diplomacy.

Four troops of the SBS, equipped with jeeps for their new mobile role and a troop of field artillery, were landed by destroyer at Heraklion on 3 December. While the troops were settling into temporary accommodation in the city, Lassen was briefed on the situation by Captain Percival of the Military Liaison Corp. The picture painted by Percival surprised the SBS commander. The Communist ELAS and Royalist EOK were moving their forces into strategical positions around Heraklion and the other important town in Free Crete, Rethymnon, as a prelude to seizing power. This situation satisfied the Germans, who had come to a non-aggression agreement with the resistance groups.

Lassen set up his headquarters in Heraklion, forty miles east of the German perimeter. Three posts were established to cover the roads the enemy could use if they decided to reoccupy the whole island, each manned by a troop of SBS, with a fourth troop stationed at Heraklion. A Royal Navy destroyer was based on the port to support the SBS.

News of Lassen's arrival in Crete spread rapidly through the city and the countryside. His exploits in the raids on airfields in the island in late 1943 had already entered Cretan folklore. On 4 December, a large and enthusiastic crowd assembled in the city's main square to welcome him back.

Later in the day, he was accorded a different welcome. He met the leaders of the principal resistance groups. These were Petrakoyeorgis, Manoli Bandouvas and the ELAS leader, Yanni Podiak. Lassen had met Bandouvas during a previous visit, but the others were unknown quantities. Captain Perkins during his briefing had warned Lassen that Podiak was the most dangerous of the three. Although the ELAS was numerically weaker, it was better organised than the others, and Podiak was clearly hostile.

Several hours after this meeting, Lassen was surprised to receive a telephone call from the German adjutant at Maleme. Lassen had not been informed the civil telephone system was still in operation and served both British and German forces. Later, he was to learn it also served the various resistance groups and that security was lax. The German officer welcomed Lassen to his new post and explained the passive role of his force. He also informed him that communications between the army and Europe were cut, their only link being a weekly flight by a Junkers 52 transport which flew from Vienna with mail and orders. Regular meetings were held between the two forces to discuss such matters as prisoner exchanges and the treatment of civilians.

Lassen had already learnt that the Germans were dependent on local sources for food supplies, a large percentage of which was supplied by the resistance forces in Free Crete.

Heraklion was the largest city on the island and Lassen, as commander of British forces, was expected to participate in civil functions. Christmas brought a flood of invitations to attend private and civic celebrations. The majority, Lassen declined. However, he did attend a Thanksgiving Service held in Heraklion Cathedral on New Year's Day, 1945. Major Lassen surprised the large congregation by wearing a private soldier's greatcoat without badges or insignia of rank, and commandos' rope-soled boots. A few days later he wore the same garb to a meeting with the German general at Georgioupolis. When the German officer expressed surprise, Lassen explained he feared an assassination attempt by Podiak's troops.

Captain Bimrose, who attended the meeting with his commanding officer, was even more surprised when the general remarked: 'It is a pity you are so few in numbers, otherwise we might consider surrendering to you. However, the Andartes are all around us—it would be suicide.' There was more than a shadow of truth in the German officer's words. During the occupation many hundreds of civilians had suffered the horror of German atrocities and sought revenge.

Relations between the SBS and the ELAS rapidly deteriorated in January 1945. Attempts to stop the British troops carrying out their duties became more prevalent. Patrols were taunted by villagers in Communist-held areas and ELAS encampments were moved into positions which overlooked the SBS control posts and barracks. Lassen warned Podiak that force would be met by force.

This continuing friction depressed the young Danish officer, and he lost much of the gaiety and ebullience which had earlier made him such a popular leader and companion. He genuinely loved the Cretans and admired the spirit they displayed during his earlier visits. The sullen receptions he now received as he moved around Free Crete bore down on him heavily.

An officer trained in civil administration would have employed more devious methods in dealing with civil disobedience and lack of respect. Lassen accepted the Cretans on face value—a dangerous philosophy in a country which thrived on political intrigue. He knew a more experienced and resolute administrator would use the conservative forces in Crete to counter the Communists, but his orders expressly forbade him from taking sides.

By late January, Podiak had increased his forces in the Heraklion area and the city was encircled by large ELAS encampments. Forty miles to the west, the Communists were billetting their troops inside Rethymnon. These moves did not pass unobserved. During this period, Lassen also discovered that Podiak had established his own border posts on the perimeter between Free and Occupied Crete. These were being used by the Communists to establish a monopoly in trading with the Germans. Lassen diverted one of his mobile patrols to police the area and the flow of food across the border was drastically reduced. The ELAS posts were soon abandoned.

Podiak turned to other methods of maintaining his profitable trade. Lassen's agents reported a heavy increase in caique and schooner trade between Free Crete and the German ports of Georgioupolis and Suda Bay. Lassen asked the Naval Officer in Charge, Crete to patrol the stretch of coastline with MLs and MTBs. The arrival of these fast vessels soon disrupted the trade, but could not completely eradicate it. It was impossible to search the hundreds of small bays and inlets which indented the coastline.

The naval presence at Heraklion provided Lassen with his only relief from his onerous duties. An evening in a British or Hellenic wardroom temporarily lifted the weight of responsibility from his mind, but unfortunately the opportunity for such evenings was rare.

Podiak now increased his war of nerves on the SBS. Patrols were obstructed by men and women in the towns and villages. ELAS troops and their supporters conducted noisy parades outside the barracks until late at night. Signs appeared on walls and buildings, exhorting 'British go home'. Demonstrations around the camps of Bandouvas sparked an interchange of shots in which several men on both sides were wounded. Lassen reacted by calling two SBS patrols into Heraklion to police the streets and to eject the ELAS troops from the city.

Podiak now directed his attention to Rethymnon. The town was seized by ELAS troops and a reign of terror was launched. Lassen realised the situation was escalating. Unless the ELAS were taught a lesson they would not forget, they would seize the island. Three patrols were despatched to Rethymnon to eject the troublemakers.

The road from Heraklion, forty miles of twisting and tortuous track winding through rugged country, was a sniper's paradise, but the jeeps travelled at high speed, their machine-guns cocked ready to fire. Not one shot was fired at them. Meanwhile, two MLs, with all guns manned, steamed into the small Venetian harbour and anchored in the stream, ready to fire at any sign of resistance.

When the jeeps thundered down the town's narrow streets, they were met by a jeering mob of civilians. Captain Bimrose, who commanded the force, saw ELAS soldiers pressing the crowd forward and ordered the machine-guns to fire high over the heads of the crowd. The reverberation of the guns in the narrow confines broke up the demonstration. A strict curfew was now placed on the town.

However, on the next day a jeep patrol was fired on by snipers in the top floor of a building near the waterfront. All windows in the three-storied factory were blasted out by machine-gun fire.

Major Lassen arrived in the town on the following morning, but found it quiet. Many of the ELAS troops had slipped out during the night believing the British would carry out a search at first light. In fact Lassen was on his way to negotiate an exchange of prisoners at the German control post some miles west of the town. The first prisoner released was the Australian war correspondent, Keith Hooper, who had accidentally strayed into enemy territory. Another prisoner in the uniform of a British major, was found to be an impostor. He was a German corporal desperate to escape, but Lassen took him.

Podiak's troops attempted to capture Rethymnon on 23 January, but were met by a strong Loyalist force commanded by Colonel Gyparis. The ELAS force was turned back after suffering heavy casualties and withdrew. Sadly, Colonel Gyparis' son was killed in the fighting. SBS patrols re-entered the town when the fighting moved into the surrounding countryside.

Most British accounts say little of the bitter struggle which was being fought in the Rethymnon area at this period. In his book, *The Cretan Runner*, George Psychoundakis writes of the period: 'In Rethymnon we had frequent parades and celebrations and torchlight processions, also rival demonstrations by the two parties. I went to several gatherings and celebrations and read some poems I had written in the mountains.'

Armed encounters between the two parties were now occurring throughout all Free Crete. On 27 January three resistance fighters were killed and many more wounded in Heraklion. Lassen signalled Athens that the position in Crete had reached dangerous proportions. Later on that day, two Nationalist leaders were kidnapped and four Loyalist soldiers ambushed and killed near Rethymnon. Free Crete was now belying its name. It was an armed camp teetering on the brink of civil war.

On 29 January Major Lassen was ordered to Athens to discuss stronger measures to be taken against the ELAS and other dissident groups.

A few hours after Lassen's aircraft took off, ELAS troops entered Heraklion in force. Fierce fighting broke out between ELAS and Loyalist forces. Captains Clynes and Bimrose immediately set out for the airfield to secure the vital link with the outside world. The party was ambushed by ELAS troops three kilometres short of the airfield. The jeep in which they were travelling and the escorting motor cycle were hit by bursts of machine-gun and rifle fire. Both vehicles careered off the road and crashed into a stone wall. The two officers and the motor cyclist were wounded. Captain Clynes and Private Cornwaite later died.

Lassen and Brigadier Barker-Benfield returned to Heraklion early next day. In the afternoon an enquiry was held into the killings, but all resistance leaders denied any involvement in the ambush. Podiak denied that the killers were ELAS, but eyewitnesses to the ambush testified otherwise. The enquiry agreed all resistance forces in Free Crete would be disarmed immediately.

The SBS ceremonially buried their dead at Heraklion on 7 February. Later in that day, the first regular troops arrived to occupy Crete. The SBS patrols handed over their posts to Brigadier Barker-Benfield's brigade without regret. Shortly before dusk, they embarked in waiting destroyers and turned their backs on the unhappy island.

Two months later, Major Anders Lassen, the young Dane who had loved Crete and its people, died in an action at Lake Commanchio in northern Italy, for which he was awarded the Victoria Cross. He was the second foreign national to receive Britain's most prestigious award for valour. The first was also a Dane.

Lassen's disarming of resistance forces saved the island from itself. His action rescued Cretans from the horrors of civil war which devastated mainland Greece. Regulars policed the island until the final surrender. Under their supervision, a national army was raised, and it was this British-disciplined force which marched into Occupied Crete when the Germans laid down their arms. It was a fitting reward that the recently promoted Lieutenant Colonel Patrick Leigh-Fermor, DSO, should be in the forefront of the officers who received the surrender. He had commanded the British SOE mission in Crete for three long years.

The surrender was taken before an audience of many thousands of wildly cheering Cretans who, long ago, had watched gallant British servicemen march into captivity from this same spot. They knew that on a hill not far distant, 5,000 German soldiers lay buried.

Resistance fighter George Psychoundakis recited the following lines at a celebration held in the Lyceum Girls' School at Rethymnon to mark that day: 'Pluck out the tares of enmity, of civil strife and hate and fear. Let us live in peace together, in a second age of gold. In honour, fame and wisdom, like the Greeks of old.'

The great day of liberation was 23 May 1945. Four years and three days after the Germans descended from the skies, Crete, the first island of the Aegean to be captured by the Germans, was the last to be freed.

The events related in this book owe a heavy debt to the Greeks of the mainland, the hardy Cretans and the Greeks of the myriad islands of the Aegean. Without their cooperation, their willingness to risk their lives and the lives of their families, there would have been few successful escapes or successful SOE, SBS and LRDG operations to record. It was their spirit which rose from the sloughs of defeat that inspired the British to return and prepare the way for final victory.

No accurate record of the number who died in this cause is available, but few areas avoided paying the price. In many regions whole villages were wiped out by the bloodthirsty occupation forces. Others, who were not executed on the hearths of their simple homes, were shipped away never to return. The golden dream of rising in great strength, as their fathers had done against the Turks, and hurling the hated oppressors out of their land was never realised. But their resistance through four long years of want and suffering sapped the strength of the German military and contributed to final victory.

In Greece there is not just one Tomb of the Unknown Warrior, there are many thousands, unmarked except in the memories of those who served alongside them. Their memorials are not carved from cold stone or cast from molten metal but implanted in the hearts of the generations. Their heroic sacrifice has become a timeless legend, not only in their native land, but in lands far removed from Greece. Age shall not weary them, nor the years condemn. Their memory is enshrined in the hearts of Britons, Australians, New Zealanders, Canadians and South Africans.

From the graves of our slain
  Shall thy valour prevail
As we greet them again—
  Hail, Liberty! Hail.

'The Greek National Anthem', 1918—Rudyard Kipling

Appendix I

The Greek Labyrinth

In the late 1970s the British government authorised the release of the first papers relating to ULTRA, under the restraints of the British Official Secrets Act. Progressively over the next ten years, further papers were released and slowly the magnitude of the British Prime Minister's most important weapon in the Second World War was made public.

One month before Winston Churchill became Prime Minister on 10 May 1940, the Government Code and Cypher School at Bletchley Park decrypted the first ULTRA code. The history-making message was in a low-order secret code transmitted through Enigma. It revealed the deployment of German Army units for the coming blitzkrieg attack on Belgium and France.

In the six months which followed this initial success, Bletchley Park progressively decrypted higher rated enemy secret codes, and on 18 December 1940 it decoded the first Führer operation plan—Directive 21. This extremely long directive was the operations plan for the German attack on Russia, code-named Operation Barbarossa. The interception of this ULTRA message was, in Churchill's words, 'the turning point of the war'.

Directive 21 was a step-by-step plan to conquer Russia and link hands with the Japanese Army on the northern border of China. It detailed the movement of more than a million troops on a front which would ultimately stretch for almost 2,000 miles. The plan was complete with an inflexible timetable. The maximum variation permissible from the crossing of the Russian border to the capture of Moscow was fourteen days.

Churchill received the directive five days after it had been approved by Hitler and the German High Command. In the weeks which followed, he studied its contents in detail. The preliminary objectives of Barbarossa were the capture of Turkey and Syria to prevent Britain launching an attack from the south. Greece was to be occupied to provide a buffer from the west, and non-intervention pacts were to be arranged diplomatically with Yugoslavia, Rumania, Hungary and Bulgaria for the passage of the German armies south.

The Prime Minister's attention was drawn to the timetable laid down by the High Command. If the attack on Russia could be delayed by more than fourteen days, he reasoned, the German armies would not reach Moscow before the first snows fell on the Russian steppes and the invading force would be trapped in a great sea of mud and slush. His mind turned to engineering such a delay.

In January 1941 the Prince Regent of Yugoslavia signed a secret non-intervention pact with Hitler. Shortly after, Bulgaria entered the war on the side of Germany and Hungary and Rumania signed the Tri-Partite Pact which ensured passage of German troops south.

Hitler ordered the attack on Greece to commence on 1 April and, when Thrace and Macedonia were seized, a two-prong attack would be launched against Turkey. Both operations were to be completed by 20 April.

These vital dates were received in an ULTRA decrypt in the first week of February. Churchill now acted on the plan he hoped would put the timetable of Directive 21 in a state of disarray.

Turkey and the United States were informed of the German plans to invade Russia. Surprisingly, President Roosevelt already knew of Operation Barbarossa—it had been leaked to him by the German Consul in New York, Captain Wiedmann, only days earlier. Turkey's President, Kemal Ataturk, expected an attack on his country by either Germany or Russia and had made plans to resist, but he preferred to remain neutral.

Churchill invited the Australian Prime Minister, R.G. Menzies, and his New Zealand counterpart, H. Fraser, to a meeting in London on 18 February to discuss the use of Australian and New Zealand troops in the defence of Greece. However, Menzies broke his journey in Cairo, where General Wavell raised the same question and the Australian Prime Minister agreed. The New Zealand Prime Minister also agreed in a message to Churchill. General Blamey, the Australian Force Commander, was absent in Libya and Menzies did not discuss the question with him before giving assent to the proposal.

On 22 February a British delegation, consisting of the Foreign Minister, Sir Anthony Eden, General Sir John Dill, General Wavell and Air Marshal Sir Arthur Longmore, arrived in Athens to offer aid to Greece should it be attacked. The timing was excellent. The Greek dictator, General Metaxas, who was an ardent admirer of Hitler, had died only a month before and the new Prime Minister, Alexander Koryzis, met the delegation. The reception was cordial but the proposal to use British troops in the defence of Greece was not received with enthusiasm. Eden offered an immediate force of three divisions, the Polish Brigade and two armoured brigades. This force would number 100,000 troops equipped with 240 field guns, 32 medium guns, 192 anti-aircraft guns and 142 tanks.

Lieutenant Colonel de Guingand, Wavell's aide, was later to write: 'It sounded pretty good, but if a real expert had carried out a detailed investigation, I doubt whether those present would have been satisfied'. The actual force sent numbered nearer to 60,000 men.

Despite doubts expressed by the Greek Commander-in-Chief, General Papagos, the Greek government accepted the offer on 23 February. Churchill was elated when he received the news. He knew from ULTRA intercepts of the great build-up of the enemy forces in Austria. By the end of March forty-one divisions were deployed for an advance either to the south or to the east.

This formidable German presence in southern Europe was also noted by the Turks. Air Vice-Marshal A.S.G. Lee, who was on loan to the Turkish Staff College from 1938 to 1941, wrote: 'The Turks feared that these forces were intended for something bigger than an attack on Greece, and were sure Turkey or Russia was to be the victim'.

Following the meeting in Athens, Sir Anthony Eden sent a telegram to the Prince Regent of Yugoslavia warning of a German threat to Salonika and agreeing on a withdrawal of Greek troops from Thrace and Macedonia to the Vermion–Olympus Line. The Regent made no reference to the non-intervention pact he had signed with Germany.

The despatch of a British army to Greece was not supported by its leaders. General

Dill remarked to General Neame, commander of British Armoured Forces in Africa, on 17 March: 'You are going to get a bloody nose here and it is not the only place where we shall get bloody noses'. Neame's subordinate, Lieutenant General Sir Gifford Martels, also shared these fears. He wrote: 'I thought we should rue the day we sent forces to fight these great German armies in Greece'.

Churchill did not share the pessimistic attitude of his field commanders. The fourteen-day delay in launching Operation Barbarossa was before his eyes. His plans to upset the timetable outlined in Directive 21 were becoming a reality.

Closer to home, on 10 March General Blamey expressed his fears of the coming campaign in a telegram to the Australian Cabinet. 'Military operation [in Greece] extremely hazardous in view of the disparity between opposing forces in numbers and training'. No action was taken by Cabinet to question the British decision and by 27 March the bulk of the expeditionary force had been landed in Greece and was being deployed with Greek forces in northern Greece.

At this time, the British Prime Minister's attention was concentrated on events in Yugoslavia. Details of the Prince Regent's non-intervention pact with Germany had reached Churchill from an undisclosed source (suspected to have been the United States) and he was now endeavouring to capitalise on the discovery. The British Ambassador in Belgrade passed the information to senior Yugoslav officers, who two days later led the coup which deposed Prince Paul as Regent. The Yugoslav armed forces then agreed to resist any German advance on their territory.

This unexpected crisis infuriated Hitler, who ordered his forces to attack and subdue Yugoslavia before attacking Greece. Unfortunately the Yugoslav Army was no match for the German Panzers. It resisted for five days before falling back on Belgrade. On 6 April, the Orthodox Church's Good Friday, Hitler ordered the Luftwaffe to destroy the city. In day-long saturation raids by fleets of bombers and dive-bombers, the old city was devastated. It is believed that 15,000 men, women and children died in the pulverised ruins. The air attack was followed by massive tank assaults and the capital of Yugoslavia fell.

Nonetheless, Yugoslav resistance resulted in Salonika being captured eight days behind the German schedule. The Greek campaign ended on the night of 29 April on the beaches at Porto Rafti and Kalamata, twenty-one days behind the rigid timetable of Directive 21.

Churchill's decision to defend Crete prevented Hitler from transferring his air fleet to Russia and cost him the elite airborne army which was an important element of the shock force intended to break the Russian lines. Crete cost the Germans ten more vital days and more than 5,000 dead. The assault on Turkey was cancelled and the lynchpin for the southern arm of the forces advancing into Russia was never secured.

Almost forty years after the last shots were fired in the Greek Campaign it was revealed that Winston Churchill knew the army he had committed to Greece could not halt the German juggernaut. The Prime Minister was buying time, and history shows his painful gamble did alter the course of the war. Franklin Delano Roosevelt signalled the British Prime Minister on 1 May 1941: 'You have done not only heroic, but very useful work in Greece. You have fought a wholly justifiable action.'

In Greece, even today, citizens refer to the battles of 1941 as 'the battles to save mankind'.

From Thrace to Crete, the Australians, New Zealanders and British who fought so valiantly against great odds are venerated as heroes, and well do they deserve the accolade. The twenty-eight days they won with their blood saved the world from an age of darkness.

The first indication that the German drive on Moscow had failed was an ULTRA intercept of a signal from the commander of a German armoured division reporting that his transport columns were immobilised in heavy snow and that the engine oil had frozen solid. The signal was transmitted on 2 December 1941.

The German victories in Greece and Crete ultimately cost them the war.

Appendix II

Allied Naval Ships in the Aegean Sea, 1940–45

Royal Navy

Abdiel (FM)
Ajax (C)
Aldenham (D)
Attacker (ECA)
Auckland (SL)
Aurora (C)
Barham (B)
Beaufort (D)
Belvoir (D)
Blencathra (D)
Bonaventure (C)
BYMS 72 (Ms)
BYMS 73 (Ms)
Calcutta (C)
Calypso (C)
Carlisle (C)
Chalka (LS)
Coventry (C)
Croome (D)
Decoy (D)
Diamond (D)
Dido (C)
Dulverton (D)
Echo (D)
Eclipse (D)
Exmoor (D)
Faulknor (D)
Fiji (C)
Flamingo (EV)
Formidable (AC)

Fury (D)
Galatea (C)
Glenearn (LSI)
Glengyle (LSI)
Glenroy (LSI)
Gloucester (C)
Greyhound (D)
Griffin (D)
Grimsby (Sl)
Gurkha (D)
Hasty (D)
Havock (D)
Hedgehog (EV)
Hereward (D)
Hermione (Cr)
Hero (D)
Hotspur (D)
Howe (B))
Hunter (D)
Hursley (D)
Hurworth (D)
Hyacinth (Cor)
Ilex (D)
Illustrious (AC)
Imperial (D)
Jackal (D)
Jaguar (D)
Janus (D)
Jervis (D)
Juno (D)
Kandahar (D)
Kashmir (D)

Kelly (D)
Kelvin (D)
Kimberley (D)
King George V (B)
Kingston (D)
Kipling (D)
Kinsley (D)
KOS 21 (Ms)
KOS 22 (Ms)
Ladybird (G)
Lanner (EV)
LCM 923 (LC)
LCT 3 (LC)
LCT 115 (LC)
Lively (D)
MGB 645 (G)
MGB 646 (G)
MGB 647 (G)
ML 285 (ML)
ML 299 (ML)
ML 308 (ML)
ML 337 (ML)
ML 340 (ML)
ML 349 (ML)
ML 354 (ML)
ML 356 (ML)
ML 357 (ML)
ML 358 (ML)
ML 359 (ML)
ML 456 (ML)
ML 461 (ML)
ML 579 (ML)

ML 835 (ML)
ML 836 (ML)
ML 1011 (ML)
ML 1015 (ML)
ML 1030 (ML)
ML 1032 (ML)
MMS 102 (Ms)
MMS 193 (Ms)
MTB 260 (TB)
MTB 263 (TB)
MTB 266 (TB)
MTB 307 (TB)
MTB 309 (TB)
MTB 313 (TB)
MTB 315 (TB)
MTB 361 (TB)
Naiad (C)
Nubian (D)
Orion (C)
Panther (D)
Parthian (D)
Pathfinder (D)
Penelope (C)
Penn (D)
Petard (D)
Phoebe (C)
Queen Elizabeth (B)
Rockwood (D)
Rorqual (Sm)
Rover (Sm)
Salvia (Cor)
Seraph (Sm)
Severn (Sm)
Shakespeare (Sm)
Sibyl (Sm)
Sickle (Sm)
Sikh (D)
Simoon (Sm)
Sirius (C)
Southampton (C)
Sportsman (Sm)
Stalker (EAC)

Surf (Sm)
Syvern (EV)
Tetcott (D)
Thrasher (Sm)
Torbay (Sm)
Trespasser (Sm)
Triton (Sm)
Triumph (Sm)
Trooper (Sm)
Tumult (D)
Una (Sm)
Unbeaten (Sm)
Unbroken (Sm)
Unruly (Sm)
Unseen (Sm)
Unsparing (Sm)
Unswerving (Sm)
Upholder (Sm)
Urge (Sm)
Valiant (B)
Warspite (B)
Welshman (FM)
Widnes (D)
Wilton (D)
Wryneck (D)
York (C)
Zulu (D)

Royal Australian Navy

Hobart (C)
Ipswich (Cor)
Napier (D)
Nestor (D)
Nizam (D)
Perth (C)
Stuart (D)
Sydney (C)
Vampire (D)
Vendetta (D)
Voyager (D)
Waterhen (D)

Royal Indian Navy

Sutlej (Sl)

Republic of France

Basque (D)
Commandant Domine (EV)
Commandant Duboc (EV)
Duguay-Trouin (C)
Duquesne (C)
Forbin (D)
La Fantasque (D)
Le Fortune (D)
Lorraine (B)

Royal Hellenic Navy

Adrias (D)
Georgios Averoff (C)
Helle (C)
Kanaris (D)
Katsonis (Sm)
Kondouriotis (D)
Miaoulis (D)
Papanikolis (Sm)
Pindos (D)
Pipinos (Sm)
Queen Olga (D)
Themistocles (D)

Polish Navy

Dzik (Sm)
Krakowiak (D)
Sokol (Sm)

Captured Italian Navy Ships

Atropo (Sm)
Euro (D)
Menotti (Sm)
Zoea (Sm)
MAS-boats (33)

Appendix III

Allied Naval Losses in the Aegean, 1940–44

12.6.1940	*Calypso* (C)	Torpedoed and sunk by the Italian submarine *Bagnolini* off Crete
19.8.1940	*Helle* (C)	Sunk by the Italian submarine *Osiro* in Tinos Harbour
26.3.1941	*York* (C)	Sunk by Italian explosive motor boats in Suda Bay, Crete
31.3.1941	*Bonaventure* (C)	Torpedoed and sunk by the Italian submarine *Dagabur* off Crete
18.4.1941	*Chakla* (LS)	Sunk by German aircraft in Suda Bay, Crete, but later raised and returned to service
24.4.1941	*Rover* (Sm)	Sunk by German aircraft in Suda Bay, Crete, but later raised and returned to service
27.4.1941	*Diamond* (D)	Sunk by German aircraft off Morea on east coast of Greece
27.4.1941	*Wryneck* (D)	Sunk by German aircraft north of Crete
20.5.1941	*Widnes* (Ms)	Beached at Suda Bay, Crete, after being damaged in air attacks. Salvaged by the Germans and renamed *UJ 2109*, she was sunk on 17 March 1943 by British destroyers in the Dodecanese
21.5.1941	*Juno* (D)	Sunk by Italian and German aircraft north of Crete
21.5.1941	*Greyhound* (D)	Sunk by German aircraft north of Crete
21.5.1941	*Gloucester* (C)	Sunk by German aircraft off Crete
21.5.1941	*Fiji* (C)	Sunk by German aircraft off Crete
22.5.1941	*Kashmir* (D)	Sunk by German aircraft off Crete
22.5.1951	*Kelly* (D)	Sunk by German aircraft off Crete
27.5.1941	*Syvern* (EV)	Sunk by German aircraft in Suda Bay, Crete
29.5.1941	*Imperial* (D)	Sunk south of Crete by German aircraft
29.5.1941	*Hereward* (D)	Sunk by German aircraft south of Crete
1.6.1941	*Calcutta* (C)	Sunk by German aircraft south of Crete
30.6.1941	*Waterhen* (D)	Sunk north of Sollum after being damaged by German aircraft. She was the first Australian warship lost in the Second World War
24.11.1941	*Barham* (B)	Torpedoed and sunk by the German submarine U 331 south of Crete
14.12.1941	*Galatea* (C)	Sunk by the German submarine *U 557* south of Crete
24.12.1941	*Salvia* (Cor)	Sunk by the German submarine *U 568* south of Crete
14.1.1942	*Triumph* (Sm)	Sunk by enemy mines off Rhodes

1.2.1942	*Welshman* (FM)	Torpedoed and sunk by the German submarine *U 617* south of Crete
11.3.1942	*Naiad* (C)	Torpedoed and sunk by the German submarine *U 565* south of Crete
6.5.1942	*Urge* (Sm)	Sunk by the Italian torpedo boat *Pegaso* in the Aegean
11.5.1942	*Lively* (D)	Sunk by Italian and German aircraft south of Crete
11.5.1942	*Kipling* (D)	Sunk by German aircraft south of Crete
11.5.1942	*Jackal* (D)	Sunk by German aircraft south of Crete
16.5.1942	*Hermione* (C)	Sunk by German submarine *U 205* off Crete
16.5.1942	*Nestor* (D)	Sunk by Italian aircraft south of Crete
14.6.1942	*Hasty* (D)	Sunk by HMS *Hotspur* after being damaged in a German submarine attack
14.9.1943	*Katsonis* (Sm)	Sunk by the German anti-submarine vessel *UJ 2101* at the entrance to Euboea Channel
26.9.1943	*Queen Olga* (D)	Sunk by German aircraft off Leros
27.9.1943	*Intrepid* (D)	Sunk by German aircraft off Leros
10.10.1943	*Euro* (D)	Sunk by German aircraft off Leros
10.10.1943	*Carlisle* (C)	Declared a constructive loss following attacks by German aircraft in Central Aegean
10.10.1943	*Panther* (D)	Sunk by German aircraft in Scarpanto Strait
18.10.1943	*Trooper* (Sm)	Sunk by enemy mines in the Aegean
21.10.1943	*Hurworth* (D)	Sunk by enemy mine off Leros
24.10.1943	*Eclipse* (D)	Sunk by enemy mine off Leros
6.11.1943	*Simoon* (Sm)	Sunk by enemy mines in northern Aegean
12.11.1943	*Rockwood* (D)	Sunk by a German aircraft-launched guided missile off Leros
13.11.1943	*Dulverton* (D)	Sunk by a German aircraft launched guided missile off Leros
12.1944	*Sickle* (Sm)	Believed sunk by an enemy mine off the east coast of Greece

Fifteen smaller vessels, including MTBs, MLs and caiques and schooners of the Levant Schooner Flotilla were also lost.

Appendix IV

The Winds of the Escapers

The Allied escapers who crossed the wide sea from the south coast of Crete to the Egyptian shores owed much of their success to the meltemi, the wind which blows in late spring and summer from the north. Without it, or the much gentler etesian, which sighs into being in the afternoon of a hot summer's day, no amount of luck would have taken them across the 380 miles of open sea.

There is no record in the accounts of those who made the dangerous crossing of meeting the simoon. This fiery, dust-laden gale sweeps from the deserts of southern Egypt and deposits hundreds of tons of red dust into the Mediterranean annually. The craft used by the escapers would have been swamped by its first blasts.

Luck was indeed with all these intrepid mariners. Two of the Australian boats were struck by summer squalls close to the Egyptian shores. These winds strike with high gusts from the west and raise high seas. Private S.L. Carroll recorded: 'At dawn on the seventh morning a strong north-wester blew up and by 1000 had developed into a gale—the boat filled and overturned and the mast smashed a hole in the bottom. It took me seven hours to reach land, swimming, floating and surfing.'

No record exists of a successful crossing being made in the winter months. Winter is the season of the ephuros, which roars out of the west and turns the peaceful Mediterranean into a maelstrom. Two destroyers were wrecked on the coast of Crete by this freezing fury. The Mediterranean has changed little since the days of the great Venetian High Admiral, Andrea Doria, who wrote in September 1638: 'This is the month when the calm conditions of summer break down in gales, violent electric storms and dangerous local phenomena like waterspouts'. Captain Horatio Nelson's flagship was blown aground on the north-east coast of Crete in a similar storm.

The Mediterranean is credited with having no tides or currents, yet two craft used by escapers made their southward passage without engine, sail or oars. Both captains recorded days of little wind which suggests a southerly drift does exist.

There is no wartime record of a successful passage north or east where a sailing vessel was used.

Appendix V

The Aegean Caique

The Aegean caique is the oldest sailing ship design still in use. Its lineage stretches unbroken from the days of the galleys of ancient Greece, Rome, Egypt, Persia and Turkey. The name is derived from the Turkish word 'kaik', a small boat or skiff, but today it refers to the small timber-built sailing vessels which still trade in the eastern Mediterranean. These fine-lined craft range from 10 to 250 tons in displacement.

Caiques may still be seen in the waters of the Aegean, the eastern Mediterranean and on the upper waters of the River Nile.

The true caique hull is low-waisted with a high rake both to stem and to stern. The rounded and extreme clipper bow are common, as is the rounded stern. A tall single mast is set well forward and the bowsprit is extremely long.

Caiques are lateen-rigged. The narrow triangular sail is set on an extended yard, the forward end bowsed well down so that it sets obliquely on the mast and produces a high peak. In strong winds it is inclined to take water in the low-waist deck and canvas strakes are commonly fitted to both sides to protect the cargo. Lateen is derived from the word 'latin', which means Mediterranean.

Caiques are now fitted with auxiliary engines, used mainly at the narrow entrances to Aegean harbours and for berthing, though they are also used occasionally for running in windless conditions. In earlier times two great sweeps mounted in the waist were used for these purposes.

Steering design has remained unaltered over the centuries. A long curved tiller bar operates a high sweeping rudder. With the introduction of engines, which were fitted towards the stern, a tall engine housing was mounted to protect the engine and the steersman. A glass window at head height provides good forward vision.

Barbarossa, the High Admiral of the Ottoman Fleet in the seventeenth century, who was born on the island of Lesbos in the Aegean, used the caique design to build his huge fleet of lateen-rigged war galleys. To supply his battle fleet and armies ashore he is reputed to have employed a thousand caiques.

During the Second World War, both British and German forces used caiques as patrol and supply vessels. More than 500 vessels were impressed for this service.

Bibliography

Bekker, C.D., *Swastika At Sea*, William Kimber, London 1957.

Brookes, Ewart, *Destroyer*, Arrow Books, London 1973.

Churchill, Winston, *The Second World War*, Cassel, London 1951.

College, J.J., *Ships of the Royal Navy*, David Charles, London 1969.

Collins, J., *HMAS Sydney*, The Naval Historical Society of Australia, Sydney 1974.

Cook, Graeme, *Silent Marauders*, Hart Davis, London 1976.

Courtney, C.B., *SBS In World War II*, Robert Hale, London 1983.

Cunningham, A.B., *A Sailor's Odyssey*, Arrow Books, London 1961.

Deacon, Richard, *The Silent War*, David Charles, London 1978.

De Guingand, Francis, *Operation Victory*, Cassel, London 1946.

Fell, W.R., *The Sea Our Shield*, Cassel, London 1956.

Gill, G. Hermon, *Royal Australian Navy, 1939–1942*, Australian War Memorial, Canberra 1957.

Gill, G. Hermon, *Royal Australian Navy, 1942–1945*, Australian War Memorial, Canberra 1968.

Granville, W. and Kelly, R.A., *Inshore Heroes*, W.H. Allen, London 1961.

Hadjipateras and Fafalios, M., *Crete 1941 Eyewitnessed*, Efatathiadis, M. and Sons, Athens, 1989.

Harrison, D.I., *These Men Are Dangerous*, Cassel, London 1957.

Hellenic Army General Staff, *Greek Sacred Squadron*, Hellenic Army, Athens 1982.

Hellenic Navy General Staff, *Aegean Operations*, Hellenic Navy, Athens 1982.

Holmes, W.J., *Double-Edged Secrets*, Berkly Publishing, New York 1970.

Howell, Edward, *Escape To Live*, Longmans Green, London 1947.

Kemp, P.K., *HM Submarines*, Herbert Jenkins, London 1952.

Lassen, Suzanne, *Anders Lassen, VC*, Frederick Muller, London 1965.

Ladd, James D., *SBS—The Silent Raiders*, Arms and Armour Press, London 1983.

Lapotier, H.A.M., *Raiders From The Sea*, William Kimber, London 1954.

Lee, A.S.G., *Special Duties*, Cassel, London 1946.

Lind, Lew, *Flowers Of Rethymnon*, Kangaroo Press, Sydney 1991

Lind, Lew, *The Royal Australian Navy*, Reed Books, Sydney 1982

Lind, L.J., and Payne, M.A., *N Class*, The Naval Historical Society of Australia, Sydney 1972

Lind, L.J., and Payne, M.A., *Scrap Iron Destroyers*, The Naval Historical Society of Australia, Sydney 1976

Lodwick, John, *The Filibusters*, Methuen, London 1947.

Long, Gavin, *Greece, Crete and Syria*, Australian War Memorial, Canberra 1953.

Manning, T.D., *The British Destroyer*, Putnam, London 1961.

Mars, Alastair, *Submarines At War, 1939–1945*, William Kimber, London 1971.

Martel, Gifford, *In Our Armoured Forces*, Cassel, London 1945.

Masters, D., *Up Periscope*, Spottiswoode, London 1942.

Ministry of Information, *The Mediterranean Fleet: Greece–Tripoli*, London 1972.

Minshall, Merlin, *Guilt-Edged*, Buchanan and Turner, London 1975.

Moulton, J.L., *The Royal Marines*, Leo Cooper, London 1972.

Naval Historical Review, 1971–93, The Naval Historical Society of Australia, Sydney.

Neame, Philip, *Playing With Strife*, Cassel, London 1947.

Payne, Alan, *HMAS Perth*, The Naval Historical Society of Australia, Sydney 1978.

Pitt, Barrie, *Special Boat Squadron*, Century Publishing, London 1983.

Rohwer, J., and Hummerchen, G., *Chronology of the War At Sea 1939–1945*, Arco Publishing, New York 1972.

Roskill, S.W., *HMS Warspite*, William Collins, London 1957.

Shankland, Peter and Hunter, Anthony, *Malta Convoy*, Collins, London 1961.

Shrubb, R. and Sainsbury, A., *The Royal Navy Day By Day*, Centaur Press, Fontwell 1979.

Singleton-Gates, *General Lord Freyberg, VC*, Michael Joseph, London 1963.

St George Saunders, Hilary, *The Green Beret*, Michael Joseph, London 1949.

St George Saunders, Hilary, *The Red Beret*, Michael Joseph, London 1950.

Stevenson, William, *A Man Called Intrepid*, Macmillan, London 1966.

Stewart, I.McD.G., *Struggle For Crete*, Oxford University Press, London 1966.

Strutton, Bill, and Pearson, M., *The Secret Invaders*, Hodder, London 1958.

Stitt, George, *Under Cunningham's Command 1940–1943*, Allen and Unwin, London 1944.

Terraine, John, *Business In Great Waters*, Leo Cooper, London 1989.

Thomas, David A., *Crete 1941—The Battle At Sea*, Andre Deutsch, London 1972.

Turner, John Frayn, *Periscope Patrol*, Harrap, London 1957.

United States Naval Institute, *Proceedings*, 1987–92, New York.

Vader, John, *The Fleet Without A Friend*, New English Library, London 1971.

Vian, Philip, Sir, *Action This Day*, Frederick Muller, London 1960.

Von der Porten, Edward P., *The German Navy in World War II*, Pan, London 1972.

Warner, Oliver, *Cunningham of Hyndhope*, John Murray, London 1967.

Wilkinson, J.B., *By Sea And By Stealth*, Coward McCann, London 1956.

Winterbotham, F.W., *The ULTRA Secret*, Widenfeld and Nicholson, London 1986.

Winter, John, *ULTRA At Sea*, Heinemann, London 1988.

Young, Peter, *Storm From The Sea*, Greenhill, London 1956.

Index